RACIAL INEQUALITY

Racial Inequality

A Political-Economic Analysis

MICHAEL REICH

PRINCETON UNIVERSITY PRESS
PRINCETON, NEW JERSEY

Contents

103694

List of Tables

List of Figures

Preface

WHAT INTEREST do different groups of whites have in the perpetuation of racism against blacks in the United States? This straightforward question, which should be distinguished at the outset from the question of the *role* various groups of whites have actually played in racism, provides the starting point for the research reported in this book. Although the distribution of benefits from racism has been much discussed, it rarely has been studied systematically in an empirical fashion. This study seeks to fill that vacuum.

Two additional concerns motivate the present study. First, neoclassical economics has not yet been able to develop a satisfactory theory of racial inequality and discrimination. Can political-economic analysis, which emphasizes collective action, conflict and power, and the interaction of political and economic variables, provide a better theory? Second, working-class whites and unions often are thought to benefit from racism. Yet unions seem to be less capable of achieving their economic and political goals in the United States than in countries with less racial and ethnic heterogeneity. How can this apparent paradox by explained?

In working on this book I have accumulated debts to many colleagues and friends. My deepest thanks go to Nancy Chodorow, Samuel Bowles, and Richard Edwards. Each provided not only helpful comments on several entire drafts, but also important support and encouragement at many stages of the enterprise. Assistance from Kenneth Arrow, David Gordon and Stephen Marglin was especially helpful at many points. Conversations with Eric Foner and Jonathan Wiener clarified aspects of nineteenth-century Southern history and David Plotke provided useful suggestions.

Many of my colleagues and students in the Department of Economics at Berkeley deserve thanks for letting me try out ideas on them and for giving me helpful comments. In particular, Bent Hansen saved me from some technical errors, Richard Sutch helped with the historical material, Lloyd Ulman provided important insights on the labor movement, and Benjamin Ward encouraged me to keep returning to the big questions.

Daniel Boothby, James Devine, Candace Howes, Charles Jeszeck, and Edward Lorenz provided able research assistance with the often laborious computations and library work. The Institute of Industrial Relations and the Institute of Business and Economic Research, both on the Berkeley campus, gave financial support to the project, for which I am also grateful.

I also wish to thank the *Journal of Human Resources* and the *American Economic Review* for permission to draw from my previously published work.

RACIAL INEQUALITY

CHAPTER ONE

Introduction

IN THE TWENTIETH CENTURY, two salient characteristics have distinguished the United States from the other developed capitalist countries in Western Europe and North America. First, political alignments are based less on class position and solidarity in the United States than in any other developed capitalist country. The United States lacks a significant socialist movement, and its labor movement is the weakest of any developed country. To many observers these unique features account for the comparatively underdeveloped character of welfare-state programs and the weak commitment to full-employment policies in the United States.

The second salient characteristic distinguishing the United States from these other developed capitalist countries concerns the long history of ethnic and racial diversity among its population. Although ethnic differences have decreased markedly over the course of the century, the United States contains a large racial minority of blacks that still remains set apart from the white majority. This feature of the United States has also developed in Western European nations since the mid-1960s, but to a lesser degree.

This book addresses these two features of American society—the relatively low level of working-class economic and political power and the continuing degree of racial inequality—and argues that they are not just parallel developments. They are inextricably linked and must be understood jointly. I show that market forces in American capitalism do not work to eliminate racial inequality and that economic and political pressures from racial minorities allied with the labor movement are required for further advances toward racial equality. I show also that racial inequality diminishes the

3

capacity of workers to organize in a solidaristic manner, thereby weakening the labor movement and hurting most white as well as black workers.

Consider, for example, the evolution of the labor and black movements since the great watershed of the 1930s. In that decade organized labor and blacks cooperated on an unprecedented scale, to the mutual advantage of both parties. However, this alliance began to unravel by the late 1940s, primarily from the side of labor. Since that time, the labor movement has not succeeded in making significant advances in organization or economic bargaining in private industry. Its gains have been limited primarily to legislative victories and to extending unionism among public employees. By the late 1970s even these gains were in danger of being rolled back. Certainly, no marked increase in class solidarity has developed. Instead, particularistic issues such as school busing have held the attention of many white working-class Americans.

Although the civil rights movement was set in motion in the 1930s, its main impact was delayed until the 1950s and 1960s. Even so, the limited support of labor constrained the economic gains of blacks. While many of the legal and some of the cultural and economic barriers to racial equality have been dismantled in the post-World War II era, most notably in the heady decade of the 1960s, racial inequality persists. I shall document in detail that while blacks have made advances both in absolute terms and relative to whites, equality has not been achieved and further relative advances are doubtful. The relative economic and political advances for blacks that did occur in the 1960s seem to have ended by the early 1970s. Both the labor movement and the civil rights movement had entered a period of decline.

In the 1970s the problems and stagnation of these movements stemmed in large part from the backlash response of many white Americans to the civil rights ferment of the 1960s, signaling a growth of selfish individualism and a turn away from collective action.[1] This hostile response notably con-

---

[1] For evidence of a reversal since 1972 in the liberalization of white racial

4

trasts with white labor's support for struggles against racism and for interracial class solidarity in the turbulent 1930s.

Why was the backlash strong and solidarity so weak? It is not my purpose here to address this important question comprehensively. I shall present briefly the principal perceptions that seemed to fuel the racial backlash among white Americans. These perceptions further suggest the connection between racial inequality and the weakness of the labor movement and indicate the starting point of my own research.[2]

First, many white Americans seemed to believe not only that racial minorities had made significant gains in recent decades, but also that these advances were so great that racial discrimination in economic life had become exceedingly rare.[3] This notion was presented frequently in mass media depictions of a newly expanded and affluent black middle class that had "made it" in economic terms to levels that exceeded average white income levels. Consequently, many whites apparently felt that further affirmative action programs were no longer needed.

Second, many white working-class and middle-class Americans seemed to believe that the gains that have occurred for racial minorities, especially those resulting from affirmative action programs in employment and education, have occurred primarily at their expense.[4] Many whites apparently felt that affirmative action programs in education and employment had taken educational opportunities, jobs, and income away from white families who had not personally created or been a party to past racial oppression, and had given these advantages to

attitudes, see John Condran, "Changes in White Attitudes Toward Blacks, 1963–1977," *Public Opinion Quarterly* (Winter 1979).

[2] The characterization below is based on accounts made in the mass media.

[3] A 1978 Gallup Poll indicated that 77 percent of whites believed that blacks are treated the same as whites. (However, only 34 percent of surveyed blacks agreed.) "Poll Shows Dramatic Drop in U.S. Bias," *San Francisco Chronicle*, 28 August 1978.

[4] For a discussion of the prevalence of conceptions of race-based politics, see Louis Bolce and Susan Gray, "Blacks, Whites and 'Race Politics'," *Public Interest* (Winter 1979).

5

underserving blacks who had not worked for them. The wide publicity given to the relatively small number of affirmative action programs instituted by government, by private corporations, and by unions, as well as the publicity given to the Bakke Supreme Court case provided a highly distorted picture of undeserved black gains to many white Americans. This perception offended many white Americans' ethic of fair treatment and led to charges of "racism in reverse." It also provided for many whites a simple and emotionally appealing explanation of one of the principal causes of the economic deterioration that many households were experiencing throughout the 1970s.

Third, many white working-class Americans apparently believed that they paid their taxes for governmental programs that mostly assisted racial minorities. Many whites felt that government spending for welfare and for public education, including school busing, consumed a major share of their tax dollars, and that these expenditures primarily benefited racial minorities. This perception was reinforced by the attention given in the mass media to accusations of welfare chiseling, usually depicting a black family on welfare. The high birth rate among black women on welfare, more a consequence of low income than of race or welfare-recipient status, validated to many whites the undeserving and unproductive nature of the recipients of these programs.

These views were formed through a combination of personal experience and observation, information and misinformation presented in the mass media, and cultural stereotypes passed on from generation to generation in white families and communities. These popular perceptions, which therefore involved a complex mixture of correct and incorrect understandings, accorded at least partly with the results of analyses undertaken by many economists, sociologists, and other social scientists. Many economists, working with massive data sets containing numerous socioeconomic variables broken down by race, concluded that racial discrimination had indeed disappeared by the end of the 1960s. What disagreements there were among economists seemed to concern primarily whether government antidiscrimination efforts or the competitive operation of the marketplace had produced this beneficial change. The neo-classical (that is, market-oriented) economic analysis and its variants that most economists in the United States work with also led them to conclude that working-class Americans indeed were the primary beneficiaries of racism. It therefore followed that black gains of the recent past had taken place at white workers' expense. Finally, conservative economists, who view government activity as generally inherently unproductive and damaging to the efficient workings of markets, proclaimed the desirability of ending government programs that interfered with individual freedom, that substituted one type of racism for another, and that did not help blacks particularly anyway. Both economic theory and econometric investigations thus tended to coincide with and underscore the common public perceptions.

These popular and scientific perceptions do contain some correct insights, and it is understandable why they are held by large segments of the public and the academic community. However, I believe that these perceptions are fundamentally flawed. In this book I sort out what I have found to be correct in these perceptions from what I have found to be incorrect. I present an alternative analysis of: the economic reality concerning the state of racial inequality in the United States today; the importance of class power in economic processes; the relation between racial inequality and class conflict; and the distribution of benefits from attempts to reduce or eliminate racial inequality.

In the chapters that follow I present the following analysis. First, it is true that blacks have made significant gains in recent decades. These changes are most evident in the areas of civil and political rights, in the depiction of blacks in the mass media, and, to a lesser extent, in black representation in elected offices. It is also true that a notable change has taken place in the black class structure. For example, the proportion of blacks employed in professional and managerial occupa-

7

tions rose from 4 percent in 1949 to 12 percent in 1969, while the proportion working in agriculture fell from about 10 percent in 1949 to about 2 percent in 1969.

Nonetheless, economic inequality for most blacks has persisted virtually unchanged in this period. Using black/white earnings ratios as a measure of racial inequality, I find that the last major era of relative gains for blacks in private industry occurred during the 1930s and 1940s, the decades of the formation and growth of the industrial union movement and World War II. Since 1949 the economic position of blacks relative to whites has not changed markedly in industry and in the major metropolitan areas.

This stagnation, I suggest, is associated with the generally stalemated position of the labor movement in private industry since the late 1940s. In this period the labor movement has not increased its strength within the sectors of the economy where it was already entrenched, and it has had very limited success in organizing low-wage sectors where it has traditionally been weak. The high-wage employment sector, moreover, has grown very slowly, while the low-wage sector has increased in relative and absolute size. Limited employment growth in the high-wage sector, where seniority-based promotion systems predominate, has delayed black advancement in those sectors, while blacks and other racial minorities have been disproportionately employed in the faster-growing but lower-wage sector. The slow growth of high-wage employment opportunities itself reflects the political weaknesses of the labor movement and the Left in the United States. Both racial equality and real income levels of most whites would have advanced further if government had been under greater pressure to expand social welfare programs and full-employment economic policy.

Second, it is also true that many economic agents act as if the gains achieved by one individual or group in the economy necessarily come at the expense of another. This behavior mirrors important aspects of American culture: a widespread individualism and narrow group insularity and identification.

8

But the gains of racial minorities, according to my empirical findings, need not and generally do not cause economic losses for most whites in the United States.

Although individualistic action is widespread, collective action among workers is also significant. Consequently, the share and level of income going to labor are not fixed by market forces alone, but depend also on economic and political bargaining processes involving labor, capital, and the state. Greater racial equality and interracial unity among workers therefore can produce gains not only for black workers, but for most white workers as well. I find that large capitalists and elite professionals are the only groups that clearly lose income from advances in racial equality. Moreover, the size of the overall economic pie is not fixed, as it is determined in large part by governmental aggregate economic policy. The institution of the traditional but still unfinished progressive full-employment and welfare-state political agendas would bring gains to blacks and to most whites.

Third, it is also true that government, on the whole and especially at the Federal and non-South state and local levels, has proven to be beneficial to racial minorities in the past two decades. But these gains have not occurred at the expense of most whites. Government employment pays a higher average wage than private industry to both black and white workers, *and* government employment patterns produce a more equitable average black/white earnings ratio than does private industry. Significantly, the state sector is also the main arena of labor movement gains in the postwar era.

Although racial minorities receive a disproportionate share of certain government transfer programs, such as welfare, whites make up the majority of the recipients. And racial minorities receive less than their share of the benefits of many programs, including social security and unemployment compensation, and even less the benefits of public higher education or weapons procurement. Despite the small benefits of tax reductions, the government cutbacks in the 1970s as well as the turn to recessionary aggregate economic policies certainly have

9

hurt minorities and most working-class and middle-class whites.

These propositions have not been wholly absent from political discourse. On the contrary, they comprise an important element in neopopulist thinking. For example, Reuben Askew, the former governor of Florida and a leading Southern politician has stated:

> Because of our persistent preoccupation with race-related issues, we have all too frequently neglected the real economic and environmental problems of the people, black and white alike. In this way, we have not been fair to ourselves. When people are divided against themselves on racial grounds, they have not time to demand a fair shake on taxes, utility bills, consumer protection, government services, environmental preservations, and other problems. In this session of the Florida legislature . . . while the legislature and the news media were focusing attention on the busing debate, lobbyists and special interests were hard at work undermining programs that would put money into people's pockets, that would help protect people and other living things which make Florida a worthwhile place in which to live.
>
> This is probably the greatest reason why the South has been lagging behind other regions on issues such as wages, distribution of the tax burden, health, medical care, and aid to the elderly and others in need. So often when someone attempts to do something about people's needs, the race issue is resurrected in one form or another.[5]

Nonetheless, these concepts remain remarkably absent from scholarly discussion, particularly among neoclassical economists.

My findings are presented and argued in this study according to the following plan. In Chapter 2 I review the long-term trends in racial economic inequality. I find that much of the

[5] Reuben Askew, "Busing Is Not the Issue," *Inequality in Education*, Harvard Graduate School of Education, no. 4 (March 1972), p. 4.

recent improvements in black incomes relative to that of whites reflects cyclical forces and a one-time structural change—the decline of the agrarian South—and that racial inequality has persisted within metropolitan areas and within private industries. This persistence is particularly striking because of the variety of demographic, economic, and political shifts of the past few decades that ought to have exerted a significant upward pressure on the relative incomes of blacks. The persistence of racial inequality in a competitive market economy further presents an anomaly for neoclassical economic analysis.

This suggests a need to look more closely at the analysis of racial inequality presented by economists working with the neoclassical paradigm. I do so in Chapter 3, where I assess the strengths and weaknesses of the various neoclassical approaches, concluding that each of the neoclassical discrimination theories is inadequate. None meets the double test of logical coherence and empirical plausibility.

In Chapter 4 I examine in detail the empirical answer to the important question: Who benefits from racism? This investigation permits a uniform econometric test of the various neoclassical discrimination theories. I develop a crosssectional model to carry out this empirical test. The results, which show that white workers lose and capitalists benefit from racial inequality, go directly against the predictions of the neoclassical theories.

In Chapter 5 I argue that the problems of neoclassical discrimination theories result from more general inadequacies of neoclassical economics. A class conflict approach to economic and political processes can be integrated with market analysis, thereby providing a coherent and superior theory of income distribution in capitalist economies. The divisive effects of racism on worker power at both the microeconomic level of the firm and the macroeconomic level of the entire economy suggests an explanation for the persistence of racial inequality in both competitive and monopsonistic market settings. Unlike neoclassical analysis, this theory is consistent

11

with the econometric evidence that is presented in Chapter 4.

In Chapter 6 I examine the changing historical relation between racial inequality and class conflict since 1865. The historical materials in this chapter provide further motivation and illustration for the hypotheses developed in the theoretical discussion.

In Chapter 7 I discuss some specific mechanisms that link racial inequality with income inequality among whites in the class conflict theory. Two mechanisms, the impact of racial inequality on unionism and on inequality in public services, are testable using the cross-sectional model developed in Chapter 4. The econometric findings indicate that these mechanisms do indeed work to hurt most white workers and benefit capitalists.

Thus, the theoretical, econometric, and historical discussions each lend support to the contention that class conflict plays an important role in economic and political processes in a capitalist economy, and that the economic basis exists for the creation of a broad interracial class alliance opposing racism in all of its forms. The theoretical and public policy implications of these findings and their significance for an era of economic stagnation are discussed further in the closing chapter.

Having outlined the analysis of this book, I also want to emphasize two important limitations of its scope. First, I examine racism here only in the context of the relationship of whites and blacks in the United States. Blacks, however, comprise only one of the racial minorities in this country. In addition to blacks the other racial minorities numerous enough to be recognized and counted by the U.S. Bureau of the Census are Indians, Japanese, Chinese, Filipinos, Koreans, and Hawaiians. These groups together constitute the census category "nonwhite," of which blacks account for about 90 percent. The census now also counts persons of Spanish origin (Mexican, Cuban, Puerto Rican, and so on) as a separate but not racial category.[6] When census enumerators classified His-

---

[6] Race itself has become as much a social as a biological category. In the Slave South, a person with one-eighth African ancestry and seven-eighths

panics into racial categories in 1970, approximately 96 percent were put in the white category.

Each of these groups has a specific history and a distinct present situation. The number of people of Spanish and Asian origin, many of whom are immigrants without proper state documents, has especially increased since the late 1960s. Since the experience of each of these groups differs, I have limited my analysis to blacks only. While I expect that many, but not all, of the conclusions presented here may remain intact with a more inclusive study, I make no claims to have undertaken such an effort. The present focus on blacks is justified not only because blacks comprise the largest racial minority, but also because the development of racism in the United States has been most bound up with the treatment of blacks. Other forms and experiences of racism in the United States must be understood in this primary context.[7]

Second, just as I do not consider the analysis here automatically generalizable to other racial minorities in the United States, I also do not consider it generalizable to race relations in other countries. Racial hostility can be observed throughout much of world history, and it continues to prevail under all sorts of regimes around the world. It frequently intertwines

---

European ancestry was considered black. Whites were required to be pure European. Although such logic has no scientific biological basis, this social definition was adopted by the entire nation and ratified in the courts. It is estimated that over 70 percent of blacks in the United States today have some white ancestry. Present-day census enumerators are instructed to follow community usage in designating persons by race. See Lerone Bennett, *Before the Mayflower* (Baltimore: Penguin Books, 1966), p. 273; Thomas Pettigrew, ed., *Racial Discrimination in the United States* (New York: Harper and Row, 1975), p. xiii.

[7] For examples of recent attempts to analyze the distinctive experience of the Chicano population, see Mario Barrera, *Race and Class in the Southwest* (South Bend, Ind.: Notre Dame University Press); Vernon Briggs et al., *The Chicano Worker* (Austin: University of Texas Press, 1977). For an ambitious recent effort to develop a comparative analysis of racial experiences in the United States, see Ronald Takaki, *Iron Cages: Race and Culture in the Nineteenth Century* (New York: Random House, 1979).

with national and religious conflicts and differences. One thinks, for example, of the experiences of the Jews in Europe, the Irish in the United Kingdom, the ethnic Chinese in Southeast Asia, the Asians in East Africa, the many national minorities in the Soviet Union, and the conflicts between Hindus and Muslims on the subcontinent of India, Pakistan, and Bangladesh. Some of these experiences reflect racial situations that stem from capitalist dynamics, but many have older and different origins.

I will not try to present the full case here, but many historians have demonstrated that modern racism against blacks in the United States did not emerge simply from the age-old patterns of oppression and marginalization of strange outsiders that sociologists frequently discuss in their analyses of racism. Rather, modern racism must be understood as originating in the context of the development of capitalism from the sixteenth century onward. The particular slave system that emerged in the Southern United States then imparted a unique character to race relations in this country.

Modern racism, as opposed to the casual color prejudice and ethnocentricity of ancient and early modern societies, began with the Atlantic slave trade and the European colonization of Africa, Asia, and Latin America. While numerous examples of racial feeling and discrimination can be observed in precapitalist societies, such as ancient Egypt, as well as in Shakespearean England (viz. Othello, the "dark Moor"), these practices differed qualitatively from the systematized oppression of one race by another that came later. Slavery in ancient Greece and Rome, for example, never produced a codified ideology that degraded and marked a person even after being freed from slave status.

On the contrary, under Roman imperialism, first Italians and later members of other conquered provinces were Romanized. They became citizens, intermarried with their Roman conquerors, filled leading positions in the army, and rose to rule in the heart of the empire. People of different ethnic and racial groups commonly could attain high social positions.[8]

In the antebellum United States, by contrast, racism against free blacks became deeply entrenched in the South and the North. And the racial-based slave system granted very limited rights and opportunities to the slaves.[9] Prejudice and economic factors interacted in determining the early development of slavery in the American colonies. Both economic and ideological factors have been employed to explain the greater brutality of racism that existed in the United States as compared with developments in other parts of the New World.[10]

Modern racism thus developed with the European colonization of the rest of the world and the subsequent systematic class

[8] On slavery and racism in antiquity, see Moses Finley, "A Critique of David Brion Davis," in Laura Foner and Eugene Genovese, eds., *Slavery in the New World* (Englewood Cliffs, New Jersey: Prentice-Hall, 1969); E. A. Brunt, "Reflections on British and Roman Imperialism," *Comparative Studies in Society and History* (1965); Gail Omvedt, "Towards a Theory of Colonialism," *Insurgent Sociologist* (Spring 1973). On the history and development of attitudes toward slavery, see David Brion Davis, *The Problem of Slavery in Western Culture* (New York: Pantheon, 1969), and Winthrop Jordan, *White Over Black* (Baltimore: Penguin Books, 1968).

Slavery within Africa also contrasts with slavery within the United States. While slavery and freedom were opposite concepts in the United States, African slavery commonly permitted substantial lifetime or intergenerational social mobility and also involved a continuum in rights-in-persons between slavery and kinship. See Suzanne Miers and Igor Kopytoff, eds., *Slavery in Africa: Historical and Anthropological Perspectives* (Madison: University of Wisconsin Press, 1977).

[9] Racism in the antebellum North is documented in Leon Litwack, *North of Slavery* (New York: Knopf, 1960). The developmental relationship between slavery, racism, and the early emergence of capitalism is discussed in Eric Williams, *Capitalism and Slavery* (New York: Capricorn, 1966); Jordan, *White Over Black*; Edmund Morgan, *American Slavery, American Freedom* (New York: Norton, 1975). Morgan and Jordan go beyond earlier debates between Oscar Handlin and Carl Degler over whether slavery caused racism or racism caused slavery; a less satisfying discussion is in Oliver Cox, *Caste, Class, and Race* (New York: Monthly Review Press, 1968).

[10] See Eugene Genovese, "The Treatment of Slaves in Different Countries," in Laura Foner and Eugene A. Genovese, eds., *Slavery in the New World*.

15

domination of people of color. Race became a central justification of the colonial system ("the white man's burden") and
the basis for the formation of class in the colonies. In North
America the clearing away of the native "Indian" population
as well as the enslavement of Africans for plantation labor led
to the transformation of previously casual racial prejudices
into a systematized and codified ideology and practice of racial
subordination of blacks. Racism in the United States origi-
nated under circumstances that produced more restrictions on
post-Emancipation blacks than on blacks living elsewhere in
the Caribbean or Latin America. The specific original conditions and the subsequent historical dynamics that perpetuated
racism (to be discussed here in Chapter 6) suggest both the
importance of understanding black-white relations in the
context of capitalist development in the United States and the
limited generality of this experience.

CHAPTER TWO

The Persistence of Racial Economic Inequality in the United States

INTRODUCTION

IN 1918, as World War I was drawing to a close, the U.S. Bureau of Labor Statistics published a report summarizing "The Economic and Social Progress of the Negro Population."[1] After extensively reviewing recent trends in the status of blacks, the authors of the report concluded that much progress had been made. Of course, complacency was not warranted, for too much inequality remained. But despair was equally unwarranted, for the progress attained in racial equality was expected to continue in succeeding decades. The next year a series of race riots swept across major cities of the United States.

In 1944, a quarter of a century later, and near the close of World War II, the Carnegie Commission published a major review of the position of blacks: Gunnar Myrdal's massive *An American Dilemma, The Negro Problem and Modern Democracy*. Myrdal's assessment was even more optimistic than the 1918 Bureau of Labor Statistics report. As he wrote in 1962, on the occasion of the reprinting of *An American Dilemma*: "The most important conclusion of my study was, however, that an era of more than half a century during which there had been no fundamental change was approaching its close . . . . 'Not since Reconstruction has there been more reason to anticipate fundamental changes in American race relations,

---

[1] Cited in Rashi Fein and Stephan Michelson, "Social and Economic Conditions of Negroes in the United States—A Critique," *Washington Post*, 14 January 1968.

changes which will involve a development towards American ideals.' "[2]

In 1967, a quarter of a century later and two more wars after the publication of *An American Dilemma*, the Bureau of Labor Statistics issued another report summarizing "The Social and Economic Conditions of Negroes in the United States." This report contains virtually the same assessment and the same language as the bureau's report that was published nearly fifty years earlier: "The facts in this report thus show a mixture of sound and substantial progress, on the one hand, and large unfulfilled needs on the other. They do not warrant complacency. Neither do they justify pessimism or despair."[3] The same year a massive black rebellion took place in Detroit. And in 1968, in the week following the assassination of Martin Luther King, Jr., black protest riots swept across most major cities of the United States.

Since 1918 race relations have changed enormously, and for the better in many respects. The reenfranchisement of black voters and the outlawing of Jim Crow segregationist laws come to mind as the most dramatic achievements. The moderation of white racist attitudes and improvements in black cultural representation seem equally visible and important.

In spite of these gains, racism, the systematic subordination of one race, remains a major problem in the United States. Economic indices show that the cautious optimism expressed in the Bureau of Labor Statistics reports and in *An American Dilemma* has proved unfounded. Instead of narrowing, important racial income differentials in the United States have persisted throughout the twentieth century. Despite the optimistic expectations of progress, the median income of black families in 1978 remained at only 57 percent of that of white families. That is, the median income of blacks was at approximately the same relative level found in the early 1950s and

[2] Gunnar Myrdal, *An American Dilemma, The Negro Problem and Modern Democracy* (New York: Harper & Row, 1962), p. xxiii.
[3] Bulletin no. 332 (Washington, D.C.: U.S. Government Printing Office, 1967), p. xii.

remarkably close to estimates of black-white income ratios in 1900.[4] Racial income inequality is still very much with us.

Despite the persistence of racial income differentials, documented in detail in this chapter, much of the public and many professional economists believe that American blacks made substantial economic gains relative to whites in the 1950s and 1960s. After all, in these decades considerable public attention and policy was directed at the elimination of racial inequalities. Not only do many economists agree that racial discrimination has diminished substantially, especially since the mid-1960s, but some economists have even claimed that racial discrimination had already disappeared from much of economic life in the United States by the early 1970s.[5] A recent debate thus focused not on whether a major movement toward racial economic equality had occurred, but rather on whether

---

[4] U.S. Bureau of the Census, *Income of Families and Persons in The United States* P-60 Series; see also Table 2.8. For 1900 estimates see Roger Ransom and Richard Sutch, "Growth and Welfare in the American South," *Explorations in Economic History* (January 1979).

[5] Studies that find substantial declines in racial discrimination or inequality include: James Gwartney, "Changes in the Nonwhite/White Income Ratio— 1939–67," *American Economic Review* (December 1970); Leonard Weiss and Jeffrey Williamson, "Black Education, Earnings and Inter-regional Migration: Some New Evidence," *American Economic Review* (June 1972); Richard Freeman, "The Changing Labor Market for Black Americans," *Brookings Papers on Economic Activity* (Summer 1973); Finis Welch, "Black-White Differences in Returns to Schooling," *American Economic Review* (March 1973); Joan Haworth, James Gwartney, and Charles Haworth, "Earnings, Productivity and Changes in Employment Discrimination during the 1960s," *American Economic Review* (March 1975); Stanley Masters, *Black-White Income Differentials* (New York: Academic Press, 1975); Wayne Vroman, "Changes in the Labor Market Position of Black Men Since 1964," *Proceedings of the Twenty-Seventh Annual Winter Meeting*, Industrial Relations Research Association, Madison (1975); James Smith and Finis Welch, "Black-White Male Wage Ratios: 1960–1970," *American Economic Review* (June 1977); Richard Freeman, *Black Elite: The New Market for Highly Qualified Black Americans* (New York: McGraw-Hill, 1977); Richard Freeman, "Black Economic Progress Since 1964," *Public Interest* (Summer 1978). Among these authors Freeman and Smith and Welch are the most assertive in claiming that racial discrimination has largely disappeared.

19

competitive market pressures or government actions caused the improvement.[6]

In this chapter I examine the evidence concerning the principal trends in racial income inequality in the United States. I begin by looking at the long-run trends since 1865. Next, I turn to the period since the Second World War in order to examine the relative importance of cyclical and secular forces on fluctuations in racial income inequality and trends within regions, urban areas, and individual industries.

On the basis of this review I conclude that racial inequalities and racial discrimination are indeed persisting in the United States. Major changes have occurred in the black class structure—most notable is the decline of blacks as an agararian class of small-holding and tenant farmers and their incorporation into the urban working class and professional and managerial strata. But these developments, registered in the changing occupational composition of the black labor force, have occurred in a manner that has not eliminated racial inequality, but instead has reproduced it in a new setting.

The persistence of racial inequality is particularly striking because of the strong forces that have been working in recent decades to equalize black and white incomes in the United States. In the final section of this chapter, these significant equalizing forces are discussed, and I conclude that the per-

---

[6] See Freeman, "The Changing Labor Market"; Vroman, "Changes in the Labor Market Position"; and Bernard Anderson and Phyllis Wallace, "Public Policy and Black Economic Progress: A Review of the Evidence," *American Economic Review* (May 1975). These authors argue that government antidiscrimination efforts have been effective. For criticisms of this view, see Robert Flanagan, "Actual vs. Potential Impact of Government Antidiscrimination Programs," *Industrial and Labor Relations Review* (July 1976); Smith and Welch, "Black-White Male Wage Ratios"; and Richard Butler and James Heckman, "The Government's Impact on the Labor Market Status of Black Americans: A Critical Review," in Leonard Hausman et al., eds., *Equal Rights and Industrial Relations* (Madison: Industrial Relations Research Association, 1977). Butler and Heckman provide a valuable survey of these and many other empirical studies of government impact on racial income inequalities.

sistence of racial inequality in the face of such pressures poses a major anomaly for conventional explanations of racial inequality.

A CENTURY OF INEQUALITY: THE LONG-RUN TRENDS

The Census Bureau began to collect income data by race only in 1946. For prior periods, particularly before 1890, one must rely on two kinds of data: scattered and incomplete records of racial wage and occupational differentials over time, and the more systematic decennial census reports of the distributions of whites and blacks across occupations.

The most striking story that the scattered records tell us about the period from 1865 to 1890 concerns the economic decline in the status of skilled blacks. Prior to Emancipation slaves had performed most of the skilled craft work in building and other trades in the South. Consequently, black workers comprised 100,000 of the 120,000 Southern artisans in 1865.[7] In the next several decades these black artisans were pushed out of or excluded from the skilled crafts, particularly in the building trades and on the railroads.[8] When new craft occupa-

[7] Charles Wesley, *The Negro Laborer* (New York, 1924), p. 142; W.E.B. DuBois, *The Negro Artisan* (Atlanta, 1902), pp. 115–120.

Slaves worked as blacksmiths, carpenters, masons, bricklayers, painters, shoemakers and harness makers. Slaves also worked in mines, iron and textile mills, and on steamboats and railroads. Many free blacks in Southern cities were employed as skilled artisans, even though in the North they were excluded from most of the skilled trades. However, after 1830 in the South, competition from a growing white urban population forced blacks out of many skilled jobs. See Richard Wade, *Slavery in the Cities* (New York, 1964), p. 275; Robert Starobin, *Industrial Slavery in the Old South* (New York: Oxford University Press, 1970); Claudia Goldin, *Urban Slavery in the American South 1820–1860* (Chicago: University of Chicago Press, 1976). See also the comments on Goldin's book as well as comments on immigration in Gavin Wright, *The Political Economy of the Cotton South* (New York: Norton, 1978), pp. 121–123.

[8] Arthur Ross, "The Negro in the American Economy," in Arthur Ross and Herbert Hill, eds., *Employment, Race and Poverty* (New York: Harcourt Brace Jovanovich, 1967), p. 10.

21

tions developed, such as that of electricians, few blacks obtained entry.[9] The number of black artisans declined both absolutely and relatively; by 1890 black workers comprised probably less than one-fifth of all Southern artisans.[10] And when the "New South" began to industrialize, beginning about 1880, blacks were excluded from many manufacturing industries, most notably that of cotton textiles.

In agriculture, where most blacks were still located, the slave labor system was replaced by an oppressive tenant and sharecropping system. Crop liens and other debt burdens became the new mechanisms that maintained black dependency on white landlords and merchants.[11] Although blacks were no longer property, thirty years after Emancipation their incomes had not significantly risen above subsistence; one writer estimated the cash value of the freedom for blacks in 1890 at less than a dollar per year.[12]

After the defeat of the interracial Southern Populist movement in the 1890s, the South developed a system of elaborate racial controls. In the 1890s Jim Crow legislation imposing segregation was instituted in all the Southern states, and between 1890 and 1910 black voters were disfranchised throughout the South. Blacks were excluded from all but the

---

[9] Richard Freeman, unpublished manuscript.

[10] Computed from Sterling Spero and Abram Harris, *The Black Worker* (New York: Atheneum, 1968), Tables 8–9, pp. 159–160, and based on U.S. census data.

[11] The sources for this period include C. Vann Woodward, *Origins of the New South, 1877–1913* (Baton Rouge: Louisiana State University Press, 1951); C. Vann Woodward, *The Strange Career of Jim Crow* (New York: Galaxy, 1966); Harold Baron, "The Demand for Black Labor: Historical Notes on the Political Economy of Racism," *Radical America* (March–April 1971); W.E.B. DuBois, *Black Reconstruction in America, 1860–1880* (New York: Harcourt Brace Jovanovich, 1935); Roger Ransom and Richard Sutch, *One Kind of Freedom* (New York: Cambridge University Press, 1977; and Jonathan Wiener, *Social Origins of the New South* (Baton Rouge: Louisiana State University Press, 1978). See Chapter 6 of the present study for a detailed discussion of this period.

[12] Cited in Woodward, *Origins of the New South*, pp. 208–209.

most menial jobs in the new factories, while Ku Klux Klan activity and the lynchings of blacks reached an all-time high. Racism became the keystone in the arch of the new social order of the South.[13]

Census Occupational Trends

In 1890 the census began collecting occupational data by race. Consequently, for the period since 1890, racial trends can be followed by using the decennial census data on occupations. These data are presented in Table 2.1. As the table shows, 61 percent of black men in 1890 were concentrated in agriculture, while 90 percent of black women were concentrated in agriculture and in domestic service. These concentrations have changed dramatically since 1890. By 1970 only 5 percent of black men worked in agriculture and 77 percent worked in blue collar or service occupations; and in 1970 only 19 percent of black women worked in agriculture or domestic service, while 49 percent worked in clerical, sales, and service occupations.

These shifts in occupational composition can be evaluated quantitatively and compared to the corresponding shifts for whites by constructing a summary statistic of the economic differences suggested by the relative occupational positions of black and white workers. A convenient index of occupational status takes the mean income in an occupation, compares the proportion of black and white workers in that occupation, and averages the results for all occupations. This index is defined by the formula:

$$I_t = \sum_i w_{it} \cdot y_i / \sum_i b_{it} \cdot y_i$$

where　w_{it} = percentage of whites in occupation i,
　　　　b_{it} = percentage of blacks in occupation i,
　　　　y_i = mean income of whites in occupation i,
　　　　　　in the base year

---

[13] In addition to the references cited in note 11, see Morgan Kousser, *The Shaping of Southern Politics, 1880–1910* (New Haven: Yale University Press, 1974).

TABLE 2.1   Occupational Distribution of Blacks in the
Labor Force, 1890–1970

Occupation	1890	1910	1930	1950	1970
Male					
Professional and managerial	.01	.02	.03	.04	.09
Clerical and sales	.01	.01	.02	.04	.10
Crafts	.03	.04	.05	.08	.15
Operatives	.07	.06	.13	.22	.30
Laborers	.20	.21	.23	.24	.16
Household workers	.05	.03	.02	.01	.00
Service workers	.02	.06	.09	.14	.16
Farmers	.26	.26	.23	.14	.01
Farm workers	.35	.32	.21	.11	.04
Female					
Professional and managerial	.01	.02	.03	.06	.13
Clerical and sales	.00	.00	.01	.05	.23
Crafts	.00	.00	.00	.01	.01
Operatives	.03	.02	.04	.15	.17
Laborers	.04	.00	.02	.02	.02
Household workers	.46	.39	.54	.42	.18
Service workers	.02	.04	.09	.19	.26
Farmers	.05	.04	.04	.02	.00
Farm workers	.39	.48	.23	.08	.01

SOURCES: U.S. Bureau of the Census, *Negro Population, 1790–1915* (1918);
U.S. *Census of the Population*, various years.

This useful index does contain some inherent imperfections.
Its main weakness arises from the abstraction in racial differences in pay within occupations. These within-occupation
differentials lower the index and might change its trend over
time. The index will also be affected by the choice of base year
used to obtain mean incomes in an occupation and by the

degree of detail employed in the occupational data. For these reasons, it is useful to compute the index with a variety of detailed techniques.

Table 2.2 presents the indices for males for each decennial year since 1890, as computed by three alternative methods. Each of the indices exhibits a similar trend: no relative progress for blacks occurred between 1890 and 1940, but there has been a modicum of improvement in more recent decades.[14] Between 1890 and 1910 rapid industrial growth occurred in both the South and the nation as a whole. However, very little of this industrial expansion provided employment for blacks. The burgeoning North absorbed a net immigration of 4.1 million persons during these two decades, and total national employment in mining, manufacturing, and construction increased from 6.3 million in 1890 to 10.3 million in 1910. But nearly all of the growth in industrial employment for blacks—from 208,000 in 1890 to 693,000 in 1910—occurred in the South, and was restricted largely to railroading, lumbering, coal mining, and other nonfactory-type work, usually in rural areas.[15]

Although blacks made some gains during the prosperous years of World War I, these were erased during the depression era of the 1930s. The greatest gains occurred during the labor shortages of World War II, when numerous manufacturing jobs were opened to blacks for the first time. Apart from that decade of improvement, however, these occupational data suggest a rather small narrowing of racial differentials during the first half of the twentieth century.

Residential segregation indices also suggest the persistence of racial inequality in the United States. It has been shown that residential segregation primarily results from racial discrimination.[16] Changes in segregation, therefore, provide an im-

[14] The different trends in the three indices reported in Table 2.2 result from the variation in the number of occupational categories. The more detailed the categories, the more the index will reflect movement *within* broad occupations.

[15] Ross, "The Negro in the American Economy"; Baron, "The Demand for Black Labor," p. 16.

[16] See Masters, *Black-White Income Differentials*, Chapter 2. See also my discussion in Chapter 7.

TABLE 2.2 The Occupational Position of Black Men Relative to White Men

	1890	1900	1910	1920	1930	1940	1950	1960	1970
North	—	—	.73	—	—	.74	.77	—	—
South	—	—	.67	—	—	.63	.65	—	—
	—	—	.78	.78	.78	.78	.81	.82	—
	.68	.69	.68	.71	.72	.68	.77	.80	.86

SOURCES: First two rows from Gary Becker, *The Economics of Discrimination*, p. 113, Table 16. Becker used three occupational categories and 1939 income weights. Third row from Dale Hiestand, *Economic Growth and Employment Opportunities for Minorities*, 1964, p. 53. Hiestand used seven occupational categories and 1949 income weights. Fourth row from Richard Freeman, "Long Term Changes in Black Labor Market Status," mimeographed (Harvard University, 1972), Table 9.2; Richard Freeman, *Black Elite*, 1977, p. 5, Table 2. Freeman used ninety occupational categories and 1959 income weights.

portant indication of changes in racism in American society as a whole.

The available data suggest that residential segregation by race has increased in most American cities since 1940, the earliest year for which indices of residential segregation by city have been computed. According to the Bureau of the Census, residential segregation increased in most large cities between 1940 and 1950, declined modestly in the North (but not in the South) between 1950 and 1960, and rose again in both regions during the 1960s. Between 1960 and 1967 both the number and the proportion of blacks living in census tracts that were predominantly black in 1960 rose in the cities surveyed by special censuses. At the same time, the number and proportion of whites rose in tracts that were already predominantly white in 1960.[17] And the trend revealed in the 1970 census seems to be toward more, not less, residential segregation by race. Residential segregation increased most in the 1960s in the largest metropolitan areas. These cities contain the greatest number of blacks as well as the highest proportion of blacks in the total population.[18]

[17] "In New Haven, for example, the Negro population in slum neighborhoods grew by nearly 30 percent between 1960 and mid-decade, while the remainder of the slum population fell by nearly the same percentage. In Louisville, the rates were $+12$ percent and -15 percent respectively." See Thomas Vietorisz and Bennet Harrison, *The Economic Development of Harlem* (New York: Praeger, 1970), pp. 59–60. See also U.S. Bureau of the Census, *Current Population Reports*, P-20 Series, no. 168, p. 1; P-23 Series, no. 19, p. 3; and P-60 Series, no. 61, p. 4; and Table E as well as Karl and Alma Taeuber, *Negroes in Cities: Residential Segregation and Neighborhood Change* (Chicago: Aldine, 1965).

[18] See Ann Schnare, "Residential Segregation by Race in U.S. Metropolitan Areas: An Analysis Across Cities and Over Time" (Washington, D.C.: Urban Institute, 1977); Annemette Sorenson, Karl Taeuber, and Leslie Hollingsworth, "Indexes of Racial Residential Segregation for 109 Cities in the United States, 1940 to 1970" *Sociological Focus* (April 1975); Thomas Van Valey, Wade Clark Roof, and Jerome Wilcox, "Trends in Residential Segregation, 1960–1970" *American Journal of Sociology* (January 1977). Valey et al. point out a downward bias in the trend indicated by Sorenson et al., introduced by the inclusion of numerous small Standard Metropolitan Statistical Areas in the Sorenson sample.

27

POSTWAR PATTERNS OF RACIAL INEQUALITY

Since World War II the Census Bureau has collected detailed income data by race to supplement the limited information given by occupational statistics. Two main sources constitute the main data base used by researchers. First, the decennial census contains a rich mine of disaggregated data; the decadal changes provide the best clues to long-term trends. Second, the annual income reports collected from data in the Current Population Survey sample contain valuable information on year-to-year fluctuations in racial income differences.

Decennial Census Trends

The decennial censuses from 1950 to 1970 give us a substantial basis for evaluating postwar patterns of racial inequality. Among the significant trends in this period, we can discern the following positive major changes in the relative economic status of nonwhites.

1. Nonwhite-white annual median income ratios rose between 1950 and 1970: from .54 to .64 for families, from .54 to .60 for males, and from .40 to .92 for females.[19]

2. Racial income differences narrowed *within* every age cohort, and by 1970 the historic pattern of widening racial income differences as a specific cohort grew older was no longer apparent.[20]

3. A number of econometric studies found that historic racial differences in the economic returns to schooling had been largely eliminated among young adults by the early 1970s.[21]

[19] U.S. Bureau of the Census, *Census of the Population, 1950 and 1970*.

[20] Freeman, "The Changing Labor Market"; Smith and Welch, "Black-White Male Wage Ratios." See also Robert Strauss and Francis Horvath, "Wage Rate Differences by Race and Sex in the U.S. Labour Market: 1960–1970," *Economica* (August 1976). However, a study by Saul Hoffman using longitudinal data found that earnings differences between comparable young black and white workers *grew* between 1967 and 1974. See Saul Hoffman, "Black-White Life Cycle Earnings Differences and the Vintage Hypothesis: A Longitudinal Analysis," *American Economic Review* (December 1979).

[21] Weiss and Williamson, "Black Education, Earnings and Inter-regional Migration"; Welch, "Black-White Differences in Returns to Schooling."

28

4. The proportion of blacks employed in professional, managerial, and clerical occupations increased dramatically, while the proportion employed in agriculture and domestic service decreased just as dramatically. These shifts occurred at a more rapid rate among blacks than among whites.

One simple statistical comparison suggests the enormous occupational changes that have taken place for black women. As recently as 1960, 49 percent of employed nonwhite women forty-five years of age and over worked as domestics, while 5 percent worked in clerical and sales occupations. By 1972 the occupational distribution for employed nonwhite women twenty-five years of age *and under* had exactly reversed. Only 5 percent of these women worked as domestics and 47 percent worked in clerical and sales occupations.[22]

The growth of black professionals and managers is indicated by the following data: 4.1 percent of nonwhite men and 6.8 percent of nonwhite women worked in professional, technical, and managerial categories in 1950; by 1970 these percentages had increased to 12.5 (8.9 among blacks only) and 12.8 percent, respectively.[23]

Numerous government press releases and reports have pointed to these advances as evidence of the easing of racism in the United States. In 1970, for example, Daniel Moynihan wrote his notorious "benign neglect" memorandum to President Richard Nixon; Moynihan claimed that "in quantitative terms, which are reliable, the American Negro is making extraordinary progress."[24] These alleged gains justified "benign neglect" by the Nixon administration to the situation of

[22] Derived from unpublished records of the Bureau of Labor Statistics and from U.S. Bureau of the Census, *Census of the Population, 1960*, U.S. Summary, PC(1)-ID, Table 204, as cited in Sar Levitan et al., *Still a Dream* (Cambridge: Harvard University Press, 1975), Table 3-3, p. 47.

[23] Computed from *Census of the Population, 1950 and 1970*.

[24] Daniel P. Moynihan, "Memo to Nixon on the Status of Negroes, January 16, 1970," *New York Times*, 1 March 1970. See also U.S. Department of Labor, Bureau of Labor Statistics, *The Social and Economic Status of Negroes in the United States, 1970*, Report no. 394 (Washington, D.C.: U.S. Government Printing Office, 1971).

29

black Americans. Once again a view was being expressed that racial inequality was soon coming to an end.

Such optimistic conclusions are not warranted by the data. The statistics presented above require qualification, for they exaggerate both the recent improvements in the relative position of blacks and the prospects for continued gains in coming years.

First, the growth of black professionals and managers has occurred primarily among the lowest-paying categories in these highly heterogeneous occupational groups and was concentrated heavily in public employment. Thus, in 1970 health technicians, nurses, precollege teachers, social workers, and vocational counselors accounted for 63 percent of all blacks in professional and technical occupations.[25] In 1970 only 1.7 percent of private sector salaried managers and administrators were black; two-thirds of black managers and administrators earned less than $10,000 in 1970, as compared to one-third of white managers.[26]

Second, the apparent gains for black women relative to white women should be evaluated in the context of both the continuing decline since 1940 in the earnings of white females relative to those of males and continuing racial differences among women in yearly hours worked as well as years in the paid labor force.[27]

Third, while relative improvements have occurred for black college graduates, comparable gains have not occurred for blacks with much less schooling. Racial differentials in unemployment and male labor force participation rates have widened since the early 1950s, suggesting that a substantial

[25] Computed from U.S. *Census of the Population, 1970*, U.S. Summary, Detailed Characteristics, Table 223.

[26] Levitan et al., *Still a Dream*, p. 163.

[27] Between 1949 and 1967 median nonwhite female incomes grew by 153 percent, median white female incomes by 81 percent, and median white male incomes by 136 percent. For racial differences between annual and hourly earnings gaps among women, see Alan King, "Labor Market Discrimination Against Black Women," *Review of Black Political Economy* (Summer 1978).

segment of the black population is falling further behind whites and more privileged blacks.

However, the most telling and serious evidence against the view that racial equality is in sight comes from consideration of the cyclical fluctuations that account for much of the observed improvements and from sectoral disaggregation of the national data that seem to show improved racial income ratios from 1950 to 1970. How much of the relative improvement registered by blacks between 1950 and 1970 reflects the effects of black migration out of the rural South to urban and northern areas? After all, it is in the rural South where the absolute and the relative income levels of blacks are lowest. How important are these intersectoral movements in relation to such other changes as business cycle fluctuations, changes within regions, metropolitan areas, and industries and changes in the degree of racial discrimination in the labor market? In the remainder of this section I take up these questions, turning first to estimates from annual data in order to consider the importance of cyclical fluctuations, and next to new calculations of racial trends in which I use heretofore unexamined sectorally disaggregated data. These innovations cast an entirely different light on the literature of racial inequality, for they indicate continuity rather than change in the structure of racial inequality for males in the postwar period.

Annual Income Data

For the postwar period median income data by race are available on an annual basis. Table 2.3 presents a convenient summary statistic, that is, the ratio of nonwhite median incomes to white median incomes, for families and for males and females separately, for the years 1945 to 1977. As Table 2.3 shows, in the postwar period this ratio for families has fluctuated between a low of .51 and a high of .65 and has averaged about .57. The same ratio for males has fluctuated between .47 and .63, averaging .56; the ratio for females has fluctuated between .46 and .92, averaging .71. Both upward trends and business cycle influences appear in Table 2.3. However, as I

31

TABLE 2.3   Ratio of Nonwhite to White Median Income
United States, 1945–1977

Year	Nonwhite Families	Black Families	Nonwhite Males	Nonwhite Females
1945	.56		n.a.	n.a.
1946	.59		.61	n.a.
1947	.51		.54	n.a.
1948	.53		.54	.49
1949	.51		.49	.51
1950	.54		.54	.49
1951	.53		.55	.46
1952	.57		.55	n.a.
1953	.56		.55	.59
1954	.56		.50	.55
1955	.55		.53	.54
1956	.53		.52	.58
1957	.54		.53	.58
1958	.51		.50	.59
1959	.52		.47	.62
1960	.55		.53	.70
1961	.53		.52	.67
1962	.53		.49	.67
1963	.53		.52	.67
1964	.56	.54	.57	.70
1965	.55	.54	.54	.73
1966	.60	.58	.55	.76
1967	.62	.59	.59	.78
1968	.63	.60	.61	.79
1969	.63	.61	.59	.85
1970	.64	.61	.60	.92
1971	.63	.60	.61	.90
1972	.62	.59	.62	.95
1973	.60	.58	.63	.93
1974	.64	.60	.63	.92
1975	.65	.61	.63	.92
1976	.63	.59	.63	.95
1977	.61	.57	.61	.88

SOURCE: U.S. Bureau of the Census, "Income of Families and Persons in the United States," *Current Population Reports*, P-60 Series (Washington, D.C.: U.S. Government Printing Office, various years).

have already suggested, disaggregation of these data are called for before a final conclusion can be reached.

The fluctuating pattern of relative nonwhite incomes of families and males in Table 2.3 correlates with each postwar business cycle. The nonwhite to white family median incomes ratio fell during the recession of 1953–1954, rose slightly during the mid–1950s, and then fell sharply during the 1957–1959 recession. Another upward movement in the ratio occurred until 1960, when the recession began, but by 1961 the ratio had fallen once again to .53. Then, during the long expansion that began in 1963, nonwhite incomes rose continually relative to white incomes particularly following the military buildup for the Vietnam War in 1966 and the urban rebellions. The ratio remained stationary at .62 during the late 1960s, rose again during the expansion years of the early 1970s, and fell in the ensuing recession. Median incomes of nonwhite families and males have risen relative to those of whites during economic expansions and have fallen during economic downturns.

The figures presented in Table 2.3 refer to ratios of annual money income. The census-defined concept of money income includes wage and salary earnings, earnings from self-employment in a small business, property income in the form of dividends, interest, and rent (but not capital gains), as well as government transfer payments such as welfare, unemployment compensation, and social security. Consideration of trends in relative earnings is of special interest. Median wage and salary earnings data of year-round full-time workers exhibit roughly the same patterns that are found for the income data in Table 2.3. Relative earnings trends for all workers also exhibit a similar pattern, although the growth rate is slightly lower.[28]

These patterns of change among the various income concepts are similar but not identical. The median income ratio is more sensitive to changes in the middle of the respective black and white income distributions, where earnings of full-time

[28] U.S. Bureau of the Census, "Incomes of Families and Persons," P-60 Series, various years.

TABLE 2.4 Ratio of Nonwhite to White Unemployment and Labor Force Participation Rates, 1948–1978

	(1) $\dfrac{UE_{NW}}{UE}$	(2) $\dfrac{1 - UE_{NW}}{1 - UE_W}$	(3)^a $\dfrac{LFPR_{NW}}{LFPR_W}$	(4) $= (3) \times (2)$
1948	1.69	0.98	1.01	0.99
1949	1.59	0.97	1.01	0.98
1950	1.84	0.96	0.99	0.95
1951	1.71	0.98	1.00	0.98
1952	1.93	0.97	1.01	0.98
1953	1.81	0.98	1.00	0.98
1954	1.98	0.95	1.00	0.95
1955	2.23	0.95	1.00	0.95
1956	2.31	0.95	0.99	0.94
1957	2.08	0.95	0.99	0.94
1958	2 07	0.93	1.00	0.93
1959	2.23	0.94	1.00	0.94
1960	2.08	0.94	1.00	0.94
1961	2.07	0.93	0.99	0.92
1962	2.22	0.94	0.98	0.92
1963	2.16	0.94	0.98	0.92
1964	2.09	0.95	0.99	0.94
1965	1.98	0.96	0.99	0.95
1966	2.21	0.96	0.98	0.94
1967	2.18	0.96	0.97	0.93
1968	2.09	0.96	0.97	0.93
1969	2.06	0.97	0.96	0.93
1970	1.82	0.96	0.96	0.92
1971	1.83	0.95	0.94	0.89
1972	2.00	0.95	0.93	0.88
1973	2.07	0.96	0.93	0.89
1974	1.98	0.95	0.92	0.87
1975	1.78	0.93	0.91	0.85
1976	1.87	0.93	0.90	0.84
1977	2.11	0.93	0.90	0.84
1978	2.29	0.92	0.92^b	0.85

Males only, civilian population sixteen years and older.
[b] October 1978.

SOURCES: U.S. Department of Labor, *Employment and Training Report of the President* (Washington, D.C.: U.S. Government Printing Office, 1976), Tables A-4, A-18; U.S. Department of Labor, *Handbook of Labor Statistics* (Washington, D.C.: U.S. Government Printing Office, 1978), Tables 4, 5b; *Monthly Labor Review* (July 1979), Table 4; *Employment and Earnings*, (November 1979), Table A-4.

workers tend to be the dominant income source, than to changes in the tails of the distribution, where government transfers and property income become more significant income sources. Consequently, median income and median earnings series tend to change in the same way.

However, simultaneous changes in the structure of the black earnings distribution have permitted the median black-white earnings ratio to grow slightly more rapidly than the income ratio. There are two factors at work here. The growth of a black professional and managerial stratum at a rate exceeding that of whites has pulled up the racial earnings ratio from the top. At the same time, a worsening of racial differentials in unemployment and labor force participation rates (see Tables 2.4) reduced to zero the earnings of many blacks who were at the bottom of the income distribution. A consequent exit from the labor market of the lowest-earning segment of black workers imparted an upward push to the trend of black median earnings.

The effects of labor demand and transfer payments on inequality are worthy of further examination. Discrimination and low demand for black labor have kept relatively more black workers out of jobs and discouraged their job search efforts. Column 1 of Table 2.4 shows that the relative unemployment rate of nonwhites worsened during the early 1950s, while column 3 shows a similar worsening since about 1966 in the nonwhite to white ratio of male labor force participation rates. (Although they are not shown in the table, relative female labor force participation rates declined even more rapidly, from about 1.5 in 1948 to 1.1 in 1974.) The cumulative effect of these developments on the relative proportion of the employed in the nonwhite and white adult populations is shown in column 4. Since 1948 the proportion of the adult population working for a wage or salary has declined more rapidly among nonwhites.

Butler and Heckman have argued that the decline in the black labor force participation rate is explained by the growth of transfer payments.[29] However, since Butler and Heckman do not control for changes in the demand for black labor, they cannot compellingly establish their asserted direction of causation. A demand-driven explanation of falling participation trends is in fact more consistent with the observations that the relative growth of transfer payments has been small in magnitude and that it occurred after the decline in participation rates. Moreover, welfare expenditures are related inversely to the level of economic activity, indicating, therefore, that welfare status often represents a response to inadequate demand for labor.

Changes in family structure can also be investigated for their effect on the family income patterns that are reported in Table 2.3. As Table 2.5 indicates, the proportion of families that are maintained by women has grown among whites from 8.7 percent in 1960 to 11.5 percent in 1978; but the comparable figures are 22.4 percent for nonwhites in 1960 and 39.2 percent for blacks in 1978. This development lowers the reported median income of nonwhite families because of the lower average income levels of women. At the same time, the more rapid growth in labor force participation among white women as compared to black women has produced a more rapid growth in the number of white families where both husband and wife earn a wage or salary.[30] This development raises the

[29] Butler and Heckman, "Government's Impact."

[30] As compared to the number of families with one or more earners, the percentage of black families with two or more earners fell from 63.9 in 1969 to 56.6 in 1977, while the percentage of white families with two or more earners rose from 58.4 to 62.8. Calculated from U.S. Bureau of the Census, "Income of Families and Persons," P-60 Series, no. 75, December 1970, Table 23; no. 101, January 1976, Table 37; no. 118, March 1979, Table 26.

TABLE 2.5   Proportion of Black and White Families
Maintained by Women, 1960–1978[a]

	Black	White
1960	22.4[b]	8.7
1965	23.7[b]	9.0
1970	28.3	9.0
1975	35.3	10.5
1978	39.2	11.5

[a] Formerly labeled by the census as female-headed households.
[b] Blacks and other races.

SOURCE: U.S. Bureau of the Census, "Household and Family Characteristics, March 1978," *Current Population Reports, Population Characteristics*, P-20 Series, 340 (Washington, D.C.: U.S. Government Printing Office, July 1979).

median income reported for white families. These two developments together lower the reported trend in the nonwhite-white family income ratio. However, income gains among black females relative to white females have apparently offset these influences, for the movement of the income ratio for families correlates nearly perfectly with the movement of this ratio for males only. We can therefore conclude that while racial income differences may have changed among specific types of families, changes in family structure have not altered the overall racial income gap.[31] Considerations of changes in income sources and in family structure do not modify the basic picture that is revealed in Table 2.3.

In addition to cyclical fluctuations the data in Table 2.3

[31] Moynihan and others who have emphasized the gains made by blacks in recent years have especially emphasized the attainment of racial parity among certain husband-wife families in the North and the West: those with husbands twenty-five to thirty-four years of age and husband and wife as earners. This development is certainly important, but it must be placed in perspective: such families account for only 5 percent of all black families in the United States. See U.S. Bureau of the Census, "Income of Families and Persons," P-60 Series, no. 101, Table 73.

37

exhibit some apparent narrowing in racial income differentials during the 1960s which continue into the 1970s.[32] For both families and males, the black/white median income ratios seem to fluctuate around a higher average in the 1970s than is observed for the 1950s or early 1960s. And much larger gains are recorded in Table 2.6 for nonwhite females.

The assessment of this apparent upward trend requires more sophisticated statistical technique. Next, I turn to econometric efforts that make the important distinction between cyclical and secular trends in racial income inequality. It should be noted, however, that the upward trends partly reflect important changes in census computing procedures instituted in 1967 and 1975 that raised reported median incomes more for blacks than for whites.[33] These effects will not be considered in the following discussion.

[32] Studies covering an earlier period observed a worsening pattern. See, for example, Alan Batchelder, "Decline in the Relative Income of Negro Men," *Quarterly Journal of Economics* (August 1964).

[33] The new processing methods, instituted when new computer capabilities became available to the Census Bureau, were designed to reduce nonresponse errors. The new procedures instituted in 1967 resulted in overestimations of the nonwhite gains between 1966 and 1967. The summary data published by the Census Bureau indicate that the ratio of black to white median male earnings rose .05 points between 1966 and 1967. The change in the ratio using procedures comparable to those in earlier years indicates only a .02 point increase. A comparable overestimation presumably confounds subsequent years as well. See Orley Ashenfelter, "Changes in Labor Market Discrimination Over Time," *Journal of Human Resources* (Fall 1970), pp. 429–430.

Revised computation procedures instituted in 1975 also produced a greater relative increase in nonwhite incomes between 1973 and 1974 than was obtained with procedures used prior to 1975. The Census Bureau presented both old and revised estimates of 1974 incomes in its P-60 Series, no. 104, *Money Income of Families and Persons in 1975.* Using these figures, I calculate that the median income ratio of black families to white families as .5971 with the revised estimates, and .5846 with the original estimates. The difference between these two estimates accounts for nearly all the observed increase in the ratio between 1973 and 1974. Without this revision the relative income ratio that is reported in Table 2.8 would have peaked in 1973, an expansion year, instead of in 1975, a recession year.

TABLE 2.6 Relative Median Income Regressions

(t-statistics in parentheses)

Equation Number	Dependent Variable	Constant	Time	Independent Variables UE	UE(−1)	%ΔGNP	R^2
1	Males, 1948–1964	.57	.00094 (0.75)	−.012 (−2.04)		.0015 (0.96)	.43
2	Males, 1948–1967	.59	.00173 (2.05)		−.022 (−3.73)	.0071 (3.57)	.51
3	Males, 1948–1974	.58	.0039 (5.44)	−.0173 (−3.24)		−.0289 (−0.15)	.61
4	Wage and salary income, males 1948–1974	.59	.0045 (5.27)	−.0112 (−1.77)		.191 (0.83)	.58
5	Family income 1947–1974	.59	.0046 (8.87)	−.0169 (−4.15)		−.174 (−1.27)	.78
6	Females, 1949–1974	.43	.0203 (13.70)	.0729 (0.88)		−.301 (−0.94)	.93
7	Wage and salary income, females 1948–1974	.39	.0209 (12.64)	−.0181 (−1.48)		−.222 (0.50)	.88

NOTES: *Time* = linear time variable, set equal to 1 in 1947.
UE = current aggregate unemployment rate, taken from *Economic Report of the President* (1975), Table C-26.
UE(−1) = previous year's unemployment rate.
%ΔGNP = percent change in real GNP from previous year, computed from *Economic Report of the President*, Table C-2.
SOURCE: Median income and wage and salary income data taken from U.S. Bureau of the Census, *Current Population Reports*, P-60 Series, various years.

Separating Cycles from Trends

In order to develop separate estimates of the magnitude of cyclical fluctuations and secular trends in racial income inequality, I have estimated for the postwar period an equation of the following form:

$$R_t = a + b_1 \cdot \text{Time} + b_2 \cdot UE_t + b_3 \cdot \%\Delta GNP_t + e_t$$

where R_t = ratio of nonwhite to white median income,

Time = linear time variable, equal to 1 in 1947,

UE_t = aggregate current unemployment rate,

$\%\Delta GNP_t$ = percent change in real *GNP* from the previous year,

e_t = error term.

The UE and $\%\Delta$GNP variables will pick up the cyclical influences, while the Time variable will capture any underlying trend. The results are presented in Table 2.4 for a variety of dependent variables and time periods.

Table 2.6 indicates that both the business cycle and underlying secular trends influence the relative incomes of nonwhites. A comparison in equations 1 to 3 of the coefficient of the Time variable indicates that the secular improvement occurs primarily after 1964. The time variable is positive but not significant in equation 1 and increases in both magnitude and significance in equations 2 and 3. In these equations the cyclical effects on relative incomes appear greater in any year than the secular trend. Over any year a percentage decline in the unemployment rate produces an increase in R of 4 to 10 times that produced by the secular trend.

The time trend estimate in equation 3 indicates that racial inequality among males is narrowing at the rate of 0.4 percent per year. At that glacial rate the .63 ratio in 1977 would not increase to 1.0, the level of racial equality, until the year 2070. If those postwar trends were to continue, it would take ninety-three years to eliminate racial inequality among men.

Equation 5 in Table 2.6 exhibits a similar story for inequality between white and nonwhite families. Again, the cyclical factors seem more powerful in the short-run than the secular trend. And according to these results, racial equality in family incomes will not occur until 2063, or eighty-five years after 1977.

Table 2.6 does contain more optimistic results on racial income inequality among women. In equations 6 and 7 the coefficient of the time trend variable is five to ten times greater than the corresponding figure in the male equations. And the underlying data suggest that by the early 1970s black and white women had come very close to attaining equality in annual incomes.

The results in Table 2.6 can be compared with studies by other economists. These studies differ somewhat from mine in the details of the technique used to capture the cyclical component of the fluctuations in relative nonwhite incomes. Tables 2.7 and 2.8 present the results of studies carried out in the late 1960s by Thurow, Gallaway, Rasmussen, and Ashenfelter, while Table 2.9 reports the results of studies in the 1970s by Freeman and by Butler and Heckman. Tables 2.7 and 2.8 provide comparisons with my results in equations 1 and 2 in Table 2.6, while Table 2.9 provides comparisons with equations 3 to 10 in Table 2.6.

Lester Thurow estimated separate equations for whites and for blacks to explain the growth of median family incomes in the years 1947 to 1964.[34] His cyclical variables are the rate of employment and the share of output going to personal income, and his trend variable is GNP per employee, a proxy for the growth of productivity. Thurow's results are shown in Table 2.7.[35]

The coefficients of the cyclical variables differ significantly in the two equations and indicate that nonwhite incomes rise relative to white incomes during expansions and fall during recessions. But the coefficients of the secular trend variable in

[34] Lester Thurow, *Poverty and Discrimination* (Washington, D.C.: Brookings Institution, 1969), pp. 58–61.

[35] Thurow, *Poverty and Discrimination*, Table 4.3, p. 59.

TABLE 2.7   Regression Results, 1947–1964

Median Income	White Family	Nonwhite Family
Constant	− 0.882	− 1.967
GNP per employee	1.140	1.172
	(0.031)	(0.070)
Percentage of labor force employed	1.209	2.285
	(0.520)	(1.157)
Ratio of personal income of GNP	2.353	1.603
	(0.462)	(1.023)
R^2	0.998	0.990

SOURCES: Derived from Lester Thurow, *Poverty and Discrimination* (Washington, D.C.: Brookings Institution, 1969), equation 4-2. Basic data are from U.S. Bureau of the Census, *Current Population Reports*, P-60 Series, no. 51, "Income in 1965 of Families and Persons in the United States" (1967), p. 3; and *Survey of Current Business*, various issues.

Figures in parentheses are the standard errors of the coefficients. All variables appear in logarithmic form.

the two equations do not differ significantly, thus indicating that no long-run improvement in black incomes was taking place. According to Thurow's results a reduction in the aggregate unemployment to 3.0 percent would leave median black family income at a level not higher than 60 percent of median white family income.

In Gallaway's study, presented in equation 1 of Table 2.8, both the cyclical and the time trend variables are statistically significant. The coefficient of the time trend variable is positive, indicating some long-term improvement in relative nonwhite incomes. The magnitude of the coefficient indicates a 0.3 percent improvement in relative incomes per year.

In Rasmussen's results (equation 2 in Table 2.8) the time trend is significant and indicates a secular improvement in relative incomes for males of 0.3 percent per year, or 5.2

TABLE 2.8 Relative Median Income Regressions

(t-statistics in parentheses)

Equation Number	Author	Dependent Variable	Constant	Time	Independent Variables				R^2
					UE	UE(−1)	%ΔGNP	U_B/U_w	
1	Gallaway	Families, 1947–1968	.591	.00367 (5.98)	−.01855 (−5.12)				.76
2	Rasmussen	Males, 1948–1964	.57	.00323 (2.15)		−.012 (−2.04)	.00984 (3.94)		.57
3	Ashenfelter	Wage and salary income, males 1950–1966	−.336	−.0013 (−0.81)	.0070 (0.10)			−.0887 (−1.74)	.35
4	Ashenfelter	Wage and salary income, year-round full-time males 1950–1966	−.127	−.0009 (−0.45)	.0147 (2.45)			−.1674 (−2.62)	.65

NOTE: Same variable definitions as in Table 2.7, except %ΔGNP = percent change in nominal GNP, U_B/U_w = ratio of black to white unemployment rates.

SOURCES: Lowell Gallaway, *Manpower Economics* (Homewood, I..; Richard D. Irwin, 1971), pp. 162–169.
David Rasmussen, "A Note on the Relative Income of Nonwhite Men, 1948–1964," *Quarterly Journal of Economics* 84 (February 1970), pp. 168–172.
Orley Ashenfelter, "Changes in Labor Market Discrimination Over Time," *Journal of Human Resources* (Fall 1970), pp. 403–429.

TABLE 2.9   Relative Median Income Regressions

(t-statistics in parentheses)

Author	Dependent Variable	Constant	Independent Variables			R^2
			Time	DGNP	EEOC	
Freeman	Wage and salary incomes, males 1947–1971	−.58	.0032 (2.67)	.91 (4.14)	.075 (3.75)	.76
Butler-Heckman	Income, males 1948–1974	−.689	.005 (3.07)	.726 (2.63)	.034 (2.76)	.69
Butler-Heckman	Wage and salary income, males 1948–1974	−.585	.004 (2.84)	.438 (1.66)	.004 (3.81)	.73
Butler-Heckman	Income, females 1948–1974	−.921	.032 (14.65)	−.278 (−0.71)	−.002 (−0.10)	.94

NOTES: Dependent variables appear in logarithmic form.

DGNP = deviation of real GNP from trend, computed by regressing the log of real GNP against time. For details, see Freeman, note 8.

EEOC = cumulated expenditure budget of the Equal Employment Opportunity Commission per nonwhite worker, based on a 1 July to 30 June fiscal-year budget for Freeman and a corrected calendar-year budget for Butler and Heckman.

SOURCES: Richard Freeman, "Changes in the Labor Market for Black Americans, 1948–72," *Brookings Papers on Economic Activity* 1 (1973), pp. 67–120.

Richard Butler and James Heckman, "The Government's Impact on the Labor Market Status of Black Americans: A critical Review," in Leonard Hausman et al., eds., *Equal Rights and Industrial Relations* (Madison: Industrial Relations Research Association, 1977).

percent over the sixteen-year period, 1948–1964. The finding replicates the Gallaway findings for families.

In Ashenfelter's study (equations 3 and 4 of Table 2.8), the racial unemployment rate ratio provides a proxy for the relative utilization of black labor, while the aggregate unemployment rate provides the cyclical control variable. Although Ashenfelter's time trend coefficients have a negative sign, they are not significantly different from zero. The coefficients of the remaining two variables are significant only in the case of full-time workers, though they have the signs expected by Ashenfelter in both equations. Ashenfelter thus finds "essentially no trend on the relative earnings of nonwhite males, substantial evidence in favor of the hypothesis that the relative extent of unemployment has a negative effect on relative nonwhite earnings, and very little evidence that aggregate labor market tightness has had any appreciable effect on relative nonwhite earnings in the postwar period."[36]

The econometric studies that employ data through the early seventies show a small upward secular trend in the relative income of nonwhite males. These results, reported in Table 2.9, also indicate the importance of the business cycle on fluctuations in relative incomes. The EEOC variable included in these equations tests the influence of government antidiscrimination policy since 1964 (through the Equal Employment Opportunity Commission). The results suggest that relative incomes of nonwhites have improved since 1964 at a rate greater than the overall postwar secular trend, but whether this improvement is due to EEOC efforts or other post-1964 changes remains an item of controversy.

The results in Table 2.9 further confirm the inferences I make from my own econometric efforts as reported in Table 2.6. Although some secular improvement is taking place in the relative income of nonwhite males, this improvement is markedly slow and continues to be small in relation to cyclical fluctuations as well.

[36] Ashenfelter, "Changes in Labor Market Discrimination," pp. 414–415.

45

Regional Differences

Until now we have looked only at national data. But the annual relative income trends for the entire United States obscure differing trends in the regions. Regional income data by race and sex are available on an annual basis for the period since 1953. These data are presented in Figure 2.1 as well as in Table 2.10 for males and in Table 2.11 for females. In every region except the South the relative income of nonwhite

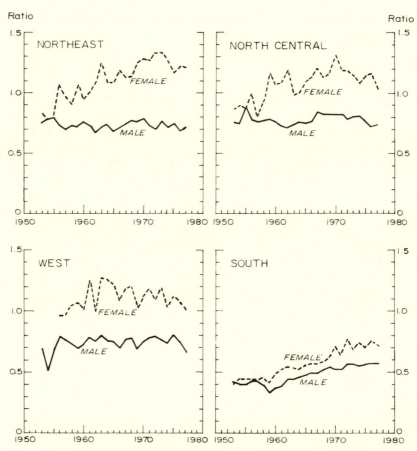

Figure 2.1. Nonwhite/White Median Income Ratios by Sex and Region

46

TABLE 2.10   Nonwhite/White Male Median Income Ratios
by Region, 1953–1977

Year	Northeast	North Central	South	West
1953	.75	.75	.42	.68
1954	.78	.74	.40	.52
1955	.79	.88	.40	.68
1956	.73	.77	.42	.79
1957	.70	.76	.42	.76
1958	.73	.77	.39	.73
1959	.72	.78	.33	.69
1960	.76	.76	.37	.73
1961	.73	.72	.38	.78
1962	.67	.71	.44	.75
1963	.72	.74	.44	.79
1964	.74	.76	.46	.76
1965	.69	.75	.47	.74
1966	.71	.76	.49	.69
1967	.75	.84	.49	.77
1968[a]	.77	.82	.52	.78
1969	.76	.82	.54	.69
1970	.78	.82	.52	.75
1971	.73	.82	.52	.78
1972	.70	.79	.56	.79
1973	.77	.80	.56	.76
1974	.72	.81	.55	.74
1975	.75	.77	.56	.80
1976	.69	.73	.57	.74
1977	.72	.74	.57	.67

[a] 1968 data for black/white ratios.

SOURCE: U.S. Bureau of the Census, *Current Population Reports*, various
years.

TABLE 2.11   Nonwhite/White Female Median Income Ratio by Region, 1953–1977

Year	Northeast	North Central	South	West
1953	.83	.86	.41	n.a.
1954	.78	.89	.44	n.a.
1955	.79	.87	.44	n.a.
1956	1.07	.99	.44	.96
1957	.97	.80	.44	.96
1958	.91	.94	.45	1.04
1959	1.06	1.16	.42	1.06
1960	.95	1.07	.48	1.01
1961	1.00	1.09	.52	1.25
1962	1.08	1.18	.54	.99
1963	1.25	.98	.53	1.27
1964	1.09	1.00	.52	1.26
1965	1.09	1.09	.56	1.21
1966	1.19	1.13	.57	1.08
1967	1.13	1.20	.57	1.17
1968[a]	1.14	1.13	.59	1.20
1969	1.25	1.16	.62	1.02
1970	1.28	1.31	.71	1.12
1971	1.26	1.18	.64	1.18
1972	1.33	1.18	.77	1.09
1973	1.33	1.14	.68	1.19
1974	1.27	1.08	.74	1.02
1975	1.17	1.14	.70	1.12
1976	1.22	1.16	.75	1.09
1977	1.20	1.02	.71	1.00

[a] 1968 data for black/white ratios.

SOURCE: U.S. Bureau of the Census, *Current Population Reports*, P-60 Series, various years.

males shows substantial cyclical fluctuations, correlated once again with the national business cycle, but show no upward trend over time. Only the South exhibits a secular reduction in racial inequality for males. After a widening of the racial gap through most of the 1950s, an improvement begins to appear about 1959 and to end by 1972. The secular national improvement noted above thus appears to result largely from an upward trend within the South and from the migration of blacks out of the South to regions that continue to have higher absolute and relative incomes for nonwhite males.

A similar pattern of differing regional trends for females appears in Table 2.11. In each region except the South, nonwhite females had achieved income inequality with white females by the late 1950s, and little secular change has occurred since that time. In the South, by contrast, nonwhite female incomes rose from about .45 of white female incomes in the 1950s to about .75 in the mid-1970s. Apparently, the national improvement for nonwhite women since 1960 is due entirely to changes within the South and to the changing regional composition of the nonwhite population.

These regional patterns, when coupled with rural-urban migration patterns documented later in this chapter, are consistent with the hypothesis that many of the recent relative gains of blacks result from their movement out of the *rural* South and into the urban and industrial areas of the North and the South. The improvement in the South may also be due to declines in labor market discrimination (most initial antidiscrimination efforts by the Equal Employment Opportunity Commission were concentrated in the South) or to improvements in the quantity and quality of black schooling there. Further disaggregation will throw some light on these hypotheses.

Urban Areas

Table 2.12 presents data indicating trends in racial inequality within urban areas of the United States. Among the urban population, the ratio of black male income to white male income rose from .600 in 1948 to .640 in 1969. Although

49

TABLE 2.12   Relative Median Income of Black Males in the
Urban U.S., Urban South, and Urban
Non-South, 1939–1969

Years	Urban U.S.	Urban South	Urban Non-South
1939[a,b]	.496	.446	.664
1949[c]	.600	.533[b]	.726[b]
1959	.583	.512	.701[b]
1969	.640	.605	.688[b]

[a] Wage and salary income of males, eighteen to sixty-four years old.
[b] One or both medians calculated by linear interpolation by the author.
[c] Data for 1949 are for nonwhites.
SOURCES: For 1939, 1949, and 1959 data, see source note, Table 2.1. Data for
1969 is from U.S. Bureau of the Census, *Census of the Population, 1970*,
vol. 1, part 1, section 2, *U.S. Summary* (Washington, D.C.: U.S. Government Printing Office), Tables 244 and 303.

significant, the urban rate of increase was not very large and
was only three-fifths of that for the United States as a whole.
Table 2.12 thus points to continuities in urban racial inequalities over two significant decades.

The aggregate national urban change, moreover, obscures
two opposing trends. While relative black male incomes rose
in the urban areas of the South, from .533 to .605, they *declined*
in the urban areas of the rest of the nation, from .726 in 1949
to .688 in 1969. By 1969 the black-white male income ratios in
these two parts of the country had moved closer together, but
the point of convergence was considerably *lower* than the 1949
urban non-South level. To illustrate, I calculated future trends,
assuming that the rate of change in the black-white income
ratio in each region continues at the 1949–1969 pace. If this
assumption were to hold, the South-non-South differential
would be eliminated in 1984, but at that time the urban black-
white income ratio would stand at .659. This pattern does not
provide a basis for optimism.

A similar picture of racial income trends emerges when we look at individual major metropolitan areas. Table 2.13 presents data for the seventeen metropolitan areas of the United States with the largest black populations in 1970. On the average, virtually no change occurred in the relative income of nonwhite males between 1949 and 1969 in these metropolitan areas. This absence of significant improvement is found for Standard Metropolitan Statistical Areas (SMSA's) in every region of the country: The nonwhite to white income ratio fell slightly in the North and West, from .71 to .69, and stayed at .56 in the South.

Individual cities showed significant changes over this period, but few systematic patterns are discernible among these cities. However, one pattern may be suggestive. The largest relative declines for blacks occurred in older industrial cities: Detroit, Pittsburgh, and Birmingham.

If this twenty-year period provides any guide, it suggests that racial inequality is not diminishing within the nation's metropolitan areas. These findings lend support to the hypothesis that improvements in the aggregate national relative position of nonwhite males result from rural to urban migration and lead to the expectation that further improvements may diminish substantially as the remaining rural population is depleted.

Industries

How have blacks fared in this period within individual, detailed industries? Since the 1940s black workers have entered industrial employment in unprecedented numbers. Total black employment in manufacturing has risen from 470,000 in 1940 to 998,000 in 1950, to 1,306,000 in 1960 and to 1,600,000 in 1970. These gains have lifted the percentage of manufacturing employment that is black from 0.5 in 1940 to 9.2 in 1970.

Although racial employment patterns by industry have been studied, there have been few quantitative studies of trends in racial income inequalities by industry. Using decennial census

51

TABLE 2.13   Ratio of Nonwhite to White Male[a] Median
Incomes, Selected SMSA's, 1949–1969

	1949	1959	1969	1949–1969
North and West				
Chicago	.714	.678	.713	−.001
Cleveland	.702	.701	.718	.016
Detroit	.808	.685	.738	−.070
Los Angeles	.704	.684	.726	.024
New York	.678	.677	.712	.034
Philadelphia	.686	.662	.689	.003
Pittsburgh	.729	n.a.	.638	−.091
San Francisco	.712	.726	.686	−.026
St. Louis	.632	.581	.583	−.049
Average	.707	.674	.689	−.018
South				
Atlanta	.520	.481	.531	.011
Baltimore	.630	.626	.631	.001
Birmingham	.531	.488	.515	−.066
Dallas	.505	.476	.550	.045
Houston	.554	.511	.551	−.003
Memphis	.484	.467	.583	.099
New Orleans	.557	.511	.507	−.050
Washington, D.C.	.627	.573	.610	−.017
Average	.557	.517	.560	.003

NOTES: [a] Fourteen years and older.

1949 data for the Standard Metropolitan Area (SMA); from the U.S. *Census of the Population, 1950, Characteristics of the Population,* Table 185.

1959 data for the Standard Metropolitan Statistical Area (SMSA); from the U.S. *Census of the Population, 1960,* state volumes, Table 133.

1969 data for the Standard Metropolitan Statistical Area (SMSA); from the U.S. *Census of the Population, 1970,* state volumes, Table 192.

data, I have calculated nonwhite-to-white ratios of median annual earnings for males in the experienced civilian labor force for detailed industries from 1949 to 1969. Table 2.14 presents the results of these calculations for all industries for which the census published relevant data in both years.

The overall pattern in Table 2.14 shows very little change in the black-white ratio over the period 1949 to 1969. In this period black employment in these industries grew from 7.4 percent to 10.4 percent of the labor force. Despite the considerable growth of black employment, the average black-white male earnings ratio in these industries increased from .71 in 1949 to only .74 in 1969. Blacks approached equality with whites by 1970 in only two industries, taxicab service (an unusual industry in that workers have greater control over their time input) and street railways and bus lines (an industry dominated by public employment). Preliminary investigation of the same industries in 1976, drawn from the 1977 Current Population Survey, indicates that these inequalities had not diminished by the mid-1970s.[37]

While some industries show the widely publicized gains for black men that occurred during these two decades, most show very small increases (the ratio rose by .1 or more in only nine industries) and a surprising number (thirteen) show declines. Declines occurred in many major industries (such as motor vehicles and equipment or meat products) that employ a large and growing number of black workers and enjoy a relatively progressive image in race relations. While black employment as a percentage of the motor-vehicle-and-parts labor force increased from 8.3 percent in 1949 to 13.8 percent in 1969, the black-white earnings ratio fell from .882 to .855. Moreover, multiple regression calculations (not shown here) indicate that labor supply variables, such as racial differences in schooling or age, do not explain the absence of greater improvement in these forty-nine industries.

---

[37] Similar results are reported in Marvin Smith, "Industrial Racial Wage Discrimination in the U.S.," *Industrial Relations* (Winter 1979).

TABLE 2.14 Black-White Male Earnings Ratios[a] By Detailed Industry 1949–1969 (n = 49)

Census Code	Industrial Label[b]	B/W 1969	B/W 1949	Differential (69–49)
	Durable Goods			
109	Miscellaneous wood products	.702	.538	+.164
118	Furniture and fixtures	.714	.581	+.133
119	Glass and glass products	.718	.751	−.033
127	Cement, concrete, gypsum, and plaster products	.697	.690	+.007
128	Structural clay products	.738	.744	−.006
138	Miscellaneous mineral and stone products	.733	.665	+.068
139	Blast furnaces, steelworks, rolling and finishing mills	.850	.807	+.043
147	Other primary iron and steel industries	.821	.802	+.019
148–49	Primary nonferrous metals	.799	.797	+.002
157–59, 167, 169	Fabricated metal industries	.749	.740	+.009
178	Farm machinery and equipment	.784	.834	−.050

199, 207–09	Household appliances, radio, television, and communication equipment	.695	.751	−.056
219	Motor vehicles and equipment	.855	.882	−.027
227	Aircraft and parts	.764	.778	−.014
228	Ship and boat building and repairing	.777	.709	+.068
229	Railroad locomotives and equipment	.858	.793	+.065
259	Miscellaneous manufacturing	.712	.649	+.063
	Nondurable Goods			
268	Meat products	.698	.797	−.099
269	Dairy products	.730	.670	+.060
278	Canning and preserving	.687	.615	+.072
279	Grain-mill products	.620	.656	−.036
287	Bakery products	.799	.682	+.117
288	Confectionery and related products	.725	.663	+.062
289	Beverage industries	.619	.504	+.115
297	Miscellaneous food preparation and kindred products	.706	.664	+.042

TABLE 2.14 (Continued)

Census Code	Industrial Label[b]	B/W 1969	B/W 1949	Differential (69-49)
	Nondurable Goods			
299	Tobacco manufactures	.789	.754	+.035
307–309, 317–318	Textile mill products	.736	.728	+.008
319–327	Apparel and other fabricated textile products	.691	.664	+.027
328	Pulp, paper, and paperboard mills	.714	.604	+.110
329	Miscellaneous paper and pulp products	.705	.730	−.025
337	Paperboard boxes and containers	.699	.704	−.005
338–339	Printing, publishing, and allied industries	.677	.647	+.030
359	Paints, varnishes, and related products	.767	.731	+.036
368–69	Miscellaneous chemicals	.703	.550	+.153
377	Petroleum refining	.713	.681	+.032
379, 387	Rubber and plastic products	.759	.800	−.041
388–89, 397	Leather and leather products	.856	1.340	−.484

	Transportation			
407	Railroads and railway express service	.753	.933	−.180
408	Street railways and bus lines	.991	.788	+.203
409	Taxicab service	1.021	.810	+.211
417	Trucking service	.691	.597	+.094
418	Warehousing and storage	.738	.672	+.066
419	Water transportation	.752	.710	+.042
427	Air transportation	.695	.627	+.068
	Communications and Utilities			
447–49	Communications	.608	.523	+.085
467–68	Electric and gas utilities	.648	.551	+.097
469	Gas and steam supply systems	.698	.646	+.052
477	Water supply	.728	.623	+.105
478	Sanitation services	.845	.801	+.044
	Unweighted Average	.742	.712	+.030

[a] Ratio of nonwhite to white annual median earnings for males in the experienced civilian labor force.
[b] Grouped industry data are reported where the census data do not permit calculations for each detailed industry.

SOURCES: U.S. Bureau of the Census, *Census of the Population, 1970, Detailed Characteristics, U.S. Summary*, 1973.
U.S. Bureau of the Census, Special Reports, *Industrial Characteristics*, PID-15 Series, 1955, Table 2.
U.S. Bureau of the Census, *Census of the Population, 1950, U.S. Summary*, vol. 1, 1953, Table 133.

Relatively small increases occurred in most industries that registered an upward trend in relative earnings. In textile mill products, an industry that has a notorious history in the South for excluding black workers, employment of blacks grew from 4.9 percent to 12.8 percent of the total industry labor force. Yet the black-white earnings ratio remained stationary at .728 in 1949 and .736 in 1969. These examples and findings indicate that black breakthrough into employment in the basic industrial sectors does not necessarily lead to the achievement of racial equality within those industries.

Finally, trends in private employment can be compared with those in the public sector. Between 1950 and 1970 employment in government increased faster than private employment, a trend which was more pronounced for nonwhites than for whites. Nonwhite workers constituted 12.3 percent of all private wage and salary workers in 1950, 10.1 percent in 1960, and 9.0 percent in 1970. In contrast, nonwhite workers accounted for 9.9 percent of government workers in 1950, 11.2 percent in 1960, and 12.7 percent in 1970.[38] The growth of government employment has thus provided considerable employment opportunities for blacks.

Both absolute and relative nonwhite earnings levels are higher in public employment than in private employment. In 1969 the median annual earnings for black civilian government employees in 1969 amounted to $5,493, as compared to $3,901 (or 29 percent less) for blacks employed in nonfarm private employment. The ratio of black to white median annual earnings among male government workers was .765, as compared to .653 among nonfarm private workers; the respective figures for females were .928 and .738.[39] The

[38] Data for 1950 from U.S. Bureau of the Census, *Census of the Population, 1950,* "General Social and Economic Characteristics," table 142; 1960 and 1970 data from U.S. Bureau of the Census, *Census of the Population, 1960 and 1970,* "Subject Reports: Occupational Characteristics."

[39] Calculated from U.S. Bureau of the Census, *Census of the Population, 1970,* "Subject Reports: Industrial Characteristics," Table 44. The nonwhite-white median income ratios in 1950 were .73 for male government workers

growth of black employment has therefore worked to raise the relative earnings levels of blacks. However, this advantage has diminished considerably since the early 1970s, as earnings and employment levels in government have fallen in relation to those in private employment.

The Persistence of Racial Discrimination

While considerable evidence indicates that racial inequality is persisting in the United States, some economists, most prominently represented by Richard Freeman, James Smith, and Finis Welch, claim that present racial discrimination in the labor market has all but disappeared.[40] Older blacks still suffer the effects of past acts of discrimination that lower their productivity and earnings. But young blacks are not so afflicted. Consequently, as young blacks, who comprise recent and new labor market entrants, replace older blacks who leave the labor market, racial inequality in earnings will also diminish. Continuing inequality is seen as merely the last vestige of a dead pattern of discrimination. This claim was given widespread publicity, and it deserves careful scrutiny.

To support their claim Freeman and Smith and Welch point to the decline during the 1960s in racial differences in the economic payoff from schooling for young people. They suggest also that black/white earnings ratios have improved for young people in every schooling and family background category.

The contentions that racial discrimination has disappeared

---

and .58 for nonfarm male private wage and salary workers; the comparable figures for females were .81 and .48. U.S. Bureau of the Census, *Census of the Population, 1950*, "General Social and Economic Characteristics," Table 142. Although these income figures are not precisely comparable to the earnings figures published for 1970, the numbers indicate that the absolute and relative earning levels of nonwhites probably increased faster in private employment than in government employment over this period. This consideration must be weighed against the employment composition factor discussed in the text.

[40] Freeman, "The Changing Labor Market"; Smith and Welch, "Black-White Male Wage Ratios."

and that racial inequalities are diminishing are not entirely supported by the evidence. First, a decline in present labor market discrimination does not imply an end to racial inequality. Many inequality-reproducing mechanisms outside the labor market, notably class background, housing, and school segregation, continue to operate.[41] Freeman and Smith and Welch discuss these issues in some of their writings, but they leave many of the inequality-generating variables substantially unexplored. Second, much of the evidence for a decline in job discrimination is based on developments that occurred during the expansionary years of the 1960s and early 1970s. More recent data capturing the patterns of the recessionary years of the 1970s point in a different direction.[42] Third, Smith and Welch's own data indicate that the greatest gains in the 1960s occurred for college-educated blacks. The relative gains for blacks in the lower schooling categories, where most blacks are still situated, ranged from much more modest to nonexistent.[43] This pattern, together with occupational evidence cited earlier in this chapter, suggests that a black professional and managerial stratum expanded significantly in recent years, but that the majority of blacks were left behind. Fourth, it is hazardous to generalize future racial differences from a study of brief labor market experiences of young workers. Much job discrimination occurs through differential promotion and training, not through initial hiring.[44] This form of discrimination may indeed grow in

[41] In his more recent work Freeman himself has been careful to discuss these sources of black disadvantage; see Freeman, "Black Economic Progress Since 1964."

[42] U.S. Bureau of the Census, "Money Income and Poverty Status of Families and Persons in the United States: 1977," P-60 Series, no. 116, (Washington, D.C.: U.S. Government Printing Office, 1978).

[43] Smith and Welch, "Black-White Male Wage Ratios." See also the similar conclusions in Christopher Jencks, *Who Gets Ahead? The Determinants of Economic Success in America* (New York: Basic Books, 1979), chapter 9, "The Effects of Race on Earnings."

[44] This pattern, found by numerous researchers, explains why black-white income ratios decline as the age cohort grows older.

importance since overt discrimination has become illegal. Finally, the decline in racial income differentials has been most dramatic among women, but this development is also diminished by several qualifications. The earnings position of the white women with whom black women are being compared has declined relative to that of white men.[45] Furthermore, black women are likely to work more hours than white women.[46] Taken together, these considerations cast considerable doubt on the thesis that racial discrimination is declining substantially for most blacks and that true racial equality will soon appear in the United States.

To conclude, we have seen that postwar patterns of racial inequality indicate that much of the fluctuations in the relative incomes of blacks occurs with the business cycle. Some secular improvement has occurred, but this change has resulted from the decline of the agrarian South and the associated movement of blacks into urban areas and industries in both the South and the North. Within these sectors relative improvements for blacks have occurred only among women.

EQUALIZING FORCES VERSUS PERSISTENT INEQUALITY

The lack of any substantial narrowing in racial income differentials contrasts sharply with several significant equalizing demographic, economic, and sociopolitical forces that have been at work in the United States, especially since World War II. These changes include the following: migration and urbanization of blacks, improvements in the quantity and quality of black schooling, changes in public opinion among whites, outlawing of legal segregation and increased government antidiscrimination efforts, greater public expenditures for programs that increase black incomes, increased antidiscrimination activity and organization among blacks, greater and more positive representation of blacks in the cultural

[45] See the data cited in note 27 above.
[46] See King, "Labor Market Discrimination Against Black Women."

arena, and an increase in black voting rates and in the number of black elected officials.

These changes ought to have exerted a significant upward effect on the relative incomes of nonwhite males and females. I examine here the most important of these equalizing forces.

Migration and Urbanization

The center of the black population has shifted from the rural and agricultural South to urban industrial areas in the North and the South. The white population has shifted in the same direction, but the changes have occurred more rapidly and to a greater extent among blacks. Blacks in the rural South receive far lower incomes, both absolutely and relatively to whites in the same geographic location, than blacks elsewhere in the United States. Therefore, the population shift ought to have had significant economic effects on improving the relative position of nonwhites.

In 1870 over 90 percent of the black population of the United States resided in the South, and 81 percent lived in the rural South.[47] From 1870 until the First World War, black migration out of the South remained quite small; Table 2.15 indicates that nearly 90 percent of all blacks still resided in the South in 1910. A substantial shift of the black population to the cities did occur during this period. By 1910 nearly 19 percent of Southern blacks lived in urban areas. This was twice the 1870 proportion. In the period 1870 to 1910 the urbanization of Southern blacks progressed at a slightly higher rate than the urbanization of Southern whites.

This pattern changed during World War I. The northward and westward migrations of blacks accelerated after 1910, and the proportion of blacks residing in the South declined continuously. By contrast, the proportion of whites in the South

---

[47] Data in this and the two succeeding paragraphs are taken from Daniel Price, *Changing Characteristics of the Negro Population* (Washington, D.C.: U.S. Government Printing Office, 1969), chapter 1, pp. 9–16.

TABLE 2.15   Proportion of the Black and White Population of the Coterminous United States in the South, By Urban and Rural Residence, 1870–1970

Years	Total		Urban		Rural	
	Black	White	Black	White	Black	White
1870	90.6	23.4	9.3	3.1	81.3	20.3
1880	90.6	24.3	9.7	3.2	80.9	21.1
1890	90.3	23.9	13.8	5.5	76.5	19.9
1900	89.7	24.7	15.4	3.3	74.2	20.2
1910	89.0	25.1	18.8	5.8	70.2	19.3
1920	85.2	25.6	21.5	7.4	63.7	18.0
1930	78.7	25.4	24.8	8.5	53.8	16.6
1940	77.0	26.8	28.1	9.9	48.9	16.9
1950	68.0	27.3	32.5	13.4	35.5	13.9
1960	59.9	27.4	35.0	16.1	24.9	11.4
1970	53.0	28.5	35.7	18.2	17.3	10.3

SOURCES: Daniel Price, *Changing Characteristics of the Negro Population*, a 1960 Census Monograph (Washington, D.C.: U.S. Government Printing Office), Tables 1–2; 1970 data from U.S. Bureau of the Census, *Census of the Population, 1970*, vol. 1, part 1, *U.S. Summary*, section 1, Table 61.

increased slightly in the sixty years from 1910 to 1970. Particularly dramatic shifts in the location of blacks occurred after 1940. In 1940, 77 percent of blacks lived in the South, and nearly 50 percent lived in rural areas of the South. In 1970, by contrast, only 53 percent of blacks lived in the South and only 17 percent lived in the rural South.

The redistribution of the black population out of the South results overwhelmingly from the decline of the Southern agricultural population. In 1940 nearly half of all black workers were engaged in agriculture; by 1970 only 4 percent

63

were still in agriculture.[48] Consequently, as Table 2.16 indicates, blacks now live predominantly in urban areas.

The redistribution of the black population into urban areas has occurred at rates far exceeding the urban population shift among whites. While the proportion of whites living in urban areas in the United States grew from 57 percent in 1940 to 72 percent in 1970, the black proportion increased from 49 percent in 1940 to 81 percent in 1970. In 1970, according to Table 2.16, in every region of the United States, blacks were far more concentrated in urban areas than were whites.

The black population clearly has shifted its location in the direction of higher incomes areas. Tables 2.13 and 2.14 indicated the lower relative incomes of nonwhites in the South as compared to the rest of the United States. The rural South remains the poorest area of the nation: with such economic payoffs to migration, the more rapid demographic shifts of blacks that we have observed should have exerted an upward force on their relative incomes.[49]

It is possible to estimate the magnitude of the change in relative incomes that would be expected from the change in the regional composition of the nonwhite population. Such a calculation has been carried out by Gwartney.[50] According to Gwartney's estimates, migration between 1940 and 1960 raised the mean income ratio of males by about 7 to 9 percent during the 1940s, and 5 to 6 percent during the 1950s. The change in regional composition therefore accounts for the *entire* observed increase in the relative male median income ratio between 1949 and 1969.[51] In the previous section of this

[48] Shifts in the geographic location of a population result from both migration and interregional differences in birth and death rates. This distinction, however, is not germane to the present discussion and is ignored in the text.

[49] For an analysis of the economic returns to out-migration from the South, see Samuel Bowles, "Migration as Investment: Empirical Tests of the Human Investment Approach," *Review of Economics and Statistics* (November 1970).

[50] Gwartney, "Changes in the Nonwhite/White Income Ratio."

[51] Ibid., p. 875.

TABLE 2.16   Percentage of the Population Residing in
Urban Areas, By Region and Race: 1880–1970

Region and Race	1880	1900	1920	1940	1950	1960	1970
United States							
White	30.3	43.0	53.4	57.4	64.3	68.5	72.4
Black	14.3	22.7	34.0	48.6	62.4	73.2	81.3
Northeast							
White	50.6	69.0	75.7	76.1	78.7	79.1	78.7
Black	62.7	78.3	86.7	90.1	94.0	95.6	97.0
North Central							
White	23.8	38.2	51.6	57.3	62.6	66.8	69.3
Black	42.5	64.4	83.4	88.8	93.8	95.7	97.3
South							
White	13.1	18.5	29.6	36.8	48.9	58.6	63.9
Black	10.6	17.2	25.3	36.5	47.7	58.5	67.4
West							
White	30.7	41.2	53.0	58.8	69.7	77.6	82.6
Black	50.8	67.4	74.0	83.1	90.3	92.7	96.9

SOURCES: Daniel Price, *Changing Characteristics;* 1970 data from U.S. Bureau of the Census, *Census of the Population, 1970*, vol. 1, part 1, *U.S. Summary*, section 1, Tables 48 and 55.

chapter I showed that most of this increase is due to cyclical economic fluctuations. The results here therefore suggest that the structural position of blacks must have worsened in some other dimensions during the postwar years. This inference is reinforced as we look more closely at other equalizing forces in this period.

Schooling

Significant improvements have occurred in both the quantity and quality of black schooling. While whites obtain more and

65

better schooling than in the past, the gains for blacks have been even greater. Inequalities still remain. But the relative gains that have occurred for blacks should have produced gains in their relative incomes.

Table 2.17 indicates racial trends in the quantity of schooling since 1890. The gap in median years of schooling completed between black and white males aged twenty-five to twenty-nine fell from 6.5 years in 1890 to 3.3 years in 1940, and 0.5 years in 1970. About 75 percent of the 1960 gap was closed between 1960 and 1970 alone.[52] The racial gap for females, which had been 7.2 years in 1890, fell to 0.3 years in 1970. These statistics understate the narrowing that has occurred. In the 1920s and 1930s black students in Southern schools attended school only two-thirds as many days as whites. By the early 1950s this difference had largely disappeared.

The dramatic increase in the quantity of black schooling as compared to that of whites should have exerted a substantial upward force on relative incomes, assuming, of course, that schooling has an economic payoff. The magnitudes involved are illustrated by two simple calculations. First, assume that blacks and whites receive the same 10 percent return to each year of schooling. Racial income differences for men then drop from 65 percent in 1870 to 5 percent in 1970, and racial differ-

---

[52] U.S. Department of Labor, Bureau of Labor Statistics, *The Social and Economic Status of Negroes in the United States, 1969*, Report no. 375 (Washington, D.C.: U.S. Government Printing Office, 1970), p. 50; Price, *Changing Characteristics*, p. 185. See also William G. Spady, "Educational Mobility and Access: Growth and Paradoxes," *American Journal of Sociology* (November 1967), Table 4.

A more unequal pattern of schooling attainment appears from data on the proportion of blacks and whites attending institutions of higher education. And a higher proportion of blacks attend community colleges and vocational schools, while a lower proportion graduate and receive degrees from higher educational institutions. In the late 1970s the proportion of black students in four-year colleges and in professional schools began to decline after earlier gains. See for example, Madelon Stent, "Education for Black Americans on the 25th Anniversary of the Brown Decision," in James Williams, ed., *The State of Black America, 1979* (New York: National Urban League, 1979).

TABLE 2.17 Median School Years Completed, by Race and Sex, Twenty-five to Twenty-nine Year Olds, 1890–1970

Year	Males			Females		
	White	Nonwhite	Difference	White	Nonwhite	Difference
1890	8.0	1.5	6.5	8.2	1.0	7.2
1900	8.2	3.7	4.5	8.3	3.8	4.5
1910	8.3	4.6	3.7	8.5	4.5	4.0
1920	8.5	5.1	3.4	8.6	5.6	3.0
1930	8.8	6.0	2.8	9.2	6.9	2.3
1940	10.7	7.4	3.3	11.2	8.1	3.1
1950	12.2	8.9	3.3	12.2	9.7	2.5
1960	12.4	10.5	1.9	12.3	11.1	1.2
1970	12.7	12.2	0.5	12.5	12.2	0.3

SOURCES: Based on U.S. *Census of the Population, 1940–1970*. Age cohorts were used to infer schooling data prior to 1940, as reported in Richard Freeman, unpublished manuscript, Table 10.1. Since life expectancy differentials by race also narrowed in this period, the use of age cohorts understates the relative increase of black schooling.

ences for women fall from 72 percent to 3 percent over the same period. Second, suppose that blacks and whites receive incomes in the proportions indicated in 1959 data on white income by schooling level. Racial income ratios would then rise from .59 in 1870 to .85 in 1960 for men, and from .65 to .96 for women. For both sexes most of this increase takes place after 1945.[53]

These calculations are only suggestive, since they omit the effects of racial differences in returns to schooling. Still, they indicate the magnitude of the upward trend in relative incomes that are expected from the developments in schooling attainment. Yet very little secular improvement has taken place.

The relative quality of black schooling has also dramatically improved in the twentieth century. The quality of schooling can be approximated by measures such as per pupil expenditures, teacher salaries, and achievement scores of pupils. Within the South both inequality by race in public school per pupil expenditures and inequality in teacher salaries by race have shown a significant secular decline. In 1917 the Southern states as a whole spent $10.32 per year on each white child in the public schools and $2.89 on each black child.[54] The inequality was even greater in counties where the black population exceeded 75 percent of the total: $22.22 per capita for white students and $1.78 per capita for black students. By contrast, in the early 1950s current expenditures per pupil in Southern states for blacks had increased to over half the figure for whites.[55] Between 1940 and 1954 the ratio of racial differences in the salaries of black Southern public-school teachers to those of Southern white teachers rose from 57.5 percent to 85.0 percent.[56] Further equalizations occurred subsequently, in response to *Brown* v. *Board of Education.*

[53] These two calculations are found in Richard Freeman, "The Role of Educational Discrimination," mimeographed (Harvard University, 1972), pp. 5–8.

[54] John Kain, ed., *Race and Poverty* (Englewood Cliffs, N.J.: Prentice-Hall, 1969), p. 16. See also Welch, "Black-White Differences in Returns to Schooling."

[55] Kain, *Race and Poverty*, p. 16.

[56] Welch, "Black-White Differences," p. 901. Organized political and

In addition, an increased proportion of blacks attend Northern schools. The racial gap in the quality of schooling is lower in the North than in the South, and the absolute level of schooling quality exceeds that of the South. The 1966 Coleman Report found that inequalities in achievement scores by race were greater in the South than in any other region.[57] Racial differences in reading test scores of third and sixth graders in New York City fell by one-third between 1957 and 1969.[58] If these improvements in the relative quality of black schooling raise the productivity of blacks relative to whites, one would expect a consequent closing of the racial income gap.

Racial Attitudes

In the last fifty years racial attitudes among whites have improved dramatically. Beginning about 1920 an important revolution took place within the social sciences, with the systematic refutation of previously dominant theories arguing the inherent inferiority of blacks.[59] In the white population as a whole, the belief that whites are inherently superior has declined in a similarly dramatic fashion.

The National Opinion Research Center has been surveying

---

legal activity among blacks promoted progress toward equality between white and black schools in Virginia in the 1940s. While annual salaries of black teachers in 1940–1941 averaged two-thirds or less the salaries of white teachers, by 1948–1949 the differential had almost completely disappeared. See Doxey A. Wilkerson, "The Negro School Movement in Virginia: From 'Equalization' to 'Integration,'" in August Meier and Elliott Rudwick, eds., *The Making of Black America* (New York: Atheneum, 1969), 2:259–273.

[57] U.S. Department of Health, Education and Welfare, Office of Education, *A Survey of Equality of Educational Opportunity* (Washington, D.C.: U.S. Government Printing Office, 1966).

[58] Welch, "Black-White Differences."

[59] See, for example, any of the following excellent historical studies: Thomas Gossett, *Race: The History of An Idea In America* (New York: Schocken, 1965); I.A. Newby, *Jim Crow's Defense: Anti-Negro Thought in America 1900–1930* (Baton Rouge: Louisiana State University Press, 1965); James Vander Zanden, "The Ideology of White Supremacy," in Barry Schwartz and Robert Disch, eds., *White Racism* (New York: Dell, 1970). On the history of Jim Crow legislation, see C. Vann Woodward, *The Strange Career of Jim Crow.*

white beliefs about racial differences in intelligence since the early 1940s. In 1942 only 42 percent of a national sample of whites answered yes to the question, "In general, do you think Negroes are as intelligent as white people—that is, can they learn just as well if they are given the same education!" Over 80 percent answered in the affirmative in the early 1950s.[60] In 1972, 84 percent of whites surveyed said they would not be disturbed if a black person with the same education and income as theirs moved to their block, as compared to 35 percent in 1942. In this same period the percentage of whites who agreed that white and black children should attend the same—not separate—schools increased from 30 to 84 percent.[61] This liberalization of racial attitudes has continued in the 1970s, in both the South and the North.[62]

When interviewed in a survey, few whites will admit to discriminatory propensities in their own fellings and behavior. Overt attitudinal racism appears to be inappropriate to most whites. Insofar as *individual*, overt racist practices are important in holding down black incomes, the decline in social approval of such behavior ought to have facilitated a closing of the racial income gap.

Government Activity

Government activity not so long ago provided one of the bulwarks of discrimination. But major changes have taken place in the stated purpose of government activity in regard to racial discrimination. The pre-World War II system of government discrimination has been gradually dismantled in the

[60] William Schuman, "Sociological Racism," *Trans-Action* (December 1969); Herbert Hyman and Paul Sheatsley, "Attitudes Toward Desegregation," *Scientific American* (July 1964). See Paul Sheatsley, "White Attitudes Toward the Negro," *Daedalus* (Winter 1966).

[61] Reynolds Farley, "Trends in Racial Inequalities: Have the Gains of the 1960s Disappeared in the 1970s?," *American Sociological Review* (April 1977).

[62] Garth Taylor, Paul Sheatsley, and Andrew Greeley, "Attitudes Toward Racial Integration," *Scientific American* (June 1978).

postwar era. Today, government constitutes a major institution that on the whole promotes racial equality.

Before World War II the Federal government countenanced segregation of public institutions, unequal protection before the law, and the disfranchisement of blacks in the South. It also maintained a segregated military, and permitted discrimination in employment among Federal contractors as well as discrimination in the disbursement of transfer payment programs. State and local governments, especially but not exclusively in the South, maintained even more rigid discriminatory practices.

Many contemporary features of racial inequality were nourished by government policy. For example, as recently as the 1950s many blacks were excluded from much of the housing subsidized by the Federal Housing Administration programs because the FHA permitted racial covenant clauses in FHA developments. These clauses constituted formal agreements not to admit blacks to predominantly white neighborhoods. Thus, the FHA helped form the highly segregated patterns of residential location in metropolitan areas that are still with us today. The continuing issue of racial inequality remains present in patterns of government employment as well.

Nevertheless, discrimination by government has been attacked and has crumbled in each of the decades since 1940. This is not the place to chronicle the turnabout, nor to account for the causes of the change. Today, most legal obstacles to racial equality, notably de jure segregation, have been ended. Voting rights for blacks are better guaranteed. Most states and the Federal government have created public agencies whose exclusive purpose concerns the enforcement of fair employment and housing legislation, and many governmental agencies have engaged in affirmative action hiring to remedy past inequities. The courts have awarded large sums in damages to plaintiffs charging major corporations with discriminatory practices.

These changes in the legal and governmental arena should

71

have decreased the racial income gap. One early study of attempts by the states to enforce equal-pay provisions in fair employment legislation estimated that these efforts raised the relative earnings of nonwhite males by 5 percent in 1959.[63] A subsequent reanalysis of this study attempted to take into account the effects of economic conditions on the incidence of fair employment legislation across states. This reanalysis finds a much greater effect (7.5 percent) of fair employment laws on nonwhite earnings.[64]

Moreover, government expenditures on transfer payments to the poor and on employment and training programs for the disadvantaged expanded substantially during the 1960s. These programs, whose budgets amount to billions of dollars per year, were meant to have a particular impact on the productivity and access to jobs of nonwhites; they have affected directly hundreds of thousands of nonwhites. These programs include the 1960s' War on Poverty, "manpower" development and training, the CETA programs of the 1970s, experiments in reorienting transit systems to connect central city ghettos with suburban employers, and subsidies for hiring and training the "hard-core unemployed." Such programs should have had some upward impact on the relative income of nonwhites.[65]

[63] See William Landes, "The Economics of Fair Employment Laws," *Journal of Political Economy* (July–August 1968), and William Landes, "The Effects of State Fair Employment Laws on the Economic Position of Nonwhites," *American Economic Review* (May 1967). See also Michael Sovern, *Government Restraints on Discrimination* (New York: Columbia University Press, 1965).

[64] James Heckman, "Simultaneous Equation Methods with and without Structural Shift in the Equations," in Steven Goldfeld and Richard Quandt, eds., *Studies in Nonlinear Estimation* (Cambridge, Mass: Ballinger, 1976). Similar studies have been carried out for the effects of Federal antidiscrimination policy, but the techniques used and the results have given rise to conflicting interpretations. For a survey concluding that Federal programs have had minimal effects, see Butler and Heckman, "Government's Impact."

[65] See Bennett Harrison, *Education, Training and the Urban Ghetto* (Baltimore: Johns Hopkins Press, 1972), chapter 6, for details on the strategy behind public programs and an assessment of their impact.

Black Political Action

Finally, and perhaps most important, the activities of blacks themselves have forced business, government, and labor to respond in some way to the cries of protest. Recall the massive civil rights movements in both the North and the South, and the urban riots during "long hot summers" in Harlem in 1964, in Watts in 1965, in Chicago and San Francisco's Hunters Point in 1966, in Detroit and Newark in 1967, and in dozens of cities across the nation after the assassination of Martin Luther King, Jr., in April 1968. Established black organizations grew and became more active and new political organizations of the poor, often led by blacks, sprang up to challenge further the existing structures of distribution and discrimination. The National Welfare Rights Organization, for example, successfully organized tens of thousands of black and white welfare mothers around the issues of welfare grants and reform. During the late 1960s the number of families receiving welfare aid increased dramatically, in a direct response to the massive protests and rebellions.[66]

Black protests and organization led to more positive cultural images of blacks both within the black community and in the nation as a whole. Blacks appeared in much greater numbers on television and other mass media, and they were more visible in professional sports and in music and other segments of the entertainment industry. These changes gave black youth positive role models and altered whites' conceptions of blacks.

Black electoral strength also grew in this period. While the proportion of voters among blacks remained relatively constant, the number of black elected officials grew from about 50 in 1960 to about 1,600 in 1970 and to 4,500 in 1978. Between 1970 and 1975 alone, the number of blacks elected to: statewide offices increased from 1 to 13; to state legislatures, from 31 to 53; to county governing bodies, from 81 to 267; and to school

[66] Frances Piven and Richard Cloward, *Regulating the Poor: The Functions of Public Welfare* (New York: Random House, 1971).

boards, from 371 to 939.[67] This increasing influence of blacks should have some upward impact on relative incomes.

CONCLUSION

Racial income inequality and discrimination persist in the United States. Long-run trends revealed by occupational statistics indicate very little narrowing of racial differentials in this century. The greatest relative gains seem to have occurred during the two world wars. Residential segregation data tell a similar story of continuing racial differentials.

Postwar trends show some advance toward racial equality, but the rate of change remains extremely slow. Much of the changes observed in national data reflect either cyclical ups and downs in the economy or the movement of blacks *between* economic sectors, out of the agrarian South and into the urban and industrial sector of the economy. Few declines in racial income inequality have been registered *within* urban areas and industries. This evidence does not warrant the view that racial discrimination has disappeared and that racial inequality will soon disappear as well.

The gains that have occurred seem especially small in comparison to the magnitude of black migrations, advances in the quantity and quality of black schooling, antidiscriminatory legislation and highly publicized affirmative action programs, as well as black struggles, protests, and gains in black political power that have taken place since the Second World War. These forces, one would expect, should have imparted con-

[67] Nonetheless, in 1978 blacks still held less than 1 percent of the elected offices in the United States. See Michael Preston, "Black Elected Officials and Public Policy: Symbolic or Substantive Representation?," *Policy Studies Journal* (Winter 1978); Joint Center for Political Studies, *Black Political Participation: A Look at the Numbers* (Washington, D.C.: December 1975); John Procope, "The New Political Power Among Blacks," *Journal of the Institute for Socioeconomic Studies* (Spring 1978); Eddie Williams, "Black Political Participation in 1978," in Williams, ed., *The State of Black America, 1979.*

74

siderable upward pressure on the relative income of blacks. This anomaly calls for a better understanding of the causes of racial inequality. The small changes that have occurred suggest that racial inequality will not be eradicated easily.

By the mid-1970s the relocation of the black population out of the agrarian South was substantially complete. Further advances toward racial equality, therefore, can only be achieved through changes in the structures that reproduce racial inequality in the urban and industrial setting.

CHAPTER THREE

Racial Inequality and Neoclassical Economics

BEFORE THE 1960s economists rarely concerned themselves with the problems of racial discrimination and racial inequality. As recently as 1967 only one sustained theoretical treatment of the subject had been published, a 1957 book by Gary Becker in which the author argued that discrimination arose from whites' dislike of physical association with blacks.[1] Becker's analysis of how discrimination adversely affects the demand for black labor at first failed to attract much attention among economists.[2] This historical resistance to the subject of discrimination reflects the structure of neoclassical economic thought.

What is this structure? The main stream of economic thought in the United States has developed within what is today called the neoclassical paradigm. The principal distinguishing features of this paradigm will be explored in detail in Chapter 5; nonetheless, a brief preliminary description can be given here. The neoclassical paradigm focuses on the interactions of individual economic agents in markets and investi-

[1] Gary Becker, *The Economics of Discrimination* (Chicago: University of Chicago Press, 1957). At the turn of the century, in the early years of the economics profession in the United States, many leading economists argued for Nordic superiority and black inferiority. See the interesting article by Robert Cherry, "Racial Thought and the Early Economics Profession," *Review of Social Economy* (October 1976).

[2] In the introduction to the second edition of *The Economics of Discrimination*, published in 1971, Becker describes the skeptical response of many of his colleagues at the University of Chicago to the first edition of his book and the reluctance of his university press to publish it. Only a few professional economic journals reviewed the book.

gates the outcomes produced by market-clearing activity under alternative conditions of supply, demand, and degree of market competition.

The emphasis on individual agents has led to the label "microeconomics" in order to distinguish this approach from "macroeconomics," the study of the movement of the economy as a whole through business cycles and longer-term fluctuations. While Keynesianism, the dominant approach to macroeconomic analysis, was once accepted by most neoclassical economists, its compatibility with neoclassical microeconomics is far from perfect. In particular, the neoclassical assumption that the labor market will clear through wage adjustments seems to contradict the existence and analysis of unemployment in Keynesian macroeconomic theory. None of the recent attempts to reformulate macroeconomic analysis in order to reconcile it with traditional microeconomics has succeeded in winning general acceptance; moreover, these attempts have tended to reject Keynes's analysis of the sources of rigidities in wages and interest rates. Therefore, it seems appropriate to define "neoclassical economics" as one approach to microeconomic analysis and to view macroeconomics as still outside the neoclassical paradigm. As we shall see, this definition is quite consistent with the approaches taken by neoclassical theorists to the analysis of racial discrimination and inequality.

The structure of the neoclassical paradigm permits a shared agreement of the methodology of market analysis while simultaneously allowing considerable debate over the optimality of market outcomes, the extent of market failures, and the desirability of government intervention to correct undesired market outcomes. Two main ideological groupings thus coexist among neoclassical economists. Conservative neoclassical economists tend to look favorably on the workings of competitive markets and unfavorably on government intervention; liberal neoclassical economists tend to share the opposite point of view. These two policy approaches are illustrated by neoclassical analyses of race.

77

Many conservative neoclassical economists consider discrimination to be an irrational phenomenon that cannot endure in a competitive capitalist economy. These economists believe that competition among employers in the labor market eliminates racial differences in wages and drives employers who refuse to hire blacks out of business. Capitalism is thus seen as the best cure for racial discrimination.

This view of the progressive nature of capitalism was articulated by Milton Friedman in a 1956 lecture, and published later in his *Capitalism and Freedom*:

It is a striking historical fact that the development of capitalism has been accompanied by a major reduction in the extent to which particular religious, racial, or social groups have operated under special handicaps in respect of their economic activities; have, as the saying goes, been discriminated against. The substitution of contract arrangements for status arrangements was the first step toward the freeing of the serfs in the Middle Ages. . . . The Southern states after the Civil War took many measures to impose legal restrictions on Negroes. One measure which was never taken on any scale was the establishment of barriers to the ownership of either real or personal property. The failure to impose such barriers clearly did not reflect any special concern to avoid restrictions on Negroes. It reflected rather, a basic belief in private property which was so strong that it overrode the desire to discriminate against Negroes. The maintenance of the general rules of private property and of capitalism have been a major source of opportunity for Negroes and have permitted them to make greater progress than they otherwise could have made.[3]

Friedman states very clearly why conservative neoclassical

[3] Milton Friedman, *Capitalism and Freedom* (Chicago: University of Chicago Press, 1962), pp. 108–109.

economists do not expect racial inequality to persist in a capitalist economy.[4]

Liberal neoclassical economists tend to express skepticism about the efficacy of the market in solving the problem of discrimination. These economists view the problem of discrimination with greater seriousness and call for government efforts to eradicate racial inequality. Liberals feel confident that such government efforts are forthcoming and that they will be efficacious. Despite the recognized depth of white racism, many liberals had been reassured by Gunnar Myrdal's classic and optimistic 1944 study, *An American Dilemma*. Myrdal had concluded that progress toward racial equality in the United States would develop rapidly because of the egalitarian spirit and democratic traditions of the American people.[5]

The growth of the civil rights movement, the black urban rebellions, and the heightened racial tensions of the 1960s forced the entire nation to reexamine the problem of racism and led to renewed attempts to analyse discrimination. The earlier resistance to the subject diminished, as studies by economists on racial discrimination and racial inequality began to appear in greater numbers. In response to a growing

[4] Friedman's optimism is shared by a long tradition of sociologists who viewed the evolution from "traditional" to "modern" society as the evolution from role assignments based on ascriptive criteria to role assignments based on individual merit. Until recently, Talcott Parsons was the leader of this tradition. This school also saw capitalism as dissolving racial discrimination.

[5] Gunnar Myrdal, *An American Dilemma*. Some Marxists, paradoxically, have maintained a similar view of the relation between capitalism and racial discrimination. Marx and Engels remarked in *The Communist Manifesto* that capitalist industrialization reduces intermediate classes and strata and homogenizes differences among workers: "The more modern industry becomes developed, the more is the labor of men superseded by that of women. Differences of age and sex have no longer any distinctive social validity for the working-class." Marx undertook a similar analysis in *Capital*, vol. 1. Following this lead, the early orthodox Marxist theoretical tradition failed to provide an analysis of the continuing racial inequality within the United States.

79

demand for an economic analysis of the subject, Becker's original book reappeared in paperback form in 1971 (in a revised edition).

The new economic literature on discrimination of the 1960s and 1970s exhibited considerable dissatisfaction with the original Becker model. Two criticisms in particular were noted. First, Becker's assumption that whites have a distaste for association with blacks was criticized for taking as exogenous what is perhaps most in need of explanation. Second, as Friedman argues, in the neoclassical view of the economy, competitive pressures work to eliminate racial differences in earnings. The Becker model does not help us understand why racial inequality persists.

These criticisms stimulated a variety of new economic analyses of racial discrimination and racial inequality. Many economists, including Becker, pointed out that racial income differentials arise not only from discrimination affecting the demand for black labor, but also from disadvantages that black workers bring to the labor market. According to this labor-supply-oriented theory, the productivity of individual workers varies with differences in investment that augment this productivity. This investment, or human capital, is supposed to account for earnings differentials among workers, with schooling and on-the-job training seen as the most important forms of human capital acquisition.

Although the human capital explanation has some merit, it has never explained more than half of the racial wage gap.[6] Nor does the theory itself account adequately for observed racial differences in human capital. Moreover, the dramatic improvements in the quantity and quality of black schooling documented in Chapter 2 make the human capital theory even less compelling today as an explanation of racial income inequality.

These considerations led economists working within the

[6] For recent surveys of such studies, see Stanley Masters, *Black-White Income Differentials;* Christopher Jencks et al., *Who Gets Ahead?*, chapter 7, "The Effect of Race on Earnings."

neoclassical paradigm to develop a number of new demand-oriented discrimination models, each attempting in a different manner to modify the theory in order to resolve Becker's theoretical contradictions. The most influential models divide into three main groups. The first group, put forward most prominently by Anne Krueger and Lester Thurow, sees economic gain rather than taste as the primary motive for discrimination by whites, and collective action as the means to achieve this objective. These authors posit that whites hold monopoly power over blacks and act as a cartel. A related effort by Barbara Bergmann views discrimination as the monopolistic crowding of blacks into a restricted number of occupations.

The second group of discrimination models, best put forward by Finis Welch and Kenneth Arrow, focuses on the relations between blacks and various categories of white workers and argues that discrimination arises from white workers' dislike of blacks. This approach begins to analyze the internal relations that are usually ignored in neoclassical theories of the firm. The third group of discrimination models, best exemplified again by the work of Kenneth Arrow, attempts to construct a theory of discrimination upon the economic analysis of personnel and information costs. This approach posits that the costs of obtaining information on a worker's true productivity account for racial wage differentials.

In this chapter I review each of these major neoclassical discrimination theories, and I consider whether each meets two criteria required of any complete theory: Is the theory logically coherent and rigorous? Is the theory empirically plausible? I show that while these theories contain important insights, each fails to meet at least one of these criteria. Therefore, racial discrimination theories based on the neoclassical paradigm do not satisfactorily explain the persistence of racial inequality. This conclusion is buttressed in Chapter 4, where I show that these theories fail perhaps the most illuminating econometric test of their empirical validity, their compatibility with the predicted distribution of gains from

81

discrimination. Nonetheless, the discussion of neoclassical discrimination theory does illuminate the nature of the analytical modifications needed for an adequate theory.

BECKER'S PSYCHIC PAIN THEORY

Becker's employer discrimination model begins by assuming there are two societies, B and W; B is relatively labor-abundant, and W is relatively capital-abundant. B and W are assumed to have identical production functions, with $f_L > 0$, $f_K > 0$; f_{LL}, $f_{KK} < 0$; $f_{KL} > 0$; B and W labor are perfect substitutes. Without discrimination, trade occurs between the two societies: B exports labor and W exports capital until the marginal product of each factor is the same in both societies. But W employers have a distaste for working with B labor, that is, the number of B laborers (L_B) working with W capital is an argument in W employers' utility functions, and $\dfrac{\partial U}{\partial L_B} < 0$.

Capital exported by W must receive a money return, $r' = r_W + d$, where r_W equals the money return on capital domestically employed, and $d = \dfrac{\partial U_W}{\partial L_B} \Big/ \dfrac{\partial U_W}{\partial \pi_W}$, where π_W is profits of white capitalists, and d is the amount by which capitalists must be compensated for employing black labor. Since $d > 0$, discrimination reduces the quantity of capital exported by W, and the quantity of labor exported by B. Markets clear in this neoclassical model, so that no capital or labor resources are unemployed.

Becker defines total white "net" income as white labor income plus total white capital times the marginal product of white capital domestically employed: $Y_W = Y_W^L + K_W \cdot f_{K_W}$. According to Becker, d, the monetary compensation for working with black labor, exactly offsets the psychic disutility of working with black labor, and should not be counted in white "net" income. Becker shows that "net" income of W

82

falls as a result of discrimination. He does not mention that the total money income of W may rise as a result of discrimination.[7]

Critique

Becker deserves much credit for bringing the subject of discrimination into the mainstream of economic analysis. However, as noted above, the Becker discrimination model is dissatisfying because of its limited analysis of preferences for discrimination and because of the instability of discrimination in the model. Here, I consider these points in more detail and discuss as well the evidential basis for Becker's model, as revealed by several investigations. I also discuss Becker's assertion that observed market discrimination is due to monopolistic imperfections in the economy.

Becker's discussion of the process of discriminatory preference formation and the stability of these discriminatory preferences is extremely limited, if not nonexistent, even though he places great emphasis on tastes. In a recent Brookings Institution panel, Paul Samuelson stated: "Becker's conceptual framework wasn't so much wrong as it was empty; tastes for discrimination are not an explanation of behavior but merely a ghost that gets blamed for observed events."[8] Becker's exogenous preference assumption deprives the economic analysis of discrimination of its most important task.

Becker's treatment of the nature of racial preferences and of black-white interaction is also unconvincing. He assumes that

---

[7] See Becker, *Economics of Discrimination*, pp. 24–26, and Krueger, "Economics of Discrimination." Becker concedes this point in his "Introduction to the Second Edition," (p. 6) but considers it irrelevant!

The effects of discrimination on W capital and W labor are also of interest: W capital's money income falls while W labor's money income rises. I present and compare the income distributional implications of the Becker and other discrimination models in Chapter 4.

[8] Quoted in a discussion following Richard Freeman, "Changes in the Labor Market for Black Americans, 1948–72," *Brookings Papers on Economic Activity*, no. 1 (1973).

white employers dislike physical association with blacks, and this is why the black proportion of a firm's work force enters the owner's utility function. But in most large corporations the owners are rarely present at the place of employment. Even when they are present, the multiple layers of management below the owners obviate physical association with most employees. Moreover, whites frequently have shown a preference for working at close quarters with blacks, as in the case of household servants.

Becker goes wrong because he misses the importance of inequality in the relation between blacks and whites when they are working in physical proximity. As Lester Thurow has emphasized, whites frequently seem more interested in maintaining a *social* rather than a *physical* distance from blacks.[9] A simple substitution of social distance for physical distance would not change the internal logic of Becker's model. But an emphasis on social distance would place less importance on the proportion of an employer's work force that is black as well as other physical proximity measures, and would direct more attention to the inequalities facing blacks in social relations with whites.

A focus on inequality also throws doubt on the relevance of the international trade analogy used by Becker. In a society in which whites seem to monopolize power, the vision of fully voluntary exchanges taking place between whites and blacks appears farfetched:

> Much of the impact of discrimination comes from the monopoly powers of the discriminator rather than from his inability to distort perfect competition with trade barriers. ... The dominant group controls much more than its willingness to trade or not to trade with the minority group. ... The minority group may have few options and certainly not the option of refusing to trade. Subsistence (social or physical) may require trade. Negroes live in a white supremacist society, not just a segregated society.[10]

[9] Lester Thurow, *Poverty and Discrimination*, chapter 7.
[10] Thurow, *Poverty and Discrimination*, p. 117.

Inequality between blacks and whites is based on more than the abundant ownership of capital among whites. But Becker's voluntary exchange model of trade between two societies does not illuminate the bases and implications of this inequality.

Moreover, this voluntary exchange model assumes that the labor market clears, so that no unemployment is present. This quintessential neoclassical assumption precludes analysis of the relation between discrimination and unemployment. Yet racial differences in unemployment are as striking and persistent as racial wage differentials.

In any case, discrimination turns out to be unstable in Becker's competitive model. As Arrow has put it, "The (Becker) employer discrimination model predicts the absence of the phenomenon it was designed to explain."[11] It is useful to consider further how this comes about. Thus far, I have been assuming implicitly that all white employers have identical tastes for discrimination. But as Becker himself shows and Arrow has emphasized, the relaxation of the assumption of identical tastes is fatal to the model.[12] If some employers have less distaste for blacks than do other employers, the effective market discrimination coefficient, d_m, must be equal to the minimum of the set of employer discrimination coefficients, $d_m = \min \{d_i ; i = 1, \ldots, N\}$.

An intuitive proof can be outlined as follows: Employers with lower than average discrimination coefficients will obtain a windfall gain by hiring black labor at the going market rate. These employers will then reinvest their above-normal profits and bid up the black wage rate or lower their output prices and drive the more discriminatory employers out of business. Therefore, if just one white employer has a zero taste for discrimination, in the long run there cannot be *any* market discrimination against black labor. Even if all employers wish

---

[11] Kenneth Arrow, "Some Mathematical Models of Racial Discrimination in the Labor Market," in Anthony Pascal, ed., *Racial Discrimination in Economic Life* (Lexington, Mass.: D.C. Heath, 1972), p. 192.

[12] Becker, *Economics of Discrimination*, pp. 36–37, and Arrow, "Some Models of Racial Discrimination."

to discriminate, so that $d_m > 0$, it will always be profitable and therefore tempting for individual employers to violate their attitudes. The competitive market works to change racist attitudes. The Becker model thus suggests that insofar as competitive market forces are operative, racial discrimination in the real world will progressively diminish and then disappear altogether!

To explain the persistence of discrimination, Becker points to the prevalence of monopólistic industries. Such industries presumably resist competitive market pressures. Indeed, Becker offers antimonopoly policy recommendations as the best strategy for ending racial discrimination. But he does not provide any empirical evidence that wage discrimination is greater in monopolistic industries than in competitive ones. He asserts that his model is correct without providing any test of its validity.

Becker does present evidence suggesting that proportionately fewer nonwhites are employed in monopolistic sectors.[13] However, the evidence that Becker cites to prove that competitive industries are less discriminatory seems open to other interpretations. Becker does not control for industry wage level, and it is well known that monopolistic industries tend to have relatively higher wage levels. Discrimination mechanisms that keep blacks out of high-wage jobs will simultaneously lead to a greater concentration of blacks in competitive industries without the operation of Becker's competitive forces.

Becker's calculations are based on a dichotomous classification of industries as either perfectly monopolistic or perfectly competitive. What happens when industries are classified less crudely? If a continuous concentration ratio variable is employed, no significant relation is found within the manufacturing sector between the proportion of nonwhite employees in an industry and the degree of industry concentration.[14]

[13] Becker, *Economics of Discrimination*, pp. 38–46.
[14] Raymond Franklin, "A Framework for the Analysis of Interurban Negro-White Economic Differentials," *Industrial and Labor Relations Review* (April 1968).

Moreover, employment discrimination against blacks is more severe in more profitable industries, contrary to the predictions of Becker's model.[15] Thus, Becker's modicum of supportive empirical evidence for his model does not buttress his case very well.

William Shepherd has attempted to resuscitate the hypothesis that monopolistic industries will be more discriminatory because they can resist competitive market pressures.[16] Shepherd examined nonwhite employment in white collar occupations in broadly defined industrial and service sectors. Having found a negative and statistically significant correlation between a sector's concentration ratio and its proportion of white collar employment this is nonwhite, Shepherd concluded that monopolistic sectors are more successful at excluding blacks from white collar occupations.

But Shepherd's simple correlation is consistent with the equally plausible alternative causational hypothesis that blacks are excluded from high-wage jobs. Wages for white collar work are much higher in manufacturing than in service industries. An examination of Shepherd's scatter diagram suggests that a simple dummy variable for the service sector explains much of the variance in his dependent variable. Given the collinearity between wage rates and industry concentration ratios, a more elaborate statistical technique is needed to distinguish the exclusion hypothesis from the monopoly hypothesis advanced by Shepherd.[17]

To summarize, Becker's discrimination model is inadequate on the grounds of logical contradictions and empirical irrelevance. Its assumptions of an international trade analogy and its focus on exogenous tastes as the motive for discrimina-

[15] William Comanor, "Racial Discrimination in American Industry," *Economica* (November 1973).

[16] William G. Shepherd, *Market Power and Economic Performance* (New York: Random House, 1970), pp. 213–220.

[17] Robert Flanagan's empirical tests of Becker's theory also failed to validate the racial employment patterns predicted by his model. See Robert Flanagan, "Racial Wage Discrimination and Employment Segregation," *Journal of Human Resources* (Fall 1973).

tion seem inappropriate and unenlightening. Becker's model assumes away unemployment, predicts the disappearance of discrimination in a competitive world, and does not adequately demonstrate that empirically observed discrimination persists because of the effects of monopoly.

THE WHITE MONOPOLISTIC CARTEL MODEL

Anne Krueger, Lester Thurow, and others have articulated discrimination models in which all whites band together against blacks. In contrast to Becker they postulate that economic gain rather than psychic preferences provides the major motive for discrimination and that collective action among whites achieves this result. How is a cartel consisting of millions of whites enforced in the absence of an apartheid-like state? The authors vary in their clarity on this crucial question. Krueger is the most forthright on this issue.

Krueger argues that "interpretations of discrimination are possible in which the motive for discrimination is economic rather than one of mere taste."[18] Like Becker, Krueger also develops an international trade analogy, with W exporting capital to B in the amount of E. Unlike Becker, Krueger looks at total money income of whites, Y_W, without psychic pain offsets:

$$(1) \qquad Y_W = f(L_W, K_W - E) + f_{K_B} \cdot E$$

White income is maximized when:

$$\frac{\partial Y_W}{\partial E} = f_{K_W} + f_{KK_B} \cdot E + f_{K_B} = 0$$

or, (2) $\qquad f_{K_W} = f_{K_B} + f_{KK_B} \cdot E$

Since $f_{KK_B} < 0$, whites maximize income by having a higher marginal product for capital exported than for capital at

[18] Anne Krueger, "The Economics of Discrimination," *Journal of Political Economy* (October 1963).

home. Whites can increase their total income by appropriate discrimination against blacks, by imposing an "optimum tariff" on exported capital. The possibility of white gain gives the cartel model an initial plausibility.

How are the cartel's discrimination gains destributed among its members? The income of white capitalists is given by:

$$(3) \qquad P = f_{K_W} \cdot (K_W - E) + f_{K_B} \cdot E$$

Capitalists' income is maximized when:

$$\frac{\partial P}{\partial E} = -f_{K_W} - f_{KK_W} \cdot (K_W - E) + f_{K_B} + f_{KK_B} \cdot E = 0$$

or, (4) $\quad f_{K_W} + f_{KK_W} \cdot (K_W - E) = f_{K_B} + f_{KK_B} \cdot E$

Comparing (4) and (2), we see that maximizing total white incomes is consistent with a maximum of white capitalists' income if, and only if, $f_{KK_W} \cdot (K_W - E) = 0$.* This condition generally will not be met. Therefore, white capitalists' income is reduced by their participation in a discriminatory "cartel" with white workers (assuming no further redivision of income occurs among whites). On the other hand, white labor's income increases so long as discrimination restricts capital exports to B, for then L_W gains by working intramarginally with more capital.

These results seem paradoxical. Why should white capitalists participate in a white cartel and discriminate against blacks if this discriminatory cartel causes them to lose potential income? And why should individual capitalists not cheat on the cartel, and gain even more? Krueger recognizes this

---

* Krueger's own calculation is somewhat different, and contains an error. She calculates, mistakenly,

$$\frac{\partial P}{\partial E} = -f_{K_B} - f_{KK_B} \cdot E + f_{KK_B} \cdot E.$$

Setting $\partial P/\partial E = 0$ then gives $f_{K_W} = f_{K_B}$, for then $f_{KK_W} = f_{KK_B}$ But her important qualitative implications are not changed by the corrections. See Krueger, "The Economics of Discrimination," p. 483.

problem and tries to resolve it by positing a relatively equal distribution of ownership of physical and human capital among whites. Then "the direct income losses of white capitalists would be relatively small" because of offsetting gains to white labor power.[19]

This reasoning might be appropriate in an economy of small independent producers. However, it is not appropriate for the United States economy, as data on the concentration of ownership and income reveal. In 1954, 1.6 percent of the adult population owned all of corporate bonds and 80 percent of corporate stock; wealth concentration data for subsequent years show similar patterns. The Gini coefficient of income from capital in 1962 was .93, as compared to a Gini coefficient of .43 for all income.[20] The variance in earnings from schooling is also substantial, just as the covariance between schooling and the ownership of financial assets is, for those who inherit financial wealth also obtain the most and best schooling.[21] With such inequality in the ownership of schooling and financial wealth among whites, Krueger's explanation for the solidarity of the white cartel must be rejected as highly implausible.

Krueger does not resolve the paradox of capitalists' discriminating for an economic motive when they lose income by so doing.

[19] Krueger, "The Economics of Discrimination."

[20] See Robert Lampman, *The Share of Top Wealth-Holders in National Wealth, 1922–1956* (New York: National Bureau of Economic Research, 1962), p. 209; J.D. Smith and S.D. Franklin, "The Concentration of Personal Wealth, 1922–1969," *American Economic Review* (May 1974), p. 166; Dorothy Weiss et al., "Survey of Financial Characteristics of Consumers," in Lee Soltow, ed., *Six Papers on the Size Distribution of Income* (New York: National Bureau of Economic Research, 1969).

[21] See Samuel Bowles, "Schooling and Inequality from Generation to Generation," *Journal of Political Economy* (May–June 1972); Samuel Bowles and Herbert Gintis, *Schooling in Capitalist America* (New York: Basic Books, 1976).

90

The White Cartel Analysis Extended

Several other authors have suggested that whites act in a monopolistic fashion against blacks. Lester Thurow's analysis of discrimination descends directly from Krueger's.[22] Like Krueger, Thurow assumes that the motive for discrimination is economic rather than one of taste. "A rational discriminator (for example, a monopolist named 'whites') is trying to maximize his gains from discrimination, including economic gains and increases in social distance."[23]

Thurow goes on to suggest seven categories of discrimination; he formalizes the objective function for each that whites would seek to maximize if they were joined together in a cartel to discriminate against blacks. Thurow's seven categories are: (1) employment discrimination (higher unemployment among blacks); (2) wage discrimination (blacks paid less than whites for performing the same work); (3) occupational discrimination (restrictions on black entry to some occupations); (4) human capital discrimination (less investment in black schooling); (5) capital discrimination (limitations on blacks in the capital market); (6) monopoly power discrimination (blacks constrained to competitive sectors of the economy); and (7) price discrimination (black buyers pay above market prices and black sellers pay below market prices). In each case whites collectively restrict the operation of free markets, thereby preventing blacks from working where their marginal productivity would dictate or from receiving their entire marginal product.

A cartel model must produce gains for whites if it is to be a logically coherent model of discrimination. Within Thurow's framework it is possible to specify under what conditions whites as a whole would lose or gain from discrimination. The gains occur because of the transfer of income from blacks to whites; the losses arise from the reduction in total output

[22] Thurow, *Poverty and Discrimination*, pp. 111–138.
[23] Ibid., p. 118.

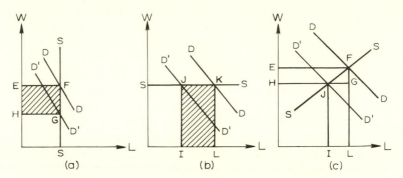

Figure 3.1. White Gains and Losses from Discrimination

created by the distortion in the efficient allocation of resources that results from discrimination. These effects are illustrated in Figure 3.1 for the case of labor market discrimination. The panels in Figure 3.1 indicate three alternative labor supply functions.

In each case discrimination lowers the demand for labor curve from DD to $D'D'$. In Panel (A) the black labor supply curve is perfectly inelastic; output is unchanged, black wages fall, and the gains to whites are measured by the shaded rectangle EFGH. In Panel (B) the labor supply is perfectly elastic. Employment and output fall by the amount IL, while the black wage remains unchanged; the losses to whites are measured by the shaded rectangle IJKL. In Panel (C), with an upwardly sloped labor supply curve, both black employment and the black wage rate fall. Net gains will occur only to the extent that trapezoid EFJH exceeds in area trapezoid IJFL.

For each type of discrimination Thurow estimates the gains versus the inefficiency losses. His calculation suggests that the overall gains exceed the overall losses by about fifteen billion dollars in 1960.[24] The implications are clear. Whites will not end discrimination voluntarily because they benefit from it: "Since discrimination produces large economic gains, there are

[24] Ibid., p. 134.

92

important vested interests in its continuation. Programs to eliminate discrimination must take these into account; economic self-interest cannot be counted on to aid in eliminating discrimination."[25]

In the political context of the late 1960s, black nationalists and their supporters were attracted to Thurow's model. Thurow, in effect, explains black economic underdevelopment in terms that recall how dependent colonies have been exploited by their imperialist masters. His model leads to the call for reparations to the black community, a demand voiced by black nationalist leaders in this period, as well as to the desirability of establishing an independent black state, also a theme of nationalist leaders in the late 1960s.

Neither these political programs nor the theoretical model on which they were based were able to gain wide adherence. Thurow's model did not win acceptance because his presentation papered over fundamental cracks in the cartel theory.

To begin with, Thurow nowhere offers sustained evidence to support his assertions. Although he marshals an impressive quantity of data from the 1960 census to estimate the magnitude of white gains from discrimination, these estimates do not validate the theory itself. They suggest the size of the effects, assuming that the theory on which they are based is correct and complete. Thurow does give several examples (such as the prevalence of black maids and garbage collectors) as anecdotal evidence for the view that whites seek to maintain social rather than physical distance from blacks. But more systematic evidence is needed to demonstrate the validity of the model. And the calculations leave us with little knowledge of the distribution of the purported gains among the members of the white cartel.

Thurow does not provide a sustained defense of the assertion that a cartel is in the interests of all whites. He simply assumes that all whites benefit because blacks are excluded from competition with them. This may well be true for some whites, but

[25] Ibid.

not for all. Because his model combines seven different kinds of discrimination, it does not contain clear implications for the distribution of gains among whites resulting from cartel discrimination. Moreover, some whites may incur costs in addition to those resulting from the output losses of inefficient resource allocation.

Finally, even if all whites benefit from the existence of a cartel, it will still be in the interests of individual whites to cheat on the cartel agreement. In the absence of an official apartheid state, resembling the current South-African type or the historic Jim Crow variety in the United States, there must be sanctions for violating the cartel if it is not to fall apart. American sociologists observed such sanction systems in the small towns of the South in the 1930s.[26] But civil rights legislation and antidiscriminatory agencies prohibit the existence of formal cartels in the United States today. Thurow does not explain how such a cartel would be policed. With these difficulties the white cartel model did not gain widespread adherents among economic theorists.

Crowding Models

Bergmann and others have emphasized monopolistic elements in the labor market that force blacks to "crowd" into a restricted number of low-paying occupations, thus limiting the supply of labor to other occupations. Unlike Krueger and Thurow, Bergmann does not state clearly the motives for this crowding. It is simply the case that "some jobs are open to Negroes and some are not."[27] We can examine the effects of occupational crowding on different groups of whites,

---

[26] See George Akerlof, "The Economics of Caste, the Rat-Race and Other Woeful Tales," *Quarterly Journal of Economics* (November 1977). On the U.S. South in the 1930s, see Allison Davis et al., *Deep South* (Chicago: University of Chicago Press, 1941).

[27] Barbara R. Bergmann, "The Effect on White Incomes of Discrimination in Employment," *Journal of Political Economy* (January–February 1971). Barbara Bergmann and Jerolyn R. Lyle, "Differences Amongst Cities and

but we cannot evaluate, except by inference, whether the discriminators are achieving their desired goals.

Bergmann analyzes the effects of crowding on whites as follows. According to the crowding hypothesis, blacks are restricted to jobs in a number of low-paying occupations. Since they are excluded from other occupations, they over-crowd the accessible ones; the excess labor employed depresses marginal products and wage rates in these occupations. Meanwhile, whites reap the benefits of working in the higher-paid occupations that are inaccessible to blacks. Wages in these high-paying occupations will rise still higher because of the reduced supply of labor to them. Moreover, some unskilled whites benefit because they would be displaced totally from those higher-paying occupations if there were no discrimination.

Bergmann thus develops a model in which black losses from discrimination produce white gains. The extent of these gains depends on the proportion of blacks in the labor force, the number of occupations in which they are restricted, the magnitude of racial educational differences, and the elasticity of substitution among different occupations and among the different factors of production. Unskilled whites in occupations that are closed to blacks stand to gain the most, for it is their occupations that most blacks would enter into in a world without labor market discrimination. Highly skilled whites are affected the least, since only a small number of blacks would be sufficiently qualified to compete with these whites in the absence of labor market discrimination. In any case since blacks are a relatively small proportion of the total labor force, they cannot be too much of a threat, and no group of whites is affected substantially. For the same reason, output

Industries in the Occupational Standing of Negroes in the Private Sector," *Journal of Human Resources* (September 1970). Barbara R. Bergmann, "Occupational Segregation, Wages and Profits When Employers Discriminate by Race or Sex," *Eastern Economic Journal* (April–July 1974).

losses due to inefficiency distortions created by discrimination are small, and do not modify significantly the above analysis.[28]

Bergmann's empirical calculations attempt to estimate the magnitude of these effects. She finds that white males with less than eight years of schooling would lose less than 10 percent of their earnings if discrimination were ended. All other white males would experience much lower losses.[29]

These estimates depend strongly, however, on the assumed elasticity of substitution among different kinds of labor. Available estimates show the elasticity of substitution to be substantially higher than the several parameters used by Bergmann in her empirical calculations.[30] This greater elasticity of substitution means that the effects of crowding on wage rates in other occupations will be much lower than Bergmann's estimates. Moreover, her one-commodity model understates substitution possibilities. Even if the elasticity of substitution for a given industry is low, substitution among products can also take place, thereby increasing the overall elasticity and further lessening the strength of the crowding mechanism.

Bergmann suggests also that the employer class does not gain from discrimination. As in the Krueger model, employers' incomes are maximized only when competitive markets are free of distortions. Bergmann's empirical results indicate that employers lose very little from discrimination because the inefficiencies created are so small that national income goes down by a very small amount.

---

[28] A similar crowding model has been elaborated by Arrow. A somewhat different model has been argued by Barry Chiswick. In his model nonwhites are better substitutes for unskilled whites than for skilled whites. A greater proportion of nonwhites produces a higher rate of return to schooling for whites, and consequently more inequality among whites. See Barry Chiswick, "Racial Discrimination in the Labor Market: A Test of Alternative Hypotheses," *Journal of Political Economy* (November–December 1973).

[29] Bergmann, "The Effect on White Incomes.

[30] For higher estimates of the elasticity of substitution among different grades of labor, see Samuel Bowles, *Planning Educational Systems for Economic Growth* (Cambridge: Harvard University Press, 1970), chapter 4.

Like Thurow, Bergmann does not systematically attempt to demonstrate the validity of her model. She begins with the important and easily documentable fact that blacks are concentrated in the lowest paying occupations and then calculates the quantitative consequences of occupational crowding on the assumption that her theory is correct. But these calculations do not constitute empirical verification.

Bergmann offers only the slightest explanation of why certain jobs are open to blacks and others are not. Like Becker, she leaves this crucial question to other disciplines and thus does not explain the *extent* of crowding. In fact, the range of jobs that are open to blacks varies substantially across regions and in different time periods. This variation remains significant after holding constant the proportion of blacks in a local labor force.[31]

The argument that blacks are restricted from some occupations does not explain how this restriction takes place, who enforces it, and why. The theoretical problems that plague Thurow's cartel model apply with equal force here. One answer to these questions may lie in the behavior of white workers and supervisors toward blacks at the workplace. In the next Section I turn to some neoclassical analyses along these lines.

Despite its failings, the cartel model does alert us to the possible significance of coalitions among groups of whites in understanding discrimination. The Krueger and Thurow models implicitly assume that the government acts as an instrument of cartel enforcement. Although this assumption is unsatisfactory now that blacks have been reenfranchised, it does suggest the importance of adding an analysis of the role of the state to the analysis of possible coalition-formations at the workplace. Finally, the brief mention of racial differentials in unemployment in Thurow's account alerts us to the importance of incorporating macroeconomic analysis into these microeconomic explanations of racial discrimination.

---

[31] See Chapter 2 of this study for a discussion of changes in the position of black artisans in the South.

DISCRIMINATION AS A RELATION AMONG WORKERS

Dissatisfaction with the distaste and cartel models led economists to revise the theory of the internal relations within the firm to explain the stability of discrimination in a competitive market economy. Economists such as Finis Welch and Kenneth Arrow began to pay more attention to friction between black and white employees. They were stimulated by a deficiency in Becker's model of employee discrimination, one of several secondary models presented in *The Economics of Discrimination*.

In Becker's employee discrimination model, employers do not discriminate, but white workers do. In order to compensate for their distaste for working with blacks, who are perfect substitutes, white workers must get higher wages. That is, as the proportion of blacks in a firm's work force increases, so too must white wages. Consequently, racially mixed work forces will be more expensive than segregated shops.

This employee discrimination model appeals because white workers have frequently exhibited racist behavior. But the model contains a serious logical difficulty. Employers with a racially mixed work force could always increase their profits and lower white wages by hiring only white workers and firing the black ones, or by firing the white workers and maintaining an all-black work force. Moreover, since employers are indifferent about hiring either an all-white or an all-black work force, black and white wage rates will be equal. Thus, employee discrimination produces segregation but not discrimination in observed wage rates. This theoretical result does not accord at all with the most evident empirical patterns.

Welch and Arrow therefore wanted to develop an employee discrimination model in which production is racially integrated, yet blacks receive lower wages, and in the long run, this discrimination is stable.[32] Such a model would resolve the inadequacies of the Becker employee discrimination model.

[32] Finis Welch, "Labor Market Discrimination: An Interpretation of Income Differences in the Rural South," *Journal of Political Economy* (June 1967).

Welch begins by assuming that workers with different amounts of schooling are complements rather than substitutes in production. The joint product of one educated and one uneducated worker will be greater than the sum of their individual products working separately. Whites have more schooling than blacks. Production complementarities, therefore, provide the incentive for employers to use both blacks and whites in production.

How does discrimination enter the model? Welch defines employee discrimination as occurring if external inefficiencies are produced when workers of different races work alongside one another. Thus, the effect of discrimination is to reduce production complementarities among racially diverse workers. It follows that the *effective* marginal product of a black worker is less than that of a white worker of the same skill level. Therefore, wages of blacks will be lower than those of equivalently skilled whites. But so long as the complementarities exceed the external inefficiencies, firms will be integrated and the marginal product and wage of educated white workers will be raised by the hiring of black workers.

Welch's discrimination model can be formalized as follows. Output (q) is a function of a physical labor input (L) and embodied schooling input (S):

$$q = f(L, S)$$

There are two groups of workers, one with average years of schooling r_1, and the other with average years of schooling r_2. In the absence of discrimination, wages are given by:

$$(5) \qquad W_1 = \frac{\partial q}{\partial L_1} = \frac{\partial q}{\partial L} + r_1 \cdot \frac{\partial q}{\partial S}$$

$$(6) \qquad W_2 = \frac{\partial q}{\partial L_2} = \frac{\partial q}{\partial L} + r_2 \cdot \frac{\partial q}{\partial S}$$

Suppose that type 1 workers are black and a numerical minority, while type 2 workers are white and a numerical majority. Then $r_1 < r_2$ and $L_1 < L_2$. Suppose further that production complementarities are maximized when each type 1

99

worker is teamed with one type 2 worker. Discrimination creates friction between the two types of workers and reduces their productivity, or effective working time. Let p_1 be the proportion of a black worker's time that is lost when he or she associates with a white worker, and let p_2 be the proportion of the white worker's time that is lost. The loss of lutput for each unit of physical labor is then $p_1 + p_2$, and the loss for each unit of schooling is $r_1 p_1 + r_2 p_2$. The effective marginal product (and wage) of the black worker is then:

$$(7) \quad W_1 = \frac{\partial q}{\partial L_1} = (1 - p_1 - p_2)\frac{\partial q}{\partial L} + (r_1 - p_1 r_1 - p_2 r_2)\frac{\partial q}{\partial S}.$$

Discrimination lowers a black worker's wage. But the wage of the more educated white worker is still:

$$(8) \qquad\qquad W_2 = \frac{\partial q}{\partial L} + r_2 \frac{\partial q}{\partial S}.$$

Black workers must absorb the full effects of the decline in labor efficiency because the addition of a black worker reduces his or her effective working time *and* that of the associated white worker. By contrast, the addition of a white worker does not increase the amount of association between the groups.

Since black workers absorb the full loss of efficiency, profits of employers are not affected by discrimination. The change in profits is given by: $\Delta \pi = \Delta q - \Delta W_1 \cdot L^1$. But $\Delta W_1 = \Delta q / L$; therefore $\Delta \pi = 0$.

To summarize, in Welch's model blacks lose income because white resentment creates friction and inefficiencies, and the decline in output is borne completely by blacks. The incomes of white workers and employers are not affected.

This surprising result depends strongly on the underlying assumptions. A slight change in the assumptions leads to different results. In a model that is similar to Welch's but more general, Arrow has considered the situation where some type 1 labor is white and some is black.[33] Type 1 white labor dislikes working under type 2 blacks, so all blacks are placed in type 1 occupations. As before, type 2 labor dislikes associating with blacks, the intensity varying with the proportion of type 1 workers who are black. In this case, as Arrow has elegantly shown, discrimination effectively transfers income from blacks to type 1 whites. Again, the incomes of type 2 whites and employers are left unchanged.

The internal logic of Welch's and Arrow's models appears to be coherent, and this achievement marks an advance over previous efforts. The empirical importance of their explanation of the forces reproducing racial inequality is another matter. Both Welch's and Arrow's models rest critically on the assumption that the workplace interactions of blacks and whites generate friction and a consequent loss in productive efficiency.[34] The empirical validity and significance of this assumption is not obvious, and neither Welch nor Arrow provides supporting evidence for it.

Some evidence suggests that their discrimination mechanism is dominated by other effects. Of the complaints regarding racial discrimination received by the Equal Employment Opportunity Commission, 85 percent are directed against employers. The remainder is split equally among government, unions, and other workers.[35]

Contrary to Welch and Arrow, it seems likely that white supervisors could extract *more* work from black subordinates than from white ones. Precisely because of discrimination, black workers have fewer job alternatives from which to choose. White supervisors may therefore be able to drive their

[33] Kenneth Arrow, "Some Models of Racial Discrimination," Technical note B, pp. 189–191.

[34] Arrow's mechanism is slightly different, but formally equivalent. Instead of external inefficiencies, he argues that type 2 whites must be compensated for associating with blacks.

[35] *1972 Annual Report*, U.S. Equal Employment Opportunity Commission (Washington, D.C.: U.S. Government Printing Office, 1972).

101

black subordinates harder, speeding up their work rate and assigning them to the heaviest and dirtiest work. These considerations, should they outweigh the inefficiencies analyzed by Welch and Arrow, cast doubt upon the empirical relevance of their models. Indeed, Arrow and other economic theorists have looked to other characteristics of employment relations within the firm to explain the stability of racial discrimination in a competitive economy. Next, I turn to these efforts.

EMPLOYMENT RELATION MODELS OF DISCRIMINATION

The most recent neoclassical attempt to explain discrimination does not invoke the "irrational" distaste for blacks of the Becker model, or the desire to exploit blacks for economic gain of the cartel model, or the friction among workers in the Welch-Arrow model. The new view instead sees discrimination as rooted in the rational attempts of employers to minimize their personnel costs. These "employment relations" theories make use of a revised theory of the firm, examining the personnel costs of hiring, training, and firing workers as well as emphasizing the costs involved in obtaining information about the productivity of applicants for employment. This group of discrimination theorists begins to scrutinize the nature of the relation between workers and employers at the workplace in much greater detail than has been customary among economists.

The several versions of the "employment relations" discrimination model can be arrayed according to their complexity. I begin with the simplest model and then introduce further elements to it. Each has been developed by a number of economic theorists; the clearest and best-known versions are due to Kenneth Arrow.[36]

The simplest model assumes that there are fixed nonzero costs of hiring, training, and firing workers and shows how the minimization of these costs works against competitive forces.

[36] Arrow, "Some Models of Racial Discrimination."

Consider an employer with an all-white work force who wants to take advantage of cheaper black labor. The paper work and other costs of firing and then hiring a new work force, as well as employer's investments in the specific training skills of the existing workers, militate against changing the work force all at once. Although the employer may find it profitable to make marginal adjustments, such as hiring black workers as vacancies occur, the inertia of existing hiring patterns will exert a substantial influence over racial employment patterns for a long time. Arrow summarizes his own presentation of such a model as follows:

> If we start from a position where black workers enter an all-white world, the social feelings of racialism by employers and by employees, both of the same and complementary types, will lead to a difference in wages. The forces of competition and the tendency to profit-maximization operate to mitigate these differences. The basic fact of a personnel investment, however, prevents these counteracting tendencies from working with full force. In the end, we remain with wage differences coupled with tendencies to segregation.[37]

Arrow's argument has some force for short-run analysis. But can it usefully explain long-run patterns of racial discrimination? With the enormous number of job changes in the economy and the growth of new firms and job structures, ordinary turnover ought to permit Arrow's counteracting tendencies of competition and profit maximization to work with significant force to reduce and eliminate labor market discrimination.[38] This simple personnel investment model does not provide a cogent explanation of persistent racial income differentials.

---

[37] Ibid., p. 96.

[38] For data on annual turnover and job changes, see Clair Vickery, "The Impact of Turnover on Group Unemployment Rates," *Review of Economics and Statistics* (November 1977).

Arrow makes his own model more complex by adding to it considerations on the cost to employers of identifying potential workers' productivity.[39] Employers must identify the productivity of different applicants in order to rank them on a queue and decide which ones to hire. But obtaining information about individuals is costly. Personnel managers, uncertain about an applicant's true productivity, must estimate it from observable characteristics. Race provides an easily observed characteristic with information content that helps to reduce personnel costs. If personnel managers believe that blacks *as a group* have lower average productivity than whites as a group, it is then cheaper to assume lower productivity for *any* individual black worker than to obtain direct information. And it is much more costly to make the mistake of hiring an inefficient worker than to make the mistake of passing over a productive one. Consequently, blacks are ranked lower in the employer's queue and not hired at all or are hired at lower wage rates. Because individual blacks are evaluated as having the characteristics of their group, this mechanism has been called "statistical discrimination."

This model explains the persistence of racial inequality in terms that relieve employers and personnel managers of any personal responsibility or motive for discrimination. Individual employers may not harbor discriminatory feelings. They are just acting rationally to minimize their costs. They can attribute the causes of low productivity among blacks to other social institutions, such as the structure of the black family, ghetto culture, the schools, the welfare system, or other alleged social roots of black disadvantage.

If the employer's belief that race is associated with low productivity is false, a feedback mechanism may nonetheless

---

[39] Additional relevant authors here include Peter Doeringer and Michael Piore, *Internal Labor Markets and Manpower Analysis* (Lexington, Mass.: D.C. Heath, 1971), chapter 7; Edwin Phelps, "The Statistical Theory of Racism and Sexism," *American Economic Review* (September 1972); and Michael Spence, *Market Signalling* (Cambridge: Harvard University Press, 1974). In what follows, I discuss mainly Arrow's statement of this approach.

104

set up a self-fulfilling prophecy that will confirm that belief. Observing employers' prejudices, blacks will invest in less schooling and other productivity-augmenting activities than whites because the black return to such investment will be lower. Rational responses by blacks thus reinforce the belief that they are unsuitable for jobs requiring considerable education. This feedback effect has been called a "signaling model" because schooling is an acquired characteristic that sends a signal to the employer. Unfortunately for the theory, however, blacks have increased their investment in schooling very rapidly. The feedback mechanism model seems deficient as an explanation.

The statistical-discrimination and signaling arguments require very strong assumptions about the unobservability of individual abilities. Most employers ask for and know much more about a job applicant than his or her race. Employers usually know at least the applicant's age, gender, address, schooling history, marital status, health status, and previous work history. They usually observe the applicant's self-presentation in a job interview, know the results of any job-related tests, and can check the applicant's references. The explanatory power of the statistical-discrimination argument is thus limited to the *additional* information that race provides to employers.

The standard personnel data just mentioned may not provide complete information about the productivity of individual workers. Most employers therefore have instituted trial or probationary periods for new employees. The probationary period most frequently ranges from thirty to ninety days, and it often lasts for six months or a year. During this time probationary employees can be fired without the usual grievance procedures, appeals, and tenure rights granted to other employees, and the employer does not contribute to probationary workers' fringe benefits. It is common to have gradations within the initial probationary period itself, so that employees who will not work out can be weeded out early. In most jobs very little formal, specific skill training is invested

105

by employers in probationary workers, since the job require-
ments are usually learned in a few hours or a few days, and
most of the training occurs informally on the job.[40]

These remarks, directed to the case of unskilled and semiskilled workers, apply just as strongly to the case of skilled
workers. Although employers have a greater training investment in their skilled employees, these workers are also subject
to probationary periods, and they are scrutinized much more
intensely before being hired. Employers obtain more information about these workers, through recommendations from
their previous employers, so that the additional information
provided by race is consequently less important.[41]

Personnel managers who believe that blacks are inferior
workers can discover quickly and cheaply whether their
prejudices are correct or mistaken. Furthermore, they face
economic incentives to do so, for the cost to employers of
identifying a worker's productivity appears to be much lower
than statistical and signaling theories of discrimination suggest. The marginal cost of determining the productivity of
black workers is even less. At the same time, the benefits of
obtaining accurate information on employees in a large
corporation would appear to be huge. The marginal revenue
derived by correcting racist misperceptions must far exceed the
marginal cost of making these corrections. These models, although logically coherent and even elegant in their structure,
do not pass the test of empirical plausibility.

Moreover, these models implicitly assume that personnel
managers in all firms are equally prejudiced. But if some
employers are less prejudiced against blacks than others, the
racial composition of employment in their firms will more
closely approximate the true (rather than the prejudiced)
racial distribution of productivity. Information-dispensing
institutions—personnel conventions, journals and associa-

---

[40] Lloyd Reynolds, *Labor Economics and Labor Relations* (Homewood,
Ill.: Richard Irwin, 1975), chapter 6.
[41] Ibid.

tions, employment agencies, and public and private civil rights organizations—will bring this information to the attention of other personnel managers. Misperceptions should not endure, for they can be corrected by simply examining the experience of other firms.

Since such corrections will increase a firm's profits, the forces of competition in the labor market ought to work to eliminate racial inequality. The misperceptions of prejudiced employers cannot explain the persistence of racial inequality.

CONCLUSION

Although the major neoclassical discrimination models give us some insights into the problem, none pass the two tests of logical coherence and empirical plausibility. The pioneering Becker model directs our attention to preferences and market imperfections. But these explanations of the persistence of racial inequality in a competitive capitalist economy are not compelling. Becker's very thin discussion of discriminatory preference structures and psychic pains fails to illuminate the source of racial inequalities. The analytical structure of his model ignores unemployment while ironically clarifying the view that capitalist competition is the best cure for racial inequality. Becker's own empirical evidence fails to demonstrate that discrimination persists because of market imperfections. However, oligopoly and monopoly may be significant variables for discrimination theory.

Becker's successors made significant advances. Thus, the cartel theorists introduced into economic analysis the important notion that discrimination may be motivated by the pursuit of economic gain. Their suggestion that collective action is employed to achieve such ends also seems fruitful. The process of coalition formation could be investigated both at the workplace and in the political arena where government policy is determined. However, Krueger, Thurow, and other cartel theorists do not present theoretical or evidential bases to underpin the crucial assumption of the existence of a cartel involving hundreds of millions of whites, nor do they inquire systematically into the determinants of government policy.

The subsequent efforts by Arrow and others to explain that discrimination is rational for individual economic agents provide a further advance over the cartel model, for no mass conspiracy needs to be proven. The revision of the internal theory of the firm to incorporate tensions among employees, personnel costs, and the costs of identifying a worker's productivity suggests further revisions that could be made. In particular, tensions among employers, white workers, and black workers could be investigated more systematically. Inflexibilities within the firm may arise more from these employment relations than from information costs.

The neoclassical efforts discussed here provide bits and pieces of a theory: the importance of imperfect market structures (Becker), economic motives for discrimination and coalitions among whites (Krueger, Thurow), employment relations within the firm (Welch, Arrow), the impact of unemployment and the role of the state (Thurow). These elements will be drawn upon in subsequent chapters. But the neoclassical theories do not individually or collectively provide a coherent and empirically plausible account of how discrimination is reproduced in a capitalist economy. After more than two decades of effort and the development of a voluminous literature, neoclassical economists have failed to produce a satisfactory theory of racial discrimination.

108

CHAPTER FOUR

Who Benefits from Racism?
An Econometric Test of
Neoclassical Discrimination Theories

RACIAL DISCRIMINATION obviously hurts blacks economically. But do whites gain from discrimination? If so, which ones do? The answers to these questions both aid our understanding of the interests served by the perpetuation of racial inequality and illuminate the empirical validity of discrimination theories.

We have already seen in Chapter 3 that none of the major neoclassical racial discrimination theories are both logically coherent and empirically plausible. A stronger empirical test of these theories can be devised by utilizing their testable implications concerning the distribution of gains and losses among whites resulting from racial inequality. These distributional implications permit a uniform test that can be applied to each theory. That is, how do the "who benefits" implications of each theory accord with empirical reality?

In this chapter I present the "who benefits" implications of each of the major neoclassical discrimination theories. In an empirical test of these implications, I find that none of the neoclassical theories appear to be consistent with the empirical evidence. Despite contrary predictions of neoclassical discrimination theories, I demonstrate empirically that white workers lose from racism while rich whites, capitalists, and a few privileged workers benefit. This finding strengthens further the empirical critique of these theories.

WHO BENEFITS FROM RACISM IN NEOCLASSICAL MODELS

The Psychic Pain Model

Recall that in the Becker model, W receives a money return on its exported capital, $r' = r_w + d$, where r_w equals the money

109

return on capital invested in W, and d, the discrimination coefficient, measures the psychic pain of associating with B labor ($d > 0$). Discrimination reduces the quantity of capital exported by W to B.

W labor. Discrimination increases the money income of W labor. By reducing the quantity of W capital exported and B labor imported, discrimination results in W labor working with more capital and W capital working with less total labor. Since $f_{LL} < 0$, and $f_{KL} > 0$, f_L ($=$ wage of W labor) rises.

Figure 4.1 illustrates the effect on W labor of a reduction in imported labor. To simplify the exposition assume temporarily that the quantity of domestically employed capital is fixed at $\overline{K}$. Without discrimination, L_T amount of labor is combined with capital $\overline{K}$. The wage rate paid to imported B labor, L_B, and to W labor, L_W, is $w = f_L(L = L_T)$ in both societies. With discrimination, the quantity of labor imported falls (to zero in the extreme case as shown in the figure). The quantity of total output also falls. But the wage rate paid to white labor,

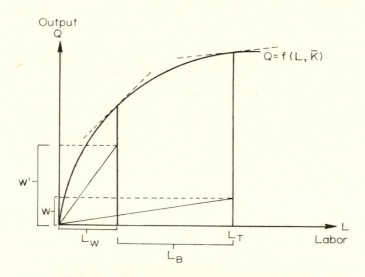

Figure 4.1. Effect of Discrimination on White Labor

110

$w^1 = f_L(L = L_W)$, rises. The income of W labor rises because of discrimination.

Now we can relax the assumption of a fixed quantity of domestically employed capital and recognize that with discrimination a greater quantity of capital will be domestically employed. Since $f_{LK} > 0$, $f_L = w$ increases with increasing K. In other words white workers gain additionally from discrimination because they are working with more capital, thereby increasing their own productivity.

W capital. Becker defines the net income of white capitalists as equal to the total quantity of white capital times the money return on white capital that is *domestically* employed:

$$(2) \qquad Y_W^K = f_{K_W} \cdot K.$$

We need only determine the effect of discrimination on f_{K_W} to obtain the change in the income of W capitalists. We know that less capital is exported to B with discrimination and more capital is employed domestically. We also know that f_{K_W}, the the money return on domestic capital , falls as more capital is employed domestically. Therefore, W capitalists' net income falls as a result of discrimination. This result accords with intuitive sense. Capitalists maximize profits by following the decision rule to invest their capital until it receives the same return everywhere; discriminatory action violates this rule, and, consequently, it should lower capitalists' income. Thus, Becker's model predicts that white capitalists lose and white labor gains from racial discrimination.

The White Monopolistic Cartel Model

Recall that unlike Becker, Krueger looks at total money income of whites, Y_W, without psychic pain offsets. In Chapter 3 we saw that white capitalists' income is reduced by their participation in a discriminatory "cartel" with white workers (assuming no further redivision of income occurs among whites). On the other hand, white labor's income increases so long as discrimination restricts capital exports to B, for then L_W gains by working intramarginally with more capital.

111

Thurow's model of seven different kinds of discrimination does not permit any uniform implications concerning the distribution of gains among whites resulting from racial discrimination. As for Bergmann's crowding model, racial barriers to entry restrict the occupations that are open to blacks; consequently, these occupations are crowded and the supply of labor to other occupations is limited. Crowding theoretically produces the greatest gains for unskilled whites—for whom blacks could otherwise easily substitute. It produces smaller gains for skilled whites, and has no effect on employers. In other words, the greater the crowding, the more compressed the white occupational wage structure and, therefore, the more equal the white income distribution.

The Employment Relation and Information Cost Theories

The employment relation theory focuses on discrimination as a relation among different workers, black and white, skilled and unskilled. In Welch's model, black workers absorb the full loss of efficiency resulting from racial antagonisms. Neither white workers' wages nor employers' profits are affected by racial discrimination. Consequently, Welch's model predicts that the effects of discrimination on the white income distribution are neutral. Discrimination in Arrow's variant of the Welch model produces gains for skilled whites while employers and unskilled whites are unaffected. This model thus predicts that increases in discrimination reduce the share of white income that is received by capitalists, while the effect on overall inequality among whites is neutral.

The information cost theories contain neutral implications concerning the effect of racial discrimination on the distribution of earnings among groups of white workers. Some individual white workers will be allocated to "wrong" job assignments, but the group distribution will be unchanged. Capitalist income is not affected. Since I have already presented an empirical critique of these theories in Chapter 3, I am passing over them here.

These neoclassical discrimination models share a common

distributional implication. They predict that racial inequality results in a less unequal income distribution among whites or has no effect at all on the white income distribution. The Becker and Krueger models predict that capitalists are hurt and white workers benefit from racial inequality; the Bergmann model has racial crowding compressing the white earnings distribution; the Thurow, Welch, and Arrow models have neutral implications. None of these models predicts that racial inequality produces increased inequality among whites.

AN ECONOMETRIC MODEL OF RACIAL INEQUALITY AND THE WHITE INCOME DISTRIBUTION

I develop here a cross-sectional econometric model to examine statistically the distribution of white gains and losses from racial discrimination. The model exploits the substantial variation that exists across metropolitan areas in the United States in both racial inequality and inequality among whites. The model is based on the general market forces that influence inequality in metropolitan areas, with the addition of the effect of racial inequality. This specification enables me to test the effects of greater racial inequality in a metropolitan area upon income inequality among whites.

In neoclassical economic theory, income distribution is determined by market forces on the demand and supply of capital and labor of various skill levels. The state of technology, initial endowments of labor, skills, and capital, and (if there are nonconstant returns to scale) individual preferences for individual commodities also play a role. However, only those market variables that vary across metropolitan areas need be included in the cross-sectional model that is developed here.

Consider the geographical boundaries of a metropolitan area (more strictly of a U.S. census-defined Standard Metropolitan Statistical Area) as defining the spatial dimensions of a distinct local urban labor market. To begin with, assume that trade in goods and services takes place between the SMSA and

113

the rest of the world, but that movement of factors—labor and capital—is restricted by the boundaries of the labor market. Later, I shall examine the effects on the model of allowing capital and labor mobility across SMSA boundaries.

As a first approximation assume that the mix of industries in the SMSA is primarily determined by considerations of geography—for example, access to raw materials or particular markets—and by accidents of history. That is, the SMSA's industrial structure is assumed to be exogenously determined.

The mix of industries, or industrial structure, of an SMSA— the distribution of employment among agriculture, construction, manufacturing, transportation, trade, finance, insurance and real estate, services and government—will be a significant determinant of the overall income distribution. These industries vary widely in their average labor earnings, in intra-industry occupational mix and earnings differentials, and in the share of industry income received by labor. If employment in an SMSA predominates, for example, in industries with narrow wage spreads and similar average wages, the SMSA will tend to have a more equal income distribution because earning inequalities among workers will be relatively low. If some cities provide relatively more employment opportunities for both blacks and unskilled whites, the industrial structure and related variables should pick up this influence.

Of course, the industrial structure of an SMSA is not strictly exogenous, and the demand for labor of different skill classes is not determined independently of the quality of the local labor supply. The substitution by firms of one "grade" of labor for another will accompany changes in the available quantities of labor of different skill levels. And the quality of the labor supply can affect the mix of industries in an SMSA as well as the choice of technologies adopted by those industries.

A cross-SMSA model of income distribution should include as variables the elasticity of substitution for different grades of labor as determined by the production function of each industry in the SMSA. Unfortunately, the data to compute

114

such elasticities are not available. The model therefore assumes that the relative supplies of labor of different educational classes are primarily determined by the industrial and occupational structure of demand. This assumption conveniently simplifies the model. Its plausibility is rooted in the following observations.

The quantity of highly schooled labor in the United States has increased over time at a percentage rate far exceeding the (negative) percentage change in relative earnings. These shifts suggest that the increase in the supply of educated labor were induced by an outward shift in demand; otherwise, the relative earnings of highly schooled labor would have fallen.[1] Second,

[1] See, for example, Zvi Griliches, "Notes on the Role of Education in Production Functions and Growth Accounting," in W. Lee Hansen, ed., *Education, Income and Human Capital* (New York: National Bureau of Economic Research 1970), and Samuel Bowles, *Planning Educational Systems for Economic Growth* (Cambridge: Harvard University Press, 1967), chapter 4, for evidence and the argument that despite the growth in the supply of schooled labor in the period 1940–1960, the high rate of return to schooling has not fallen, indicating, therefore, that an outward movement of the demand curve for schooled labor occurred during the period. The supply of schooled labor did not increase autonomously, but adjusted to the growth of demand for it in the economy.

It has recently been argued that schooled labor became oversupplied by the late 1960s, thereby depressing the rate of return to schooling; see Richard Freeman, "Overinvestment in College Training?," *Journal of Human Resources* (Summer 1975). For a critique, showing that Freeman observed cyclical rather than secular effects, see Peter Meyer, *The Reproduction of the Distribution of Income* (Ph.D. diss., University of California, Berkeley, 1979).

For many years the dominant school of educational history argued that the expansion of the educational system occurred as a result of the victorious political struggles of the middle and working classes against the upper classes. Educational reform and expansion of schooling were wanted because they were seen to be instruments of upward social mobility. Recently, this school has been challenged by a revisionist view that stresses the role of schools in socializing and disciplining a labor force for the capitalist class. For the orthodox view, see Frank Carleton, *Economic Influences Upon Educational Progress in the United States, 1920–50* (New York, 1908), and Lawrence Cremin, *The Transformation of the School* (New York: Knopf, 1964). For the revisionist view, see Samuel Bowles and Herbert Gintis, *Schooling in Cap-*

the rise of mass education is more likely a response to the rise of manufacturing rather than vice versa. By contrast, the development of mass education in the South was impeded by the antipathy of planters to manufacturing.[2]

Many cross-sectional income distribution models include as an additional variable the average level of income. The authors of these models frequently offer little theoretical justification for inclusion of this variable; most writers refer only to Kuznets's speculation that income inequality tends to decrease with economic growth. Thompson and Matilla justify inclusion of an average income variable on the grounds that affluence creates a noblesse oblige, an altruism for the poor. This rationale seems implausible.

The inclusion of an average income variable in a model of income distribution can be justified as follows. First, the average income level may reflect aspects of the industrial structure that are not captured by other industrial structure variables. Second, the effects of the migration of labor and the mobility of capital on the white income distribution (and on the degree of racial inequality) are related to the average level of income. Labor migrates from low-income areas to high-

---

italist America; Michael Katz, *The Irony of Early School Reform* (Cambridge: Harvard University Press, 1968); David Cohen and Marvin Lazerson, "Education and the Modern Labor Force," in Richard Edwards, Michael Reich, and Thomas Weisskopf, eds., *The Capitalist System* (New York: Prentice-Hall, 1972); and Samuel Bowles, "Unequal Education and the Reproduction of the Social Division of Labor," in Martin Carnoy, ed., *Schooling in a Corporate Society* (New York: McKay, 1972), and the numerous references cited in the latter two essays. Considerable present-day statistical evidence for this thesis is reported in Herbert Gintis, "Education, Attitudes and Worker Productivity," *American Economic Review* (May 1971).

[2] The antagonistic relationship of the slaveholders to manufacturing interests is analyzed in Eugene Genovese, *The Political Economy of Slavery* (New York: Random House, 1965), chapter 7. The backwardness of schooling in the South in the decades following the Civil War is described and analyzed in Horace Mann Bond, *Negro Education in Alabama, A study in Cotton and Steel* (New York: Atheneum, 1969).

116

income areas.[3] The effects of the net migration of labor out of agriculture and out of the South may be more reasonably controlled for by including an average income variable rather than including a geographic Mason-Dixon line dummy variable for the South. Migration can also be controlled for by using direct data on migration.

SPECIFICATION OF THE VARIABLES

The sample chosen contains the fifty most populous Standard Metropolitan Statistical Areas in 1960 and 1970.[4] With a sample size of forty-eight SMSAs, the smallest SMSA had a population of over 570,000 in 1960. SMSAs were chosen in preference to the more commonly used state units because SMSAs comprise a coherent metropolitan economy and labor market, whereas state boundaries reflect historically arbitrary political divisions. Moreover, the states contain large rural sectors that are not germane to the present study.

Dependent Variables

The appropriate variable in an empirical study derives from the theory and hypotheses underlying the empirical analysis and from the nature of the questions to which the empirical effort is being addressed. In this study I am concerned with the relation between the extent of racial inequality in an SMSA and the distribution of income among whites in the SMSA.

---

[3] In another cross-SMSA study, David Kaun found that median income was significantly and positively correlated with the rate of in-migration. David Kaun, "Negro Migration and Unemployment," *Journal of Human Resources* (Spring 1970).

[4] The sample chosen originally contained fifty SMSAs. But during the course of data collection and processing, it was discovered that the data published in the census for two SMSAs contained internal inconsistencies, presumably because of computational or typographical errors. These two SMSAs were dropped, leaving forty-eight in the sample. There is no a priori reason to believe the exclusion of these two SMSAs will bias the results.

Therefore, the dependent variables should measure the relative shares of SMSA income going to white labor and to capital and the extent of inequality among whites as a whole.

Unfortunately, data on the functional shares of income are not available on an SMSA basis. Nor are detailed earnings distributions by race. The data that are available by SMSA report frequency distribution of *personal* incomes, therefore limiting the dependent variables used here to measures of personal income inequality. The personal income data are themselves imperfect because the concept of income used by the Census Bureau excludes much of the income received by the very rich.[5]

However, these limitations are not very severe. First, the share received by capital can be estimated adequately for purposes here from the personal income data. Second, income and earnings inequalities are highly correlated across SMSAs and the two variables are highly interchangeable. I shall exploit the especially high correlation that obtains for workers above the twentieth percentile. Finally, a related effort by Albert Szymanski (see footnote 41 below) uses states rather than SMSAs as the unit of analysis, thus permitting him to make use of earnings data that are available on a state but not an SMSA basis. His results with earnings inequality variables are generally similar to those reported here.

From the wide variety of income inequality measures available, I make use of the Gini coefficient and various decile and percentile shares. The Gini coefficient was chosen to fill several needs.[6] First, it is the most commonly used measure of

[5] Selma Goldsmith, "Changes in the Size Distribution of Income Since the Mid-Thirties," *American Economic Review* (May 1957); John Gurley, "Federal Tax Policy," *National Tax Journal* (September 1967); Roger Herriott and Herman Miller, "Who Paid the Taxes in 1968?," *Conference Board Record* (1972).

[6] The relative merits of alternative summary measures of inequality has been the subject of a long-standing debate. An early contribution by Hugh Dalton, "The Measurement of the Inequality of Income," *Economic Journal* (September 1920) sought to relate measures of inequality to measures of aggregate social utility. Until recently, most of the subsequent discussion

118

personal income inequality and so allows comparison with other studies. Second, the Gini coefficient measures the *overall* degree of inequality, and so it does not require that one know beforehand *which* part of the income distribution is most likely to be affected by variations in the independent variables.[7] The Gini coefficient varies between 0 and 1, with 0 indicating complete equality, and 1 indicating complete inequality.

The decile and percentile share measures were chosen to

tended to be narrowly empiricist, concerned with such issues as the sensitivity of alternative measures to changes in the underlying distribution, ease of computation and presentation, and the associated issue of the choice of recipient unit. This empirical discussion is reviewed by Harold Lydall, *The Structure of Earnings* (Oxford: Oxford University Press, 1968), chapters 2–3, and by Mary Jean Bowman, "A Graphical Analysis of Personal Income Distribution in the United States," reprinted in American Economic Association, *Readings in the Theory of Income Distribution* (Philadelphia: Blakiston, 1946).

The theoretical issues raised earlier by Dalton have been revived by Aigner and Heins, by Theil, and by Atkinson, in a paper that has stimulated a series of responses. Atkinson criticized the Gini coefficient for not being consistent with any additive individualistic social welfare function. Sheshinski responded that additivity has no particular normative significance, but the additivity property was then supported as compelling by Rothschild and Stiglitz. While this debate is of some interest, it is not germane to the present study, as I am not attaching any normative significance to my measures of inequality. Moreover, I find much too restrictive the assumptions that are needed for an "individualistic social welfare function." These assumptions include no externalities or interdependencies in utility functions, as well as exogenous preference structures.

See Henri Theil, *Economics and Information Theory* (Amsterdam: North-Holland, 1967), pp. 121–128; Dennis Aigner and A. J. Heins, "A Social Welfare View of the Measurement of Income Equality," *Review of Income and Wealth* (March 1967), pp. 12–23; A.B. Atkinson, "On the Measurement of Inequality," *Journal of Economic Theory* 2 (1970); D.M.G. Newberry, "A Theorem on the Measurement of Inequality," *Journal of Economic Theory* 2 (1970); Eytan Sheshinski, "The Relation Between a Social Welfare Function and the Gini Index of Inequality," *Journal of Economic Theory* 4 (1972); Michael Rothschild and Joseph Stiglitz, "Some Further Results on the Measurement of Inequality," *Journal of Economic Theory* 6 (1973).

[7] For a comparison of the sensitivity of the Gini coefficient with other measures, see Aigner and Heins, "Social Welfare View."

probe what the Gini coefficient cannot reveal. That is, at what parts of the income distribution are the independent variables having their greatest impact? One of the dependent variables measures the percentile share of income that is received by the top 1 percent of white families. Although the data are on personal incomes, this variable provides a fair proxy for income from capital; among the top 1 percent of the population, income from capital amounts to at least two-thirds of total income.[8] This variable will therefore test the critical implications of racial inequality for capital. This variable will systematically understate capital income because of the exclusion of capital gains from the census money income concept. However, there is no reason to expect that this downward bias on the mean will bias the variance across SMSAs.

Besides the top 1 percent variable, I use several additional dependent variables. The share received by the top 5 and 10 percent of white families further measures the effect on the top tail of the income distribution. The share received by the bottom 20 and bottom 40 percent of white families investi-

---

[8] This calculation is based on the wage and salary share of total taxable income, as reported in the Internal Revenue Service, *Statistics of Income, 1966: Individual Income Tax Returns*, Tables 7, 11, and 19. Gurley estimates that returns to property (including all capital gains) account for 80 percent of the income for the top one-third of 1 percent of all families. See John Gurley, "Federal Tax Policy."

Since owners of capital do not necessarily reside in the same SMSA as the physical capital they own, the top 1 percent variable will include some returns to capital located elsewhere and will omit some returns to capital located in the SMSA. However, studies of financial interest groups have shown that controlling interests of many major corporations are located in the same city as the corporation. This suggests that some of the variance in the location of physical capital is related to the variance in the location of the capital owners. If the remaining variance is random, the top 1 percent variable retains usefulness as a proxy for capital income in the SMSA. Although it would be preferable to separate income more directly into property income, earnings, and transfers, such data are not available at the level of disaggregation used here. See Peter Dooley, "The Interlocking Directorate," *American Economic Review* (June 1969); S. Menshikov, *Millionaires and Managers* (Moscow: Progress Publishers), 1969.

gates the bottom tail of the income distribution. However, the bottom 20 percent variable will record the effects of transfer payments as well as earnings. Finally, the share of income received by white families who fall between the second and seventh deciles of income probes the effect on "middle America." This variable will best pick up the effects on workers' earnings.

No one has previously computed inequality measures for SMSAs *for whites only*. While the data themselves are readily available, the computations required some innovations in technique. The following description of the computation technique is detailed in order to explain fully the method of obtaining race-specific income distributions.[9]

The first problem that arises concerns the estimation of mean incomes for each of the closed income intervals and for the open-ended highest income interval. Many writers have simply assumed that the midpoint of a closed income interval is also the mean of the interval.[10] Yet these two numbers often differ substantially, particularly in the higher intervals. Many writers also assume that the highest two intervals contain sufficient information to generate the parameters of a Pareto curve and thereby provide a reliable estimate of the mean income in the upper open-ended interval.[11] This technique does not utilize all the available information about the other intervals which, if used effectively, can substantially increase the reliability of the estimates.

[9] The basic source for the 1960 data is the *United States Census of the Population, 1960.* In Parts 2-51, Table 76 presents the total number of families in an SMSA in each of thirteen income classes; Table 78 presents the same data for nonwhites only. The 1970 data are found in *United States Census of the Population, 1970,* State volumes, Table 198. The white income distribution was obtained by subtracting data for nonwhites from the total.

[10] Examples of studies that make this error include: Herman Miller, *Income Distribution in the United States* (Washington, D.C.: Government Printing Office, 1966); Ahmad Al-Samarrie and Herman Miller, "State Differentials in Income Concentration," *American Economic Review* (March 1967).

[11] Miller, *Income Distribution in the United States.*

121

Since the method of computing the interval means in the upper intervals can significantly affect the ranking of SMSAs according to the Gini coefficient, care must be taken in estimating these class means.[12] The method I employ involves using all the information on the above-median income intervals to generate a Pareto distribution for each SMSA. See the Appendix to this chapter for a full description of the technique used to estimate class means.

Once the interval mean incomes are estimated, the total income received by families in each interval can be calculated, permitting as well calculation of a cumulative Lorenz distribution. The Gini coefficient was then obtained from the Lorenz distribution according to the formula:

$$G_W = 1.0 - \sum_i f_i(z_i + z_{i-1})$$

where f_i = percent of families in income interval i

z_i = percent of total income received by families in interval i and all lower intervals.

The interval means Lorenz distribution also permit calculation of the income share of each decile by linear interpolation. The income shares received by the highest decile, by the top 5 percent and top 1 percent of white families, were calculated, using the formula:

$$S_j = \frac{m_j \times N_j}{TOTAL\ INCOME}$$

---

[12] This point is illustrated clearly in Harry Oshima and Mitsuo Ono, "The Size Distribution of Family Incomes, by States and Industries" (Paper prepared for the Conference on Income and Wealth, National Bureau of Economic Research, March 1967).

An older study that avoids these errors is Maurice Liebenberg and Hyman Kaitz, "An Income Size Distribution From Income Tax and Survey Data, 1944," in *Studies in Income and Wealth*, vol. 13 (New York: National Bureau of Economic Research, 1951). The studies in this volume comprise the most technically careful and competent set of essays in the literature, and they surpass the quality of later census studies.

where $N_j = \left(\dfrac{1}{100}\right) \times (j) \times$ (number of families in SMSA)

$$m_j = \left(\frac{1}{a+1}\right) \times \left(\frac{.01 \times j}{k}\right)^{1/a} = \text{interval mean income}$$

a and k are the two estimated parameters of the Pareto distribution for the SMSA (see Appendix)

$j = 1, 5,$ or 10

All the dependent variables are listed in Table 6.1.

Racial Inequality Variables

The measurement of racial inequality in this model requires some discussion. Economists often attempt to separate the various forms of racial discrimination and analyze them in isolation from one another. For example, pure wage discrimination is defined as the racial differential in wages paid to workers of equal productivity. This approach assumes that the various forms of discrimination can be calculated separately and then added up.

But the various forms of discrimination are not separable nor additive. The different components of racial inequality interact with and reinforce each other in suppressing black incomes. To account for the effects of racial inequality on whites in a unified manner, it is necessary to employ a single index of the extent of inequality. The unadjusted ratio of median black to median white family incomes is therefore used here as a measure of racial inequality.

Although racial differences in personal earnings might be more relevant for labor market analysis, family incomes are used here for reasons of data availability and computational convenience. The analysis following Table 2.3 in Chapter 2 indicated that trends in these two measures are extremely similar. The same conclusion applies to cross-sectional analysis. Black families are more likely to be maintained by a woman, to have more than one wage earner, and to receive

123

transfer payments. But the variance across SMSAs in racial differences in these dimensions is not substantial and unlikely to be correlated with other variables; therefore, the mean B/W level will be affected but the coefficients will not be biased in one direction or another.[13]

If blacks and whites differentially obtained schooling and other income-related characteristics in the past and in other locations, the black-white income ratio may not fully reflect the degree of current racial discrimination where these persons now reside. This problem is also minor. Migration effects are controlled for in large part by including migration and median income variables on the right-hand side of these equations. It is not clear, moreover, that past discrimination could be so easily separated from present discrimination or that it should be excluded from tests of discrimination models. Finally, the effects of SMSA and regional differences in patterns of schooling inequality are investigated in the empirical analysis that follows.

Notice that the racial inequality variable as defined here varies inversely with the level of racial inequality; the *higher* the ratio of median black to median white incomes, or B/W, the lower the extent of racial inequality. Therefore, the hypotheses discussed earlier in this chapter predict a negative sign on the coefficient of this variable in an equation explaining white income inequality; that is, when B/W is higher, the measure of white inequality (the Gini coefficient) will be lower.[14]

The degree of residential segregation in a city also provides

[13] The 1960 data on median family incomes by race and SMSA are taken from *United States Census of the Population, 1960*, part 1 "Detailed Characteristics," Table 301. The 1970 data are from *United States Census of the Population, 1970*, "Detailed Characteristics," Table 366.

[14] Here, and in the ensuing discussion, I will refer to an equation with the white Gini coefficient as the dependent variable when I indicate the predicted sign of an independent variable. The same sign is expected in equations with upper-tail percentile shares as dependent variables, and the opposite sign is expected in equations with middle and lower-tail percentile shares as dependent variables.

a measure of racial discrimination.[15] A number of studies have shown that very little of the variance in residential segregation both within and between cities can be explained by socioeconomic variables or by voluntary self-segregation.[16] In other words, residential segregation by race primarily results from racial discrimination in the housing market, and so it measures in part the extent of overall racial discrimination in the SMSA.

[15] The 1960 index was calculated for central cities by Taeuber and Taeuber, using data from *United States Census of the Population, 1960*. See Karl Taeuber and Alma Taeuber, *Negroes in Cities: Residential Segregation and Neighborhood Change* (Chicago: Aldine, 1965), Table 1, pp. 32–34.

The 1970 segregation index is taken from Annemette Sorenson, Karl Taeuber, and Leslie Hollingsworth, "Indexes of Racial Residential Segregation," Table 1.

[16] Taeuber and Taeuber examined the extent to which such socioeconomic variables as family income, education, and occupational status explained the variance in the proportion of nonwhites living in different census tracts of a central city in 1960. Using 1960 census data, they analyzed census tracts in fifteen different cities and found that in most of their cities, economic factors (rather than racial ones) explained less than 10 percent of the variance in percent nonwhite population by census tract; in none of the cities did economic factors explain more than 18 percent of the variance. The Taeubers concluded that "the net effect of economic factors in explaining residential segregation is slight," and that the variation in residential segregation indices *between* cities has extremely little to do with economic factors. See Karl Taeuber and Alma Taeuber, p. 94 and pass. Moreover, whereas family income levels and the location of the household head's employment adequately explain the residential distribution of white families, these variables do not account for the extent of black concentration and segregation. See John Kain, "The Journey-to-Work as a Determinant of Residential Location," *Papers and Proceedings of the Regional Science Association* (1962), and Anthony Pascal, *The Economics of Housing Segregation* (Santa Monica, Calif.: RAND Corporation, November 1967) Memorandum RM-5510-RC; Stanley Masters, *Black-White Income Differentials*, pp. 31–36.

Finally, the residential segregation of blacks cannot be explained by a desire for self-segregation, at least as compared with the propensity of members of various ethnic groups to live near one another. (See Pascal, *Economics of Housing Segregation*.) It should be noted that this analysis of voluntary self-segregation is based on the data and situation of 1960. That is, the growing cultural nationalist sentiment among black communities that began in the late 1960s may invalidate this point for later years.

125

The residential segregation index that is used here varies from 0 to 100, with 100 indicating complete segregation. The index was calculated by Taeuber and Taeuber, who used city block data for the central city only. The Taeuber index is used widely in studies of discrimination. The hypotheses of this study predict a positive coefficient on this variable.

The residential segregation index provides an interesting alternative measure of racial inequality, but it is different from and subsidiary to B/W. The housing market does not involve the same configuration of economic agents and institutions as does the entire SMSA economy. Racial discrimination in housing, therefore, may not accurately reflect the actual extent of overall racial discrimination and inequality in the SMSA. And the segregation index that is available covers only the central city of the metropolitan area; however, the inclusion of a proportion nonwhite variable ameliorates this problem to some extent.

Writers on discrimination frequently discuss the importance of the relative proportion of nonwhites in the population as a measure of the frequency of racial contact and the intensity of racial antagonisms. Becker, for example, hypothesizes that discrimination against any minority group will increase as the relative size of the group increases. Crowding models also predict that the proportion of the labor force that is nonwhite affects the crowding of nonwhite occupations, and thereby affects the white income distribution. Another approach suggests that white Americans' fears of blacks may be greater if more blacks are around to set off and intensify such fears. Since these white fears are usually only loosely related to the actual reality, it may be argued that racist feelings among whites vary only marginally with the greater presence of racial minorities in the population.

In order to test these hypotheses, I include a percentage nonwhite variable in some of the equations.[17] If the crowding hypothesis is valid, the greater the proportion of nonwhites,

[17] The source for these data is *United States Census of the Population, 1960*, parts 1–51, Tables 76 and 78.

126

the narrower will be the white wage distribution. The co-efficient of the proportion nonwhite variable will be negative.

Market Control Variables

Market variables must be included in order to control the various influences on SMSA income inequality that are distinct from the influence of racial inequality. Some of these variables work on the demand side of the labor market, others on the supply side.

The industrial and occupational compositions of an SMSA influence the demand for labor. A number of different variables measure the industrial and occupational structures.

An approximate although easily computed measure of the industrial structure of an SMSA can be obtained by calculating the percentage of total SMSA employment in manufacturing industries.[18] Manufacturing is singled out because wages and the wage determination process tend to be more homogeneous within this sector than in others. For example, Henle found that Gini coefficients were lower in manufacturing than in any other employment sector.[19] Therefore, I expect a negative sign for this coefficient.

The manufacturing sector can also be analyzed more closely. The variables that are used here include measures of the average quantity of capital per worker in manufacturing, and the extent of concentration of manufacturing employment in durable goods industries.[20] Since these variables are associated with unionism and uniform wage rates, I expect the signs of these coefficients to be negative.

[18] Data sources, *U.S. Census of the Population*, "General Social and Economic Characteristics," Table 142 (1960) and Table 184 (1970).

[19] Peter Henle, "Exploring the Distribution of Earned Income," *Monthly Labor Review* (December 1972). A percent manufacturing variable appeared highly significant in Thompson and Matilla's cross-SMSA study of inequality. See Wilbur Thompson and John Matilla, "Toward an Econometric Model of Urban Development," in Harvey Perloff and Lowdon Wingo, eds., *Issues in Urban Economics* (Baltimore: Johns Hopkins University Press, 1968).

[20] The basic data sources for these industrial structure variables are *United States Census of the Population, 1960*, and the *U.S. Census of Manufacturing, 1963*. The immediate source was from the tabulations of Thompson and

Employment in the public sector of the urban economy deserves separate treatment. The income distribution in Washington, D.C., and the several SMSAs in the sample that are state capitals may be influenced by the large number of government workers. This effect can be captured by including the percentage of employees who are government workers in some of the equations.[21] Since the entry wage in public employment is relatively high, while a preponderant number of public employees are low- and middle-level white collar workers, a large public sector is likely to exert a narrowing influence on earnings inequalities. I therefore expect this variable to have a negative sign.

For each SMSA I also constructed an industrial structure index that would be a measure of the income distribution "expected," given the industrial composition of the SMSA. This index is computed by combining data on the local industrial mix with national data on the frequency distribution of earnings by industry.[22] The "expected" frequency distribution of income for the SMSA is:

$$
\begin{bmatrix} f_1 \\ \vdots \\ f_{12} \end{bmatrix} = \begin{bmatrix} q_{1,1} & \cdots & q_{1,13} \\ \vdots & & \vdots \\ q_{12,1} & \cdots & q_{12,13} \end{bmatrix} \times \begin{bmatrix} I_1 \\ \vdots \\ I_{13} \end{bmatrix}
$$

Matilla, who had used these variables in their cross-SMSA study of urban structure, growth, and distribution. The Thompson and Matilla sample differed somewhat from my own and required adjustments. They included as single observations the New York-New Jersey Consolidated Area and the Chicago Consolidated Area; these areas each contain several distinct SMSAs in my sample. For these SMSAs, I computed the variable estimates from the underlying census data.

[21] This variable is computed from data in *U.S. Census of the Population, 1960*, "General Social and Economic Characteristics, Table 142.

[22] The report, U.S. Census Bureau, "Trends in the Incomes of Families and Persons, 1947–64," *Technical Paper No. 17* (1968) presents tabulations for 1960 of frequency distributions of income for thirteen industries and twelve income intervals. The employment weights for each industry and SMSA are taken from *U.S. Census of the Population, 1960*, "General Social and Economic Characteristics. Table 147.

where f_i = percent of SMSA population in income interval
  $i, i = 1, 12;$

I_j = percent of SMSA employment in industry j,
  $j = 1, 13;$

q_{ij} = percent of national employment of industry j in income interval i.

The "expected" Gini coefficient can be computed from this frequency distribution of income. The index has the advantage of utilizing detailed information on the dispersion of earnings within industries. However, the usefulness of this index is limited because the industrial breakdowns are still highly aggregated. I expect the coefficient of this variable to appear with a positive sign.

The occupational composition of an SMSA also influences the distribution of income in the SMSA. To control this factor it is important to examine directly the SMSA occupational structure. I include a variable measuring the share of SMSA employment in the white collar occupations.[23] Although white collar workers receive higher salaries than blue collar workers, there are large differences among white collar workers. The expected sign of this variable is therefore ambiguous.

It seems desirable to disaggregate the white collar variable. In pay and in working conditions, lower level white collar work in the clerical and sales occupations resembles blue collar work more than professional or managerical jobs.[24] I

---

[23] From *U.S. Census of the Population*, "General Social and Economic Characteristics," Table 142(1960) and Table 184(1970).

[24] For arguments along these lines, see David Gordon, "From Steam Whistles to Coffee Breaks," *Dissent* (Winter 1972); Michael Reich, "The Development of the Wage Labor Force," in R. Edwards, M. Reich, and T. Weisskopf, eds., *The Capitalist System* 2d ed. (Englewood Cliffs, N.J.: Prentice-Hall, 1978); Harry Braverman, *Labor and Monopoly Capital* (New York: Monthly Review Press, 1974); Richard Edwards, *Contested Terrain* (New York; Basic Books, 1979).

therefore include a variable on the share of employment in the managerial and professional occupations alone.[25] The expected sign of the coefficient of this variable is positive.

The occupational distribution may influence family income inequality through its effect on the proportion of women working in the SMSA. In their comprehensive cross-SMSA study of labor force participation, Bowen and Finnegan found that a demand-side variable—the proportion of employment in occupations that are predominantly female in composition—provided the major determinant for explaining the proportion of married women who worked for a wage or salary outside their home.[26] In order to control for this indirect influence of the occupational structure as well as the direct influence of working women, I include as a control variable the SMSA percentage of females, fourteen years and older, in the labor force.[27]

The expected sign of this female labor force participation rate variable is ambiguous. On the one hand, working women from low-income families augment their husbands' incomes, tending to narrow the income distribution among families. On the other hand, female heads of households are more likely to be in the labor force and to have low family incomes as well, and well-educated women from higher income families are more likely to be in the labor force. These factors tend to widen the income distribution among families.

Finally, to capture some of the effects of the industrial and occupational structure of the SMSA that are not contained in the above variables, I also include the median white family income as a control variable.[28] Kuznets has hypothesized

[25] Computed from U.S. Census of the Population, 1960, "General Social and Economic Characteristics," Table 146.

[26] William Bowen and T. Aldrich Finegan, The Economics of Labor Force Participation (Princeton: Princeton University Press, 1969).

[27] Data from U.S. Census of the Population, 1960, "General Social and Economic Characteristics," Table 142.

[28] Median income of white families, in thousands of dollars. Source: U.S. Census of Population, "Detailed Characteristics," Table 301 (1960), Table 366 (1970).

130

that economic development is associated with a reduction in the overall level of inequality. Therefore, I expect this variable to have a negative sign.

The supply side control variable included in the model is concerned with the effect of migration on labor supply. The female labor force participation rate that has already been discussed could also be included under this heading. A migration variable is included in order to control for disequilibrium effects on the wage structures of SMSA's. As a migration variable I use the percentage of persons in the SMSA, five years or older, who lived in different counties in 1955 and 1960.[29] This variable captures the effects only imperfectly, for most intercounty household moves remain within the same SMSA. Nevertheless, this variable will capture some of the relevant effects. Moreover, it is the only measure of migration that is available for SMSAs. Neither existing theoretical analyses nor empirical research provide clear results on the nature of possible disequilibria in SMSAs. Consequently, it is not apparent whether this variable should have a positive or a negative coefficient.

The following chart summarizes the variable definitions presented here and the symbols used for these variables in the next section.

Symbol	Explanation
G_w	Gini coefficient of white family income
S1, S5, S10	Income share received by top 1, 5, or 10 percent of white families
B20, B40	Income share received by bottom 20 or 40 percent of white families
SMID50	Income share received by white families in twentieth to seventieth percentiles
B/W	Ratio of nonwhite to white median family income
SEGR	Residential racial segregation index

[29] The data source is *U.S. Census of the Population, 1960*, "General Social and Economic Characteristics," Table 141.

PCTNW   Percentage nonwhite in population
PCTMFG   Percentage of employment in manufacturing
KPERL   Capital-labor ratio in manufacturing
SPECMFG   Specialization in a few manufacturing
                industries
DURMFG   Percentage of employment in durable goods
                manufacturing
WHICOL   Percentage of employment in white collar
                occupations
MGPROF   Percentage of employment in managerial and
                professional occupations
PCTGOVT   Percentage of employment in public sector
FLFPR   Female labor force participation rate
MIGRANT   Percentage of households with intercounty
                moves

ECONOMETRIC RESULTS

In this section I present the econometric results, beginning with equation estimates with G_w, S1, and S5 as the dependent variables and data drawn from the 1960 census. I then consider the effects of including additional control variables in the equations and the estimates of equations with the alternative inequality measures as the dependent variables. I also report results when PCTNW is added to the equation and estimates for a non-Southern subsample. Finally, I present results of similar tests using data drawn from the 1970 census, comparing the results to those obtained for 1960.

The simple correlation coefficient between the two variables, B/W and G_w, is $-.47$ in 1960. This strong negative correlation contradicts the predictions of the neoclassical discrimination theories. Of course, this evidence by itself cannot carry much weight, since it is necessary to control for other independent forces that may be simultaneously influencing both variables in the same manner. To allow more confidence in inferences about causality from these statistical results, one must introduce such control variables in a multivariate model specified

132

from theoretical principles. This econometric technique will minimize the spuriousness of the simple correlation.

Linear regression estimates for 1960 are presented in Table 4.1 for a model that is based on the theoretical and data discussions in the previous sections. The equations contain, as independent variables, a racial inequality variable, industrial-structure variables, and a median white income variable. Results are reported for three different variables, G_w, S1, and S5.

In equation 1, with G_w as the dependent variable, the coefficient of B/W, the racial inequality variable, has a negative sign, the opposite of neoclassical predictions, and is significant at the 1 percent level. At the sample means of the variables, a 1 percent increase in B/W (a decrease in racial inequality) is associated with a 0.2 percent decrease in the Gini coefficient of white income (a decrease in white inequality).

The control variables are also significant and have their expected signs. The coefficients of PCTMFG and MDWINC are significant at the 1 percent level, and the coefficient of WHICOL is significant at the 10 percent level. As expected, the negative coefficient of PCTMFG indicates that specialization in manufacturing is associated with less inequality because of the narrower range of wage differentials in manufacturing. The positive coefficient of WHICOL indicates that concentration in white collar employment tends to increase income inequality. The inverse association between the level of income (MDWINC) and the Gini coefficient is consistent with the Kuznets hypothesis that associates economic development with a reduction in the overall level of income inequality.

Finally, the magnitude of the beta coefficients for the B/W variable is of the same order as for the market control variables; a decline of one standard deviation in racial inequality reduces the white Gini coefficient by three-tenths of a standard deviation.

These results encourage confidence in the model. Over two-thirds of the variance is "explained," indeed, a high proportion for cross-sectional analyses. The results compare

TABLE 4.1 Explanation of Inequality: Total Sample, 1960 (n = 48)

Equation Number	Dependent Variable	Constant	B/W	SEGR	PCTMFG	WHICOL	MDWINC	R^2
1	G_w	.492	−.097 (−3.29) −.19 −.31		−.134 (−5.50) −.11 −.50	.066 (1.89) .09 .25	−.012 (−3.49) −.21 −.29	.685
2	G_w	.370		.069 (2.09)	−.153 (−6.01)	.055 (1.50)	−.010 (−2.58)	.642
3	G_w	.266		.108 (3.45)	−.170 (−6.58)	.074 (1.91)		.587
4	S1	.094	−.059 (−4.32) −.55 −.48		−.043 (−3.80) −.19 −.44	.029 (1.81) .19 .19	.001 (0.72) .10 .07	.511
5	S5	.229	−.099 (−4.09) −.35		−.078 (−4.01) −.13	.049 (1.77) .13	−.00 (−0.02) −0.0	.538

NOTE: In this and succeeding tables in which regression estimates are reported, numbers in parentheses refer to the t-statistic, elasticity at the mean is given below the t-statistic, and the beta coefficient is below the elasticity.

well with other cross-SMSA or cross-state income inequality studies: the R^2's are slightly lower than those reported by Thompson and Matilla and slightly higher than those of Aigner and Heins or Al-Samarrie and Miller.[30] Moreover, the coefficients of the individual variables that are also included in these other studies appear with the same sign as here. It seems safe to conclude that the most important market determinants of SMSA income distribution are incorporated in this simple equation, and it is doubtful that a major systematic although unidentified control factor has been omitted. This conclusion is reinforced by an examination of the results, reported later in this section, when additional control variables are included in the regression.

The correlation matrix in Table 4.2 indicates a moderate level of simple correlations between B/W and the other independent variables. Such a moderate level of multicollinearity among the independent variables makes it doubtful that the racial inequality variable is picking up the effects of one or more of the included control variables. Indeed, when B/W is excluded from the equation, the remaining coefficients and their standard errors remain stable.[31]

[30] Wilbur Thompson and John Matilla, "Toward an Econometric Model; Ahmad Al-Samarrie and Herman Miller, "State Differentials;" Dennis Aigner and A. J. Heins, "On the Determinants of Income Equality," *American Economic Review* (March 1972).

[31] I examined the residuals in equation 1 to see if any pattern could be discerned. The actual value of G_w exceeded the predicted value by .01 or more in eleven SMSAs: Los Angeles, San Jose, San Antonio, New York, Birmingham, Miami, Tampa, Newark, Portland, Cincinnati, and Cleveland. The actual value of G_w fell short of the predicted value by .01 or more, also in eleven SMSAs: Sacramento, San Bernardino, Albany, Buffalo, Fort Worth, Akron, Denver, Minneapolis, Jersey City, Memphis, and Kansas City. The magnitude of the largest residual was .036, for Newark.

The large positive residuals for Los Angeles, San Jose, San Antonio, and New York may be caused by the large number of Hispanics in those SMSAs. The presence of such groups probably tends to raise B/W above its "true" value and to increase G/W. The large positive residuals for Miami and Tampa may be caused by the large proportion of elderly retired persons with low incomes in these SMSAs, adding to the overall degree of inequality among whites.

135

The estimate of the equation using an alternative measure of racism, the Taeuber residential-segregation index, is reported in equations 2 and 3 of Table 4.1. The simple correlation coefficient between the B/W variable and the residential-segregation variable is $-.65$. In these equations the SEGR variable is significant at the 1 percent level. Its positive sign is inconsistent with neoclassical discrimination theories: the greater the degree of residential segregation, the greater the income inequality among whites.

These results further support my model specification. The high correlation between B/W and SEGR supports the use of a racial income inequality variable as the main measure of racism. The significance of the SEGR variable casts further doubt on the possibility of spuriousness in the observed partial correlation between G_w and B/W, which may be influenced by an omitted class-based factor affecting both variables. The SEGR variable is not likely to be influenced by class variables. Consequently, the significance of these results also lends support to the adequacy of the control variables in the equations that use B/W as the racism variable.

Equations 4 and 5 in Table 4.1 present results with S1 and S5 as the dependent variables. In these equations the coefficient of B/W is significant at the 1 percent level, and WHICOL is significant at the 1 percent level. With the exception of MDWINC, the signs of the coefficients are the same as in equation 1. The R^2, although lower, is still high for a cross-sectional study. Again, the results are high for this type of study. Again, the results are inconsistent with neoclassical discrimination hypotheses.

The relative importance of the racial inequality variable, as

---

The negative residuals for Sacramento and Albany might be explained by their status as state capitals; I discuss this hypothesis further below, using a PCTGOVT variable. The large negative residuals for Buffalo, Akron, and Jersey City might be explained by the high level of specialization in a few manufacturing industries in these SMSAs; I discuss this hypothesis below, using other industrial-structure variables.

TABLE 4.2 Correlation Matrix, Total Sample, 1960 (n = 48)

	S1	S5	B/W	PCTMFG	WHICOL	MDWINC	SEGR
G_w	.85	.88	−.47	−.68	.17	−.55	.36
S1		−.99	−.55	−.54	.11	−.18	.30
S5			−.55	−.57	.12	−.24	n.a.
B/W				.25	.20	.23	−.65
PCTMFG					−.04	.29	−.08
WHICOL						−.12	−.14
MDWINC							−.43

measured by the beta coefficient or by its elasticity at the mean, is greater in the S1 and S5 equations than in the G_w equation. In the S1 equation the elasticity at the mean is 100 percent greater, and the beta coefficient 50 percent greater than the comparable figures in the G_w equation. In other words, the unequalizing effect of racial inequality on whites is concentrated in redistribution to the top 1 percent (and, to a lesser degree, the top 5 percent) of white families. This finding is examined further in this chapter, when I use alternative dependent variables to measure the impact of racial inequality on the lower and middle ranges of the white income distribution.

The lack of significance of MDWINC in the S1 and S5 equations is surprising, especially given the significance of this variable in the G_w equation. Apparently, the lessened degree of inequality associated with increasing median income levels does not affect the share of the uppermost income groups. In other words, the more affluent SMSAs tend to have greater equality *among* the nonrich, without any loss in the *relative* position of the very rich.

The results for the S1 and S5 equations indicate that the extent of variance explained and the robustness of the coefficients when the racial inequality variable is excluded are similar to that of the G_w equation and need not be repeated in detail. Again, the apparent adequacy of included control variables and the stability of the coefficients suggest that the observed relations between B/W and S1 or S5 are not spurious.

Additional Control Variables

How are the results thus far affected by including additional control variables into the equation? I consider first the effects of using more elaborate measures of industrial structure; these results are presented in Table 4.3. The first two equations in the table show that, with the addition of PCTGOVT, the magnitude of the racial inequality variable falls somewhat, but it is still significant at the 1 percent level. PCTGOVT appears with a negative sign, as expected by the relatively narrow range

138

of pay scales in government and the absence of profit income. The inclusion of PCTGOVT renders WHICOL insignificant and adds somewhat to the overall explanatory power of the equation, but it does not significantly affect the coefficients of the remaining variables. Surprisingly, PCTGOVT and WHICOL are negatively correlated; I have no explanation for this result.

Equations 3 to 5 in Table 4.3 report the effects of including additional measures of the structure of the manufacturing sector in the equation. None of these variables appears to be significant. Nor do they add explanatory power that is not already incorporated in PCTMFG. The addition of these variables does not affect the racial inequality variable.

Equations 6 to 10 in Table 4.3 indicate the effects of including these additional industrial-structure variables when PCTGOVT is included in the equation instead of WHICOL. The coefficient and t-statistic of B/W remain unchanged. The t-statistic of the PCTGOVT coefficient increases substantially, perhaps because of the exclusion of WHICOL. The KPERL and KPERL2 variables are each significant at the 10 percent level in the G_w equation (see equations 6 and 10), and, as I expected, the signs are negative. KPERL is not significant in the S1 equation. None of these structural variables add significantly to the overall explanatory power of the equations.

Another method of capturing industrial structure effects involves using the Gini and percentile income share variables that are "expected" from the industrial mix of the SMSA, and computed by the technique described in the previous section. Table 4.4 presents the estimated equations using these variables. Once again, the more complex measures do not affect the B/W variable. The variables EXPGINI and EXPS1 do not enter the equations significantly. The results are surprising, particularly because PCTMFG, a cruder measure of the industrial structure, appears highly significant when it is included in the equations.

An explanation for this insignificance appears in the correlation coefficient matrix of Table 4.4. The low simple

139

TABLE 4.3 Total Sample, 1960: Additional Variables

Equation Number	Dependent Variable	Constant	B/W	PCTMFG	WHICOL	PCTGOVT	MDWINC	KPERL	KPERL2	R^2
1	G_w	.468	-.0727 (-2.14)	-.230 (-6.35)	.0013 (.03)	-.233 (-2.87)				.661
2	S1	.116	-.041 (-2.89)	-.067 (-4.43)	-.0016 (-.09)	-.081 (-2.39)				.563
3	G_w	.466	-.112 (-3.29)	-.155 (-5.58)				-.0019 (-1.09)		.564
4	"	.457	-.103 (-3.12)	-.158 (-5.71)					-.0016 (-0.79) DURMFG	.558
5	"	.454	-.099 (-2.84)	-.157 (-5.50)					-811×10^{-4} (.40)	.554
6	"	.489	-.083 (-2.77)	-.229 (-7.59)		-.248 (-4.04)		-.0027 (-1.75)		.684
7	"	.531	-.075 (-2.67)	-.197 (-6.51)		-.194 (-2.79)	-.0093 (-2.79)	-.0023 (-1.61)		.733

								KPERL2	
8	S1	.118	−.042 (−3.27)	−.067 (−5.10)	−.081 (−3.04)	.0003 (−0.40)			.564
9	"	.107	−.045 (−3.47)	−.075 (−5.38)	−.094 (−3.42)	−.0004 (−0.55)	.0024 (1.56)		.588
10	G	.479	−.071 (−2.40)	−.235 (−7.79)	−.257 (−4.13)			−.0031 (−1.74)	.684

DEFINITIONS: *KPERL*: The capital-labor ratio used in manufacturing; more precisely (total value added − all employees payroll) ÷ (total manufacturing employment, in thousands, 1960).

KPERL2: An alternate measure of capital per worker in manufacturing; more precisely (plant and equipment expenditures, 1958 + 1959 + 1960) ÷ (number of production workers, in thousands).

SPECMFG: The degree of SMSA specialization in a few industries; more precisely, total employment in four largest manufacturing industries in the SMSA, as a percentage of total manufacturing employment.

DURMFG: The percent of total manufacturing employment in durable goods industries.

SOURCES: Estimates of these variables, based on data in the *U.S. Census of the Population, 1960* and the *U.S. Census of Manufacturing, 1963*, were kindly made available by Professor Wilbur Thompson, Department of Economics, Wayne State University. See Wilbur Thompson and John Matilla, "Toward an Econometric Model of Urban Economic Development," in Harvey Perloff and Lowdon Wingo, eds., *Issues in Urban Economics* (Baltimore: Johns Hopkins University Press, 1968). Since Thompson and Matilla combined certain SMSAs into consolidated areas, I computed estimates for the following SMSAs: New York, Jersey City, Newark, Paterson, Chicago, Gary, and Washington, D.C.

TABLE 4.4 Total Sample, 1960: Additional Variables

Dependent Variable	Constant	B/W	EXPGINI	EXPS1	MDWINC	R^2
G_w	.542	-.116 (-3.08)	-.034 (-0.07)		-.018 (-4.02)	.428
S1	.142	-.064 (-4.16)		-0.549 (-0.71)	-0.008 (-0.40)	.308

Correlation Matrix, 1960

	EXPGINI	S1	EXPS1	PCTMFG	MDWINC
G_w	.03	.85	-.02	-.68	-.55
EXPGINI		-.02	.94	.07	-.03
S1			-.07	-.54	-.18
EXPS1				.13	-.01

correlation between the expected and actual Gini coefficients and percentile shares suggests that the use of *national* data on income distribution by industry at the two-digit level of aggregation does not appear appropriate. Apparently, the distribution of earnings by two-digit industry varies so greatly across SMSAs that it is not helpful to compute a measure that abstracts from these differences.

Next, I turn to the effects of introducing several additional control variables that were discussed earlier: FLFPR, MGPROF, and MIGRANT. The results of including these variables are given in Table 4.5. In every case, the addition of any of these variables has no significant downward effect on the racial inequality variable. FLFPR is negative and significant at the 10 percent level in equation 1, but positive and not significant in equation 2. MGPROF has the expected positive sign in equation 2 and is also significant at the 10 percent level. In addition, though not reported here, MGPROF is not significant at all if it is entered simultaneously with WHICOL. Neither FLFPR nor MGPROF adds substantially to the explanatory power of the equations. These additional attempts to incorporate demand-side market variables do not improve the statistical results.

The MIGRANT variable is included in equation 3 of Table 4.5. The results are not significant, and the inclusion of this variable does not affect the racial inequality variable or the other independent variables. These results suggest that very little inequality in white incomes is produced by labor market adjustments that are associated with migration from rural labor surplus areas to SMSAs. This inference is consistent with Hall's finding that labor surplus adjustment models do not significantly explain intra-SMSA wage differentials.[32]

Finally, but not shown here, the SMSA unemployment rate and an SMSA schooling inequality variable, the Gini coefficient of years of schooling completed among whites twenty-five

---

[32] Robert E. Hall, "Why Is the Unemployment Rate So High at Full Employment?," *Brookings Papers on Economic Activity*, no. 1 (1969).

TABLE 4.5 Total Sample, 1960: Additional Variables

Equation Number	Dependent Variable	Constant	B/W	PCTMFG	MDWINC	FLFPR	WHICOL	MGPROF	MIGRANT	R^2
1	G_w	.48	−0.117 (−3.69)	−.168 (−6.13)		−.152 (−1.83)	.080 (2.12)			.625
2	G_w	.48	−0.12 (−3.45)	−.079 (−2.08)	−.020 (−4.08)	.253 (1.33)		.218 (1.77)		.689
3	G_w	.52	−.087 (−2.54)	−.132 (−3.51)	−.0134 (−3.67)				.0069 (0.16)	

Correlation Matrix

	S1	B/W	PCTMFG	FLFPR	WHICOL	MDWINC
G_w	.85	−.47	−.68	.02	−.17	−.55
S1		−.55	.25	.25	.20	.23
B/W			.25	−.07	−.05	.37
FLFPR			−.29			

to twenty-nine years of age, were also included as independent variables. The unemployment rate did not appear significantly, reflecting perhaps the low variance in unemployment rates across SMSAs, and the remaining coefficients were unaffected. The schooling inequality variable did appear significantly and with a positive coefficient. The inclusion of this variable lowered the coefficients of B/W, PCTMFG, and MDWINC, but these variables remained significant.[33]

To summarize the econometric results up to this point, these findings indicate that greater racial inequality is associated with greater inequality among whites, a result that is generally inconsistent with neoclassical discrimination hypotheses. The main finding holds even with the inclusion of a variety of control variables. The best results are obtained with the simplest model, equations 1 to 3 in Table 4.1. The inclusion of additional variables neither affects the B/W variable nor increases the explanatory power of the model. In further statistical work, therefore, I drop the additional control variables and estimate equations with the independent variables: B/W, PCTMFG, MDWINC, and WHICOL.

Alternative Inequality Measures as the Dependent Variable

In addition to using G_w, S1, and S5 as dependent variables, the basic equation was estimated using dependent variables that are more sensitive to the shares received by the lower and middle ranges of the income distribution: B20, B40, and SMID50. These equation estimates are presented in Table 4.6.

In the B20 equation the coefficient of the racial inequality variable is positive, as expected, but it is not significant at the usual standards. WHICOL has the expected negative sign in this equation, but it also is not significant. Only PCTMFG and MDWINC enter into the equation significantly; they do so at the 1 percent level and with the expected signs.

---

[33] See Chapter 7 for a fuller discussion of the schooling inequality variable, including details of its definition and data sources. The schooling inequality variable is generally excluded from the results presented here because it is a function of B/W itself. This argument is presented in Chapter 7.

TABLE 4.6 Alternative Dependent Variables

Equation Number	Dependent Variable	Constant	B/W	PCTMFG	WHICOL	MDWINC	R^2
1	B20	.020	.010 (1.20)	.0363 (5.10)	−.0137 (−1.35)	.0049 (4.94)	.666
	elasticity		.105				
2	B40	.112	.028 (1.83)	.0770 (6.02)	−.0247 (−1.35)	.0078 (4.36)	.694
	elasticity		.110				
3	SMID50	.353	.059 (3.13)	−.0536 (3.48)	−.0536 (−2.43)	.0033 (1.54)	.510
	elasticity		.095				

Correlation Matrix

	B20	B40	SMID50	B/W	PCTMFG	WHICOL	MDWINC
G_w	−.89	−.97	−.92	− 47	−.68	.17	−.55
B20		.96	.67	.31	.65	−.17	.64
B40			.83	.37	.70	−.15	.60
SMID50				.45	.55	−.23	.40

In the B40 equation the coefficient of the racial inequality variable increases in magnitude and becomes significant at the 10 percent level. The elasticity of B/W at the mean is the same as in the B20 equation. The signs and t-statistics of the remaining variables are similar to those in the B20 equation. Apparently, racial inequality does not exert a significant effect on the income share received by the lowest quintile of whites but does moderately affect the second quintile. These findings are consistent with the crowding hypothesis suggested by Bergmann.

As equation 3 indicates, the effect of racial inequality on "middle America," the half of the white population in the second to seventh deciles, is significant: the coefficient of the B/W variable in this equation is positive and is significant at the 1 percent level. The elasticity is the same as in the previous two equations: a 1 percent decrease in racial income inequality is associated with an increase of 0.1 percent in the income share of the middle-income families. When compared with the results in Table 4.1, this elasticity is about half of that obtained in the G_w equation and one-fifth the elasticity of B/W in the S1 equation.

These results reinforce an observation made earlier. An increase in racial inequality (a decrease in B/W) is associated with a substantial improvement in the share of the richest 1 percent of white families, with a lesser increase in white inequality overall and with smaller decreases in the share of middle- and lower-income whites. On the basis of these findings, it appears that the redistributive effect of racial inequality is concentrated among the very rich; they are the primary beneficiaries.

Including the Percentage-Nonwhite Variable

A simple occupation-crowding model suggests that the relative income of nonwhites will be inversely related to the proportion of the population that is nonwhite. In fact, the simple correlation coefficient between B/W and PCTNW is −.71. Once again, however, a multivariate model permits

147

greater confidence in making inferences than do these simple correlations. And with this much collinearity, care must be taken, both in adding the PCTNW variable to a multivariate model and in interpreting the results.

Table 4.7 shows the effects of adding the PCTNW variable to the equations that were estimated earlier. While the simple correlation coefficient between PCTNW and G_w is .37, as compared to $-.47$ between G_w and B/W, the addition of PCTNW does not significantly increase the proportion of the explained variance in any of the equations.

In equations 1 to 3, PCTNW does not enter significantly. In equations 1 and 2, with MDWINC excluded from the equation, the addition of the PCTNW variable has a small effect on the racial inequality variable. While the sign and magnitude of the coefficient of B/W are unaffected, the t-statistic drops slightly, from 3.29 in equation 1, Table 4.1, to 2.66 in equation 1, Table 4.7. In equation 3, with MDWINC in the equation, the magnitude and t-statistic of the racial inequality coefficient decline in the S1 equations (equations 4 and 5 in Table 4.7), but the B/W variable remains significant at the 5 percent level and with the expected sign. The PCTNW variable itself becomes significant at the 10 percent level only in equation 5. The introduction of PCTNW apparently picks up only a small part of the influence of B/W.[34]

These results are striking, in view of the high degree of intercorrelation among the two variables, B/W and PCTNW. Generally, multicollinearity among independent variables produces unstable coefficients for these variables, with standard errors rising substantially as intercorrelated variables are added to the equation. The considerable stability in both the coefficient of the racial inequality variable and its standard error therefore contrasts sharply with the instability of the PCTNW variable (which is negative in equations 1 and 2 and positive in equation 3) and its high standard error.

---

[34] PCTNW does appear significantly in equation estimates (not reported in Table 4.7) that omit the B/W variable.

TABLE 4.7 Including PCTNW

Equation Number	Dependent Variable	Constant	B/W	PCTMFG	WHICOL	MDWINC	PCTNW	R^2
1	G_w	0.47	−0.12 (−2.66)	−0.16 (−5.75)			−.030 (−0.60)	.556
2	"	0.42	−0.12 (−2.70)	−0.15 (−5.58)	0.084 (2.07)		−.020 (−0.04)	.596
3	"	0.48	−0.076 (−1.79)	−0.130 (−4.74)	0.073 (1.99)	−0.0123 (−2.92)	.038 (0.74)	.690
4	S1	0.10	−0.038 (−2.10)	−0.040 (−3.56)			.024 (1.09)	.485
5	"	0.08	−0.037 (−2.12)	−0.040 (−3.33)	0.035 (2.16)		.036 (1.68)	.535

Simple Correlation Coefficients

	G_w	S1	B/W	PCTMFG	WHICOL	MDWINC
PCTNW	.37	.53	−.71	−.31	−.31	−.02

Such joint behavior between two intercorrelated variables implies that the two differ substantially in how well they represent the underlying phenomenon. Within the framework of this study, the behavior of the PCTNW variable suggests that it is inferior to B/W as a proxy for the extent of racism in an SMSA. Insofar as racism has effects on white inequality, the severity of those effects seems more closely related to the severity of racial income inequality than to the relative size of the nonwhite population.

The crowding model suggests that B/W is itself a function of PCTNW and therefore is only an intervening variable between PCTNW or G_w or S1. If the crowding model is correct, the inclusion of PCTNW should substantially reduce the magnitude of the coefficient of B/W. This reduction does occur, but to such a slight extent that it cannot support the crowding hypothesis.

Results for the Non-South Subsample

It is possible that the empirical results reported thus far reflect only regional differences between the South and the rest of the nation. This would occur if the independent variables are proxies for regional differences, with most of the variance in white-income inequality falling between and not within regions. By 1960 one might expect the differences between the South and the rest of the nation to reflect primarily parallel differences among all the SMSAs. In fact, there is substantial variation in both G_w and B/W within just the non-South. But of the eleven SMSAs ranking lowest in B/W, nine are Southern (the exceptions are St. Louis and Washington, D.C.).

I test for regional differences by estimating the equations for a non-South subsample, rather than by adding a dummy variable for regions. The subsample estimates will provide socioeconomic explanations that identify the underlying processes that distinguish the two regions. It is not enough to say that the South is different; one must specify the important differences and the difference they make. To check for regional differences, I therefore estimated the regression equations for a

150

subsample of thirty-six non-Southern SMSAs in the sample. The results are presented in Table 4.8 and are compared here with the results presented in Table 4.1 for the entire sample.

In both the G_w and S1 equations in Table 4.1, the sign and magnitude of the coefficient of the racial inequality variable are unaffected by the exclusion of the southern SMSAs. The t-statistic of B/W is somewhat lower than for the entire sample, but it is still significant at the 5 percent level in the G_w equation and at the 1 percent level in the S1 equation. These results provide further disconfirmation of neoclassical discrimination hypotheses. Racial inequality has a strong unequalizing effect on whites even within the more limited variance of the non-South.[35]

A comparison of equations 1 to 3 in Table 4.8 with equations 1 to 2 in Table 4.1 also indicates that the proportion of the total variance explained is lower for the non-South sample than for the entire sample. The R^2's range between .51 and .69 in Table 4.1 and between .32 and .40 in Table 4.8. Such a result is to be expected when the variation in the independent variables is reduced.

As for the industrial-structure variables, the coefficient of PCTMFG falls somewhat in this subsample, as does the t-statistic. though the statistical significance remains above the 1 percent level. At the same time, the coefficient and t-statistic of WHICOL rise slightly. Concentration in manufacturing has less of an impact on the income distribution in the non-South, while the importance of the white collar employment variable increases. Different components of the industrial structure apparently exert different influences in each region on the white-income distribution.

The results for the MDWINC variable are particularly surprising. MDWINC is not significant in the G_w equation, although it remains positive and significant at the 10 percent level in the S1 equation. The opposite pattern appeared for the

[35] However, SEGR does not appear significantly in a G_w equation for the non-South subsample.

151

TABLE 4.8 Non-Southern SMSAs, 1960 (n = 36)

Equation Number	Dependent Variable	Constant	B/W	PCTMFG	WHICOL	MDWINC	PCTNW	PCTGOVT	R^2
1	G_w	.400	−.098 (−2.10)	−.088 (−3.00)	.078 (2.14)	−.0022 (−0.46)			.319
2	``	.459	−.080 (−1.93)	−.174 (−4.38)		1.001 (−0.09)		−.222 (−3.02)	.396
3	S1	.067	−.062 (−2.80)	.028 (−2.0)	.034 (2.0)	.0043 (1.9)			.355
4	B40	.159	.029 (1.27)	.051 (3.56)	−.030 (−1.70)	.0026 (1.11)			.340
5	SMID50	.403	.065 (2.37)	.027 (1.57)	−.063 (−2.93)	−.0027 (−0.95)			.304
6	G_w	0.37	−.080 (−1.5)	−.080 (−2.7)	−.089 (2.3)		.043 (0.64)		.323
7	S1	.074	−.041 (−1.6)	−.026 (−1.9)	.042 (2.3)		.062 (1.9)		.355

entire forty-eight SMSA sample: MDWINC was negative and significant in the G_w equation and insignificant in the S1 equation. The insignificance of MDWINC in the G_w equation for the non-South subsample may result from the exclusion of much of the variance of MDWINC; the Kuznets hypothesis, after all, refers to grossly different levels of economic development.

Reasons for the significance of MDWINC in the S1 equation are indicated by an examination of the raw data. The SMSAs with highest values for S1 tend to be regional corporate capitals: New York, Boston, Chicago, Los Angeles, and San Francisco. The MDWINC variable may be picking up the concentration of highly paid executives and of profit income that is characteristic of cities containing corporate and financial headquarters.

Turning next to the B40 and SMID50 equations in Table 4.8, the results are again comparable to those for the entire sample (see Table 4.6). The R^2's are somewhat lower, as are the t-statistics, but, in general, the coefficients have the same signs and are still highly significant. Two exceptions should be noted. First, the B/W coefficient is not significant in the B40 equation; however, B/W was significant only at the 10 percent level in the B40 equation for the entire sample. Second, the t-statistic of the WHICOL coefficient in the SMID50 equations increases in the non-South subsample.

Finally, equations 6 and 7 present the effect of including PCTNW in the equation.[36] In the G_w equation, the t-statistic of B/W drops, but it is still much higher than the t-statistic of PCTNW. In the S1 equation, however, the t-statistic of PCTNW is higher than that of B/W. Interpretation remains difficult, since the two variables are so highly correlated with each other. The results suggest that the proportion of blacks in the SMSA population has more of an impact on the white income distribution in the non-South sample than in the entire sample.

[36] MDWINC has been omitted in these estimates because it did not appear significantly in the previous equations.

Further Evidence from 1970

The 1960s proved to be a turbulent decade, with especially dramatic developments in race relations. Census data also indicate that the relative position of various SMSAs on key variables changed during the 1960s. For example, the ranking of Northern SMSAs fell on PCTMFG and rose on PCTNW. The B/W variable rose in many Southern SMSAs and fell in many non-Southern SMSAs. It is therefore important to consider to what extent the structure of distributional effects revealed by the empirical investigations for 1960 remained in place at the end of the decade. Using data drawn largely from the 1970 census and the same forty-eight SMSA sample, I have repeated the previous analysis for 1970.

Econometric results are presented in Table 4.9 for both the total sample and the non-Southern subsample of thirty-six SMSAs. As equation 1 in Table 4.9 reports, the B/W variable has a negative sign (more racial inequality is associated with more inequality among whites), and it is significant at the 10 percent level. At the sample means, an increase of 1 percent in B/W is associated with a decrease of 0.15 percent in the white Gini coefficient. The control variables all have their expected signs, but only the PCTMFG variable is significant. The proportion of variance explained again compares favorably with other cross-sectional studies. Compared to the results that use 1960 data, the sign and magnitude of the coefficients are virtually the same, while their significance level is decreased somewhat.[37]

In equation 2, with S1 (the income share of the top 1 percent of white families) as the dependent variable, the coefficient of the B/W variable again is negative, as expected, and is significant at the 5 percent level.[38] An increase in racial inequality in 1970 increases the share received by the richest whites. The

[37] With the exception of MDWINC, which appeared significantly with 1960 data.

[38] One difference from the 1960 results is: the positive and highly significant coefficient of MDWINC, which was not significant in the S1 equation for 1960.

154

TABLE 4.9 1970 SMSA Equations

Equation Number	Dependent Variable	Constant	B/W	PCTMFG	WHICOL	MDWINC	R^2
1	G_w	.404	-.079 (-1.66)	-.159 (-4.20)	.087 (1.45)	-.0017 (-0.66)	.449
2	S1	.059	-.059 (-2.03)	-.079 (-3.39)	.035 (0.96)	.0048 (2.97)	.386
3	B20	.041	.004 (0.47)	.032 (3.91)	-.017 (-1.32)	.0016 (2.84)	.471
4	SMID50	.419	.062 (1.94)	.071 (3.77)	-.056 (-1.46)	-.0040 (-2.41)	.413
5[a]	G_w	.379	-.118 (-1.88)	-.129 (-3.16)	.078 (1.15)	.0023 (0.67)	.412
6[a]	S1	.039	-.079 (-2.14)	-0.62 (-2.61)	.020 (0.51)	.0079 (4.00)	.533
7[a]	B20	.038	.014 (0.090)	.028 (2.87)	-.018 (-1.07)	.0014 (1.76)	.343
8[a]	SMID50	.449	.081 (2.25)	.063 (2.64)	-.065 (-1.67)	-.0066 (-3.39)	.555

NOTE: [a] indicates non-Southern subsample; n = 48 in the total sample and 36 in the subsample.

elasticity at the means of the B/W coefficient in this equation is .52, more than three times that of B/W in the Gini equation. As was the case with the 1960 results, the redistributive effects of racial inequality in 1970 appear to be concentrated in the top 1 percent of white families.[39]

In the B20 equation in Table 4.9, the B/W coefficient appears positively, as expected, but it is not significant; this was also the case with the 1960 results. The effect of racial inequality on the income share of white families in the second to seventh deciles (SMID50) is indicated in equation 4. B/W appears positively and significantly, and its elasticity at the means is .10, about two-thirds of the elasticity found in the G_w equation and one-fifth the elasticity of B/W in the S1 equation. Again, as I found with 1960 data, the effects of an increase in racial inequality (decline in B/W) are concentrated disproportionately in the upper tail of the white income distribution. The gains to the highest 1 percent exceed by far the losses to the majority of low- and middle-income whites.

To control again for possible regional differences, the same model was estimated for the subsample of thirty-six non-Southern SMSAs. (See equations 5 to 8 in Table 4.9.) In every non-South equation, the coefficient of B/W becomes more significant and has a larger absolute magnitude than in the total sample, while the magnitude and significance of the remaining coefficients remain substantially stable. Compared to the 1960 non-Southern results, the 1970 B/W coefficient in each case again increases slightly in magnitude, while the t-statistic falls slightly. The magnitude and significance of the coefficients of the control variables remain virtually the same as in 1960, while the proportion of the variance explained is somewhat higher. Racial inequality continues to have un-equalizing effects, even within the more limited variance of the non-South.

---

[39] Similar results were obtained when the shares of the top five and top ten percentiles were used as dependent variables.

Thus, the 1970 results in Table 4.9 can be summarized as significantly inconsistent with the neoclassical hypotheses. The coefficients are remarkably similar to those found with 1960 data, indicating that the same structure appears for both the beginning and the end of the 1960s.[40] Despite the dramatic civil rights developments of the decade, the considerable urban migration of blacks, the rapid growth of southern cities, and the tighter labor market in 1969 (which might have diminished racial divisions between black and white workers), the 1960 results are replicated in 1970.[41] Racial inequality in metropolitan areas continued to benefit rich whites and to hurt most white as well as black workers.

[40] In one important respect, concerning the use of the residential-segregation variable as a measure of racial discrimination, the 1960 model was not replicated with 1970 data. I estimated an equation with a Taeuber block residential-segregation index for central cities (SEGR) substituted for B/W. The 1970 segregation index was taken from Annemette Sorensen, Karl Taeuber, and Leslie Hollingsworth, "Indexes of Racial Residential Segregation," Table 1. The coefficient of the SEGR variable appeared with the expected sign, but it was not significant, as had been the case in the full sample in 1960. (For the non-South subsample, SEGR appeared insignificantly but with the correct sign in both 1960 and 1970.)

The higher proportion of blacks in central city populations and the smaller proportion of the SMSA populations residing in central cities in 1970 may render the Taeuber segregation variable a less valid measure of overall SMSA discrimination. This speculation is supported by the contrast between the decline in segregation from 1960 to 1970, as noted by Sorensen et al., and the increase over the same period, as found by Schnare, using census tract data for the entire SMSA. See Ann Schnare, "Residential Segregation by Race in U.S. Metropolitan Areas: An Analysis Across Cities and Over Time, (Washington, D.C.: Urban Institute, 1977).

[41] Using a different statistical methodology, states as his unit of observation, and data for 1970, Szymanski has also attempted to replicate my earlier study. His findings generally point in the same direction as mine. Although Szymanski's methodology leaves some important statistical issues unresolved, the criticisms made by Villemez appear to be insubstantial. See Albert Szymanski, "Racial Discrimination and White Gain," *American Sociological Review* (June 1976), and the exchange between Szymanski and Wayne Villemez in the *American Sociological Review* (October 1978).

Summary and Implications of Empirical Results

The empirical results of this chapter can be summarized as follows. In both 1960 and 1970 the findings are inconsistent with the neoclassical hypothesis that racial inequality does not have an unequalizing effect on the white income distribution. In both years the unequalizing effect of racial inequality is most pronounced at the upper tail of the white distribution and least pronounced at the lower tail, suggesting that high-income whites benefit most from racial inequality. The same findings are obtained (for 1960 only) both when a residential segregation variable is substituted for B/W and when the equations are estimated within the more limited variance of the non-South.

The empirical results presented here consistently suggest that most white workers lose from racism and that rich whites benefit. None of the neoclassical discrimination theories predict these empirical findings. Only the Thurow model, which does not specify any clear distributional implications, is not inconsistent with these findings. Thus, the empirical results in this chapter further support the argument of Chapter 3: neoclassical discrimination theories are inadequate to the task of explaining racial inequality.

Can the finding that white workers lose from racism and rich whites benefit be explained in a coherent theoretical fashion? In the following chapters of this book I argue that the problems of neoclassical discrimination theories stem from fundamental problems in the neoclassical economic paradigm. An alternative and theoretically coherent economic paradigm emphasizing class conflict in capitalist economies better explains both the observed distribution of benefits from racism and the persistence of racial inequality in the United States.

APPENDIX TO CHAPTER FOUR

Estimation of Interval Means of White Income

Interval mean incomes were estimated by the following method. For income intervals below the median interval (that is, the income interval containing the median income), the interval mean was assumed to be equal (for all SMSAs) to the mean incomes that were estimated by Oshima and Ono from a 5 percent sample of urban whites in the 1960 census.[42] These means are presented below:

income interval (000)	mean income (000)
0–1	0.50
1–2	1.50
2–3	2.50
3–4	3.50
4–5	4.50
5–6	5.40
6–7	6.40

The assumption that the mean of each interval is the same for all SMSAs is not entirely correct. A correct approach would be to fit a parabola to each interval by using data on the adjoining intervals. Then compute the mean by dividing the area under the parabolic segment into its first moment.[43] This method would be repeated for each SMSA. However, experimentation by Oshima and Ono indicated that only a negligible

[42] Harry Oshima and Mitsuo Ono, "The Size Distribution of Family Income."

[43] The parabolic estimation is developed in Dennis Aigner, "On a Calculation Technique for the Moments of Frequency Distribution in Grouped Forms," *Proceedings of the American Statistical Association* (August 1966), and Dennis Aigner, "A Linear Approximator for the Class Marks of a Grouped Frequency Distribution with Special Reference to the Unequal Interval Case" (Systems Formulation, Methodology, and Policy Workshop Paper 6708, University of Wisconsin, 1967).

error is introduced into computations of Gini coefficients and percentile shares, by using a close approximation of the mean. The errors introduced are small because of the low weights of the lower-income intervals in these inequality measures. For this reason, I used the Oshima and Ono estimates for the lower intervals, rather than applying the more cumbersome parabolic estimation method.

For the six income intervals above the national median, I did fit a Pareto distribution to the data for each of the forty-eight SMSAs.[44] The Pareto distribution is:

$$\log N = k + a \log Z$$

where Z = income level

N = number of recipients with incomes $\geq Z$

The fits were excellent, with the average R^2 for the forty-eight SMSAs in 1960 equal to .997; the lowest R^2 was .989. This method of estimating the Pareto coefficient, a, by using six observations, appears to be much more reliable than the two-point method used by Miller.[45]

The interval mean $m(x, y)$ for each closed interval (x, y) is calculated as follows:

$$m(x, y) = \int_x^y N \, dZ \Big/ \int_x^y N' \, dZ$$

$$= \left(\frac{a}{a+1}\right) \cdot \left[\frac{x^{a+1} - y^{a+1}}{x^a - y^a}\right]$$

where x is the lower bound of the interval, and y its upper bound.

---

[44] This procedure was suggested in Maurice Leibenberg and Hyman Kaitz. "An Income Size Distribution." See also Dennis Aigner and A.J. Heins, "A Social Welfare View of the Measurement of Income Equality," *Review of Income and Wealth* (March 1967).

[45] Herman Miller, *Income Distribution in the United States*, A Census Monograph (Washington, D.C.: U.S. Government Printing Office), 1966.

The interval mean for the open-ended interval (x, ∞) is:

$$m(x, \infty) = \left(\frac{a}{a + 1}\right) \cdot x$$

The estimated interval means for the Boston SMSA in 1960 are shown for illustrative purposes:

interval (000)	class mean (000)
7–8	7.46
8–9	8.47
9–10	9.47
10–15	11.93
15–25	18.57
25 and over	42.51

The mean for the highest interval ranged from $36,900 to $44,200 over the forty-eight SMSAs in the sample. These estimates of the interval means for the upper brackets differ significantly from those given by Miller for national data.

TABLE 4A.1 Correlation Matrix (n = 48)

	S1	B/W	PCTMFG	WHICOL	PCTGOVT	KPERL	KPERL2	DURMFG	MDWINC
G_w	.85	−.47	−.68	.17	.07	−.08	−.11	−.32	−.55
S1		−.55	−.54	.11	−.02	.06	−.18	−.38	−.18
B/W			.25	.20	.07	−.22	−.01	.34	.23
PCTMFG				−.04	−.58	.08	.05	.29	.29
WHICOL					−.41	−.04	−.06	.12	−.12
PCTGOVT						−.19	−.20	−.17	.10
KPERL							.28	−.01	.03
KPERL2								.27	−.10

TABLE 4A.2 Correlation Matrix for Non-Southern Sample, 1960 (n = 36)

	Mean	Standard Deviation	S1	B/W	PCTMFG	WHICOL	MDWINC	PCTNW
G_w	.3302	.0172	.86	−.15	−.41	.24	−.003	.14
S1	.0618	.0084		−.32	−.14	.09	.34	.38
B/W	.6634	.0596			−.12	.37	−.11	−.55
PCTMFG	.3196	.0898				−.01	−.20	−.14
WHICOL	.4459	.0762					−.18	−.49
MDWINC	6.879	.552						.45
PCTNW	.081	.050						

NOTE: The twelve SMSAs excluded to form the Non-South subsample are Dallas, Fort Worth, Houston, San Antonio, Birmingham, Miami, Tampa-St. Petersburg, Atlanta, Louisville, New Orleans, Memphis, and Norfolk. The twelve out of forty-eight, or 25 percent proportion of Southern SMSAs in the overall sample, corresponds extremely closely to the proportion of the overall population of the nation that is Southern.

CHAPTER FIVE

Economic Theory and
Class Conflict

NEOCLASSICAL DISCRIMINATION theories predict that white workers gain from racism, but this prediction does not accord with empirical reality. In the remainder of this book I argue that a class conflict view of the economy, in which racial inequality works to divide and weaken workers and reduce their strength relative to capitalists, does accord not only with a logically coherent theory, but with historical and econometric evidence as well. The theoretical argument is introduced in this chapter, the historical evidence in Chapter 6, and the econometric evidence in Chapter 7.

The omission from neoclassical discrimination analysis of such a perspective on racism will not surprise anyone conversant with neoclassical economic theory. Emphasizing the effects of racism on class divisions itself presupposes a perspective on economic processes in which class conflict and bargaining power are important determinants of the overall distribution of income between labor and capital. Such a perspective does not fit congenially into the neoclassical paradigm. On the contrary, the neoclassical model of the economy denies by its own logic any possible role for class conflict. Furthermore, neoclassical economists often argue that there is little compelling evidence suggesting that the operation of class power and class conflict plays a significant role in the economy.

In this chapter I argue that conflict and power do play a significant role in the determination of the distribution of income in a capitalist economy. I begin by presenting the neoclassical model of a competitive economy and indicate how it eliminates class conflict and power from its purview, thereby reducing profoundly its relevance for the analysis of a capitalist economy. I then present an alternative theory of a capitalist economy. This theory emphasizes the central significance of power and class conflict in the operation of capitalist institutions. The hierarchical and inherently conflictual relation between capitalists and workers provides the starting point of the analysis. I sketch a theory of the competitive capitalist firm that is consistent with this viewpoint, and yet quite different from the standard neoclassical theory of the firm.

Finally, in an appendix I show how capitalists benefit from stratifications among workers that limit worker solidarity. This theoretical analysis indicates that racial inequality will be reproduced, not eliminated, in a perfectly competitive capitalist economy because individual capitalists gain from it. The relaxation of the assumption of perfect competition reinforces this theoretical argument.

THE NEOCLASSICAL PARADIGM OF ECONOMICS

A characterization of the neoclassical paradigm can begin by contrasting it briefly with other approaches to economics. Among economists in the United States today, one can identify at least three broad schools of thought. An institutionalist school emphasizes the importance of institutions in economic life and focuses its initial efforts on the accretion of descriptive material on these institutions, reserving the development of specific hypotheses and broader theories until after the distinguishing institutional features have been identified. Institutionalists have a long tradition in American economic thought and have contributed important work in a variety of areas. Perhaps the most influential product of the institutionalist school has been in the area of labor economics, under the rubric of "industrial relations research."

A second school, Marxist or radical political economics, emphasizes the central importance of power in the determination of economic variables and therefore sees political and economic variables as inherently interrelated. Power is exercised in the first instance by classes competing over production and distribution. But the historical evolution of capitalist economies has involved the development of particular institutions that mediate conflict and organize class power. The most important of these institutions include the system of industrial relations and the structure of the state. Radical political economists thus draw on the work of the institutionalists to study the structure and dynamics of these institutions. This school of thought also recognizes that much of economic life in a capitalist society is organized through markets and that class power and conflict must be analyzed in relation to market behavior. However, markets do not completely determine outcomes as they do in the neoclassical approach.

The third, and by far the most influential, is the neoclassical school. This school emphasizes individual economic agents who interact in competitive markets and takes the allocation of resources in static competition as the norm or starting point. Monopoly, imperfect information, risk, disequilibrium dynamics, and so forth are increasingly analyzed by neoclassical economists, but primarily in terms of deviation from the competitive norm. Considerable debate takes place over the extent and causes of market failures as well as the desirability of reforms involving government intervention in markets. These debates indicate important internal cleavages between conservatives and liberals within the neoclassical school.

Such differences also suggest that neoclassical economics constitutes only a set of neutral methodological tools to investigate the behavior of economic agents under alternative constraints. But the neoclassical paradigm is more than a set of tools. It also involves a distinct angle of vision on the economic process.[1]

---

[1] The relation of microeconomics to macroeconomics has posed difficult problems for neoclassicals. Liberal neoclassical economists accept Keynesian macroeconomic analysis despite the evident inconsistencies with neoclassical microeconomic theory, notably the theory of unemployment. Yet considerable

Many mainstream economists object to the notion of the existence of a neoclassical paradigm to which they are alleged to belong. They argue that so much of their own recent theoretical efforts have involved relaxing the assumptions of perfect competition, equilibrium, complete information, zero risk, no externalities, and so forth, and that they moreover welcome such broadening work. How can one speak of a coherent paradigm when such heterogeneity exists? A perusal of recent issues of the leading professional journals bears out this view.

However, these laudable and diverse efforts constitute precisely the kind of normal scientific research that one expects to be taking place in an ongoing scientific paradigm. They do not invalidate the view that distinct paradigms exist. Although the institutionalist, radical political economy and neoclassical paradigms have borrowed from one another to some extent, they remain quite different. Proof of the existence and dominance of a coherent neoclassical paradigm comes from examination of the common ideas that are taught in colleges and universities throughout the country to first-year graduate and advanced undergraduate students of economic theory. The overwhelming proportion of these courses and textbooks are virtually identical, and they fit the brief characterization of the neoclassical paradigm presented here. (However, these teaching materials do tend to understate the

---

neoclassical work continues to assume that labor markets clear. Recent attempts to reconcile the two approaches have tended to depart from Keynes's own analysis and have tried to derive macroeconomic variables from microeconomic maximizing activity rather than the other way around. Consequently, a group of so-called post-Keynesian economists have organized to maintain and develop Keynes's insights without accepting neoclassical microeconomics. Conservative neoclassical economists generally attribute unemployment either to government mismanagement of monetary policy or to workers' voluntary behavior rather than to Keynesian explanations. There is less theoretical inconsistency as a result, but the macroeconomic analysis remains underdeveloped. In what follows I characterize the neoclassical paradigm as a microeconomic theory, preferring to view macroeconomic theory as a relatively distinct approach to economic analysis.

allocative inefficiency, instability, and inequity properties of competitive market economies that are put forward in professional journals and other advanced research outlets.)

Does the existence of a distinct neoclassical paradigm tend to foreclose recognition by its adherents of important contributions that have been made in other paradigms? Although I cannot fully answer this question here, I shall suggest that the research program generated by the neoclassical paradigm tends to direct the attention of its practitioners to market processes rather than to processes of conflict and bargaining power. The clarifying effect of the angle of vision of the neoclassical paradigm on markets simultaneously blurs questions of power. These effects are illustrated by the way in which neoclassical economists have analyzed racial inequality.

It is true that the neoclassical paradigm is flexible enough to permit modifications such as imperfect competition or the operation of class power, just as the Ptolemaic geocentric view of the motions of heavenly bodies permitted epicycle analysis to be added to account for observed anomalies to the theory. But as the Copernican revolution in astronomy taught, such modifications may be more fruitfully analyzed by adopting an entirely different approach. Consequently, it is important to view the neoclassical approach as constituting one of several alternative paradigms in economics. Having suggested that neoclassical economics constitutes a coherent and distinct paradigm, we can turn to considering further its internal structure.

The Structure of Neoclassical Economics

Modern neoclassical economic theory begins with atomistic, individual economic agents who interact through markets. Provided certain conditions are met, these interactions result in market-clearing equilibrium prices and quantities for every commodity that is bought and sold. The theory articulates the necessary and sufficient conditions for the existence, uniqueness, and stability of such equilibria. This approach to eco-

168

nomic theory (more precisely, to microeconomic theory) was first developed systematically in the 1870s, and is known throughout the world today as "the neoclassical theory of economics."[2]

In this theory the unique character of a particular factor (input) or product (output) is suppressed to permit a general theory and to illuminate the interdependence of the input and output markets. The neoclassical theory of the distribution of income therefore forms a subset of the general theory of the determination of equilibrium prices and quantities. This characteristic of neoclassical theory contrasts strongly with the dominant approach which preceded it, that is, classical economics. For this reason, and because some important insights were lost in the transition from classical to neoclassical theory, it is useful to contrast the classical approach explicitly with its neoclassical successor.

In the classical approach to income distribution, as typified by the work of Adam Smith, David Ricardo, and Karl Marx, a distinctive theory was developed for each of the separate factors of production, labor, capital, and land. Hence, the classical economists obtained quite different determinants for the prices of each factor. The wage rate, the profit rate, and rent not only had unique determinants, but also were determined differently from the prices of the output of firms.

The classical economists stated their theories in terms of the behavior of social groups in relation to one other. Classes rather than individuals provided the analytical starting point,

---

[2] For recent rigorous statements of the neoclassical theory, see Kenneth Arrow and Frank Hahn, *General Competitive Analysis* (San Francisco: Holden Day, 1971); Hal Varian, *Microeconomic Analysis* (New York: Norton, 1978).

The conditions required for existence, uniqueness, and stability of equilibrium are presented clearly in Arrow and Hahn. These conditions are quite strict. The stability requirement, especially, is unlikely to be satisfied in the real world. Benjamin Ward, *The Ideal Worlds of Economics* (New York: Basic Books, 1979), emphasizes this neglected point and elaborates the damage it causes for the neoclassical world view.

and capitalists, workers, and landowners were deemed to be distinct groups with fundamentally differing relations to the economic system. The classical economists argued, though not always explicitly or consistently, that these socioeconomic class relations determined, together with the technical conditions of production, the relations between profits, wages, and rent. These class relations and technical conditions were deemed causally anterior to the determination of the relative prices of produced commodities, in the sense that such prices themselves were not determinants of the causal variables.

The classical school also insisted that economic processes be viewed in dynamic terms. Smith, Richardo, and Marx identified the accumulation of capital as the principal driving force that over time both changed the conditions of production and the relations among the three classes in a capitalist economy. The distribution of income, therefore, could not be understood in a timeless, static framework.[3]

The neoclassical economists drew on and accepted some of the suggestions made by the classical school. They particularly utilized and developed further the insight that the economic system could be analyzed as a set of interrelated processes. Neoclassicals also accepted the Richardian view that land and other nonreproducible inputs received rents related more to their scarcity than to their productivity.

In most respects, however, the neoclassical approach departed from the classical tradition and would better be termed "anticlassical."[4] The neoclassical view of distribution

---

[3] Histories of economic thought that review the classical school include Mark Blaug, *Economic Theory in Retrospect*, 3d ed. (New York: Cambridge University Press, 1978); Maurice Dobb, *Theories of Value and Distribution Since Smith* (New York: Cambridge University Press, 1973); Joseph Schumpeter, *History of Economic Analysis* (New York: Oxford University Press, 1951).

A sticky point for the classical economists was the precise relation between the incomes received by each class and the relative prices of the commodities that were produced. Smith seemed only dimly aware of this problem, while Ricardo and Marx struggled with it explicitly. See Dobb's account, for example.

[4] This label has been suggested by Joan Robinson.

170

thus sees the payments of reproducible inputs as determined not by specific institutional mechanisms, but by the general mechanism of market interactions among atomistic individuals. Instead of beginning with the relations among classes, neoclassical theory began with individual economic agents, namely households and firms (which are owned by households), who engage in optimizing consumption and profit-maximizing behavior that is subject to budget constraints. Households supply factors of production while demanding commodities, and firms demand factors while supplying commodities. Factor incomes are a return for a productive service and express the opportunity cost of the leisure or present consumption forgone by individuals supplying those factors. No particular assumptions are made on the distribution of ownership of the factors of production among the households, no single economic relation is viewed as more causal than any other, and static rather than dynamic analysis tends to prevail.

The neoclassical distribution argument proceeds as follows. Consider a competitive economy with two factors of production: labor and capital; one or both factors are used in the production of every output. Competition insures that a uniform wage rate and a uniform profit rate will be formed when markets are in equilibrium. The income of any individual then depends on the *quantity* of the factors of production he or she owns—the initial factor endowment—and on the *prices* that those factors command on the market. Given the stock of assets and the size of the adult population, the price of each factor and the quantity that will be exchanged are determined by the interaction of supply and demand for factors.

The demand for factors derives from their productive services to firms. Profit-maximizing firms minimize their costs by hiring inputs up to the point where the price of the input equals the output price multiplied by the marginal physical product of the input. The aggregate schedule of demand for each factor of production therefore depends on the production function, the statement of existing technology that connects

171

inputs and outputs in each industry, on the determinants of the price of each output, and on the weight of each output in the total product. The possibilities of substituting one factor for another in production are included in the technological data that make up the production function. Substitution possibilities among different products and the other product market conditions affect the demand for factors and indicate the interdependence of product and factor markets.

Individual households can supply each factor. Labor services are offered by individuals according to their preferences for income for consumption goods versus their preference for leisure. Individuals offer their savings to the capital market according to intertemporal preferences for consumption goods. Initial asset endowments are important here not only in influencing the consumption-saving tradeoff, but also in influencing the labor-leisure tradeoff.

In this static model the competitive market equilibrium configuration of prices and resource allocation has several efficient properties. Production is efficient in the sense that firms will be operating with optimal plant sizes, input costs per unit of output will be at a minimum, and excess profits will be competed away. Consumption is efficient in the very narrow sense that resources have been allocated to each individual's consumption preferences and possibilities in such a way that he or she could be made no better off without someone else being made worse off. Given preferences, technology, and initial endowments, the allocation of resources will be efficient in the two senses that have just been defined.

The advent of the competitive neoclassical model is generally dated from the 1870s onward. Ironically, the efforts of the neoclassical pioneers relegated the analysis of imperfect competition (by Cournot and others) to the sidelines of economics just as the major capitalist economies were experiencing a major transformation toward oligopolistic market structure. Oligopoly and monopolistic competition were not important topics in mainstream economics until the late 1920s. Keynes's own neglect of imperfect competition once again relegated this topic to the periphery of economic theory.

172

The modern statement of the competitive model is due to Arrow and Debreu, who greatly clarified the stringent assumptions that are necessary for existence, uniqueness, attainment, and stability of general market equilibrium. Recent work in the Arrow-Debreu tradition has primarily focused on properties of the model under conditions of uncertainty and incomplete information.[5] While these efforts to make the model more realistic can certainly be applauded, it is still fair to conclude that imperfect competition models remain underdeveloped and on the periphery of the theoretical apparatus of neoclassical economics.

Neoclassical Growth Models

While the neoclassical general equilibrium model is static, dynamic models have been developed within the neoclassical traditions.[6] The main attempt along these lines, by von Neumann and others, involves balanced growth of all sectors. This attempt hardly represents a significant contribution, for it cannot account for the most evident developments of the past two centuries—major increases in per capita consumption and capital, the evolution of a wage-labor based class structure, the evolution of giant, oligopolistic corporations, the appearance of unionism, and the increasing intervention of the state in economic life. Moreover, the "everything depends on everything else" conclusion of general equilibrium analysis precludes any significant conclusions. Efforts to dynamize the model, to indicate the directions of change of the variables in a general equilibrium framework where the economy grows over time, have not been very successful.

The neoclassical models of dynamic growth that have produced more substantive results contain a single sector or two sectors. This aggregate or partial equilibrium approach, which owes more to Marshall than to Walras, has been devel-

[5] See, for example, the survey in Varian, *Microeconomic Analysis*, chapter 8, "Topics in the Economics of Information."

[6] For a recent survey, see G.C. Harcourt and N. Laing, eds., *Capital and Growth* (Baltimore: Penguin), 1972.

173

oped and extended by Solow, Uzawa, and others in recent decades. Aggregate growth models purport to show how the growth of capital per worker, although requiring abstinence from consumption and payment of profit to capital owners today, increases not only output per worker, but consumption in the future. Together with an associated discussion of productivity-augmenting technical change, this theory accounts for the dramatic increase in consumption levels of the past two hundred years. By indicating how economic growth presupposes payments to capital owners to compensate them for their abstinence, this version of neoclassical theory also is able to provide an ideological rationale for the contribution of capital owners to economic welfare. As we shall see, however, the aggregate production function approach of this theory contains internal logical inconsistencies that invalidate its basic results.

Failures of the Competitive Market

The efficiency property of competitive markets generally leads neoclassical economists to view competitive structures as preferable to oligopolistic or monopolistic market structures. However, neoclassical economists recognize important reasons why the competitive market fails to allocate resources in an optimal manner so that government action is called for. These failures involve externalities, public goods, "natural" monopolies, and equity. Externalities arise in situations where interdependencies among economic agents are not reflected in market prices, as in the case of pollution. Public goods occur in situations where it is difficult to exclude any individual from the consumption of the good. Such goods cannot be produced profitably by private producers because they cannot prevent free riders; no one will voluntarily pay a positive price for the good. Natural monopolies arise where economies of scale are such that one large producer can supply the good more cheaply than any multiplicity of firms. These generally agreed-upon cases of market failure provide a need for state taxation and expenditures. Market failure may also arise because uncer-

174

tainty and information costs make attainment of efficient equilibrium difficult.

Neoclassical welfare economics recognizes that, in addition to efficiency, equity also constitutes one of the objectives of economic organization. But the market does not necessarily produce maximum equity. There is little consensus among neoclassical economists on how alternative income distributions rank according to measures of aggregate social welfare, and even less consensus on how to obtain agreed-upon measures of aggregate social welfare. The neoclassical assumption that the government seeks to maximize aggregate social welfare is also questionable. Nonetheless, it is clear that policies that might be thought to improve efficiency could also involve a reduction in equity. A classic example is the removal of government subsidies to declining economic areas. A move toward freer markets may not result in a more desirable social outcome.

Much of the scientific and ideological debates among conservative and liberal neoclassical economists concern whether existing problems result from government interference with what otherwise would be well-working competitive markets or from market failures that justify government intervention. For example, conservative economists tend to be more hostile to antitrust activity or government regulation of industries on the grounds that the cure is worse than the disease. They point to the harmful effects of government intervention and to evidence suggesting that big business's conduct and performance are more competitive than liberals believe.

An additional important cause of market failure has received less recognition among neoclassical economists. This problem arises from the doubtful assumption that individual preferences for consumption, income, and leisure can be taken as individually determined, exogenous, and relatively stable. Once consumer preferences are seen as endogenous and interdependent among individuals, whether from the perspective of Galbraith's views on the effects of advertising, or from a

175

sociological perspective that sees tastes and personality characteristics developing in relation to the economic system, the optimality property of a competitive market system no longer follows.

It might be replied that such a theory of preferences need not be anathema to neoclassical economics, for the analytical properties of market outcomes can be obtained by starting with given demand curves for products and supply curves for factors without inquiring into the utility or preference structure supposedly lying behind them. Although this view is perfectly tenable, it must be recognized as one that precludes any possibility for making policy prescriptions from the economic theory. Moreover, it still leaves open the nature of the social theory that would explain why demand and supply curves have their observed shape and position. It is significant that efforts to introduce interdependencies and endogenous preferences have never made much headway among neoclassical economists and that individual preferences remain as a starting point for the teaching of microeconomic theory.

A recent finding in neoclassical economics questions the standard policy prescription that government can always improve efficiency by setting up side-payment markets (or new property rights) to internalize externalities or by breaking up oligopolies and "unnatural" monopolies. But so long as there remain some other distortions from the competitive market in the system, attempts to reduce noncompetitive distortions in another part of the system may actually involve movements away from efficiency. This remarkable finding, known within the profession as the theory of the second-best, has nonetheless been given little attention in standard curricula or discussions of economic policy.

These comments indicate both the openness of neoclassical theory to debate about the optimality of competitive markets and the limits of the theory's policy implications. But even if one accepts these criticisms, it might still be said that neoclassical theory provides a useful analytical approach to how markets operate. The scientific and descriptive value of the

176

theory is separate from the value of its prescriptive implications. This view contains some merit. Yet there remain substantial problems in the competitive neoclassical paradigm's ability to analyze scientifically the structure and dynamics of capitalist economies.

The well-known problems include: the fallacious assumption that macroeconomic relationships will permit all markets to clear; the clear evidence that technical, financial, and market power economies of scale in modern capitalism promote oligopolistic and monopolistic market structures rather than competitive ones; the observed capacity of economically powerful groups to enlist the state for their own ends. Each of these realities, but particularly the process of imperfect competition, has been the subject of insightful theoretical and empirical analysis by neoclassically oriented economists. However, the results only further undermine the coherence of the paradigm as a whole, and they have not relieved the widespread doubts on the capacity of neoclassical economics to capture the main historical forces at work in capitalist economies. These issues indicate the importance of a pluralistic dialogue with institutionalist, Marxist, and Keynesian traditions of economic discourse.

But the most serious weaknesses of the neoclassical paradigm stem from its neglect of the important processes of class conflict that characterize capitalist economies. These omissions are much less widely recognized within the neoclassical school and profoundly affect its relevance. Next, I turn to a discussion of these limitations.

CRITIQUE OF THE NEOCLASSICAL PARADIGM

Four principal weaknesses involving processes of class conflict characterize the neoclassical paradigm. (1) The neoclassical approach is logically incomplete. Despite claims to the contrary, it is not a determinate theory, and it does not show the impossibility of class conflict in a market economy. (2) The neoclassical approach lacks a theory of the distribution

177

of factor endowments. It therefore incorrectly specifies the institutional class relations that distinguish capitalist economies from other market economies. (3) The neoclassical approach incorrectly construes labor to be a commodity, failing to see that workers sell only their capacity to work, that is, their labor power, to capitalists. It therefore obscures the character of the labor process in capitalist production, failing to distinguish between capitalist and other forms of commodity production. (4) The neoclassical approach neglects collective action by workers and capitalists. Its incorrect individualistic assumptions about human behavior obscure the bases of widespread collective behavior not only in regard to the determinants of government action, but also in regard to economic activity inside and outside the workplace. Of these four points, the first constitutes only a technical criticism; the remaining three contain much greater significance, both as critiques and as indicators of the elements of an alternative theory.

The Logical Incompleteness of Neoclassical Theory

Neoclassical economics suggests that there is no role for class conflict in the determination of the distribution of income between wages and profits. The operation of markets alone determines these variables. Of course, conflict exists among individuals in the marketplace; sellers prefer higher prices and buyers prefer lower prices. But such conflict is settled by the market. The theory is said to be closed to additional determining factors. How then can class conflict be an important part of our understanding of economic processes?

The general equilibrium theorists have suggested one answer to this question. The work of Arrow and Debreu rigorously showed the conditions in which multiple equilibrium states, rather than only one possible market-clearing set of prices and quantities, are possible in a market economy. These theorists showed that a unique equilibrium emerges under a much narrower set of assumptions than was previously

178

believed.[7] This finding opens the door for additional determinants of economic variables, such as class conflict, which work to select one equilibrium configuration from the feasible set.

Piero Sraffa, Joan Robinson, and other economic theorists in England and Italy have argued that the partial equilibrium Marshallian model is also not closed to nonmarket variables. This criticism was made in a famous debate with American neoclassical economists that centered on technical issues.[8] But behind the technical debate lurked a larger set of questions.

The technical debate concerned the validity of the connection made in neoclassical theory between the rate of profit and the marginal productivity of capital. Neoclassical theorists had argued that the marginal productivity of capital declines as capital becomes more abundant relative to labor. Since a declining marginal productivity of capital implies a decline in the rate of profit, a rising capital-labor ratio would be associated with a monotonically falling ratio of profit rate to wage rate. This view has been shown to be erroneous. The value of capital cannot be determined independently of the rate of profit, and the marginal productivity of capital is therefore not a well-defined concept. More precisely, in the neoclassical model it is possible that the same method of production may be the most profitable of a number of production methods at more than one rate of profit, although other methods are profitable at intermediate profit rates. This phemonenon is known as "reswitching." The same physical capital goods may have more than one value, since a different real wage rate and set of relative prices will be associated with each rate of profit,

[7] Kenneth Arrow and Gerard Debreu, "Existence of Equilibrium for a Competitive Economy," *Econometrica* (1954); Gerard Debreu, *A Theory of Value* (New York: Wiley, 1959).

[8] See "Symposium," *Quarterly Journal of Economics* (November 1966). The controversy is discussed ably in G.C. Harcourt, *Theory of Capital: Some Cambridge Controversies* (New York: Cambridge University Press, 1972). See also E.K. Hunt and Jesse Schwartz, eds., *A Critique of Economic Theory* (Baltimore: Penguin, 1972).

and the capital goods have to be valued at their appropriate set of prices.

The Anglo-Italian critics argued that the possibility of reswitching was fatal to the neoclassical model. No longer could the neoclassicals speak of the "marginal productivity of capital." No longer could one tell the simple parable of the developing economy in which the accumulation of capital makes production more capital-intensive, thus causing the wage rate to rise while the profit rate falls. Without a strictly downward sloping demand curve for capital, the price of capital could no longer be taken as an index of its scarcity.

There were several neoclassical replies to the criticism. One reply conceded the mistake. But another pointed out that the Arrow-Debreu-Walras general equilibrium theory does not require a macroeconomic aggregate concept of capital. General equilibrium theory needs only a uniform rate of return to investment in different industries, and the Anglo-Italian criticism does not apply. Since the possibility of multiple equilibrium solutions in the Walrasian model had long been recognized, the discovery of reswitching did not seem to add very much.

Logical consistency did demand a price. The general equilibrium attempts to make neoclassical theory logically consistent have also rendered it intellectually vacuous. In general equilibrium theory, nothing specific can be said about the state of the income distribution or of its trend over time.

But the model remains logically consistent. Income distribution is determined, albeit not uniquely, once factor supplies, tastes, and technological substitution possibilities are given. For the neoclassicals, the neoclassical general equilibrium model of a competitive economy is still logically sound.[9]

The resilience of the neoclassical theory reveals that the reswitching debate focused on a relatively minor issue. The critics correctly pointed out an important internal incon-

[9] For a discussion along these lines, see Bob Rowthorn, "Neo-Classicism, Neo-Richardianism and Marxism," *New Left Review* (July–August 1974).

sistency in the partial equilibrium version of the neoclassical model, thereby invalidating its substantive argument on the relation between economic growth and the necessity of payments to capital. But while the critics successfully opened some chinks in the neoclassical armor, they did not show that the general equilibrium version of the neoclassical model was logically inconsistent.

The critics would have done better to stay closer to the more fundamental issues lying behind the technical debate. These concern the neoclassicals' claim to have a theory of value and distribution that applies universally to all market economies, with no mention of the particular institutional conditions of a capitalist economy.

The Institutional Incompleteness of Neoclassical Theory

Neoclassical economics purports to apply to any market economy, whatever its distribution of wealth. The neoclassical assumption of equal and voluntary exchange among free producers may be appropriate for some historical situations, such as that prevailing in the northeastern sections of the United States in the eighteenth and early nineteenth centuries. Most households at that time were, or could easily become, independent small producers who received payment for a completed product they sold in a market exchange. The voluntary nature of market participation is revealed by the fact that many independently subsisting households in this period could and sometimes did choose to refrain from participating in market exchanges.

In present-day capitalism, however, control and ownership of production are highly concentrated. Most producers are workers who are paid a wage or salary for their labor power; they are dependent on this market activity for their income because they own little, if any, income-producing property.[10]

[10] For documentation of these statements, see Michael Reich, "The Development of the Wage Labor Force," and Frank Ackerman and Andrew Zimbalist, "Capitalism and Inequality in the United States," both in Richard Edwards, Michael Reich, and Thomas Weisskopf, eds., *The Capitalist System.*

Their participation in the labor market is not entirely voluntary. This characteristic of highly unequal endowment distributions is a feature that distinguishes capitalist economies from other market-organized economies. Yet neoclassical theory neither specifies the initial distribution of factor endowments nor indicates how the endowment distribution will change over time.

Some theorists in the neoclassical tradition, such as Arrow and Hahn, label their theories in terms of the analysis of general competitive economies, not as the analysis of a capitalist economy only. That is, these neoclassical theorists believe that a single theory applies to a Yugoslav-type market socialist economy, to Tom Paine's eighteenth-century ideal of a society of equal property holders and to the United States in the twentieth century, since all these economies have competitive economies with decentralized decision-making.

This alleged universality of neoclassical theory is inaccurate. Wealth is highly concentrated among a few in every capitalist economy, and this inequality is reproduced consistently over time. Neoclassical theory incorrectly suggests that any distribution of endowments and income can be achieved in a capitalist economy. But capitalists can appropriate a share of the total product only if the conditions of existence for the mass of households require them to sell their labor power to a capitalist at a wage less than the average product per worker.[11] Not all endowment distributions appear to be feasible. This observation suggests that "general competitive analysis" is too general for many important questions.

The Incorrect Construction of Labor as a Commodity

Neoclassical theory fails to see the noncommodity character of labor. Workers sell to capitalists not an agreed-upon amount of labor, but only their capacity to work, their labor power, for an agreed-upon period of time. The amount and conditions of work remain to be specified, with workers and

[11] See p. 188 for a further elaboration of this point.

employers holding opposing interests. When workers are paid piece rates instead of time rates, the length of time that the workers are expected to take to produce a unit of output is not determined. Labor contracts under piece payments are also incomplete.

This fundamental incompleteness of the labor contract is resolved primarily by conflict and bargaining at the workplace between workers and capitalists. The imperative of minimizing workers' bargaining strength suggests why capitalists organize work along hierarchical rather than cooperative lines. Neoclassical theory, by contrast, does not comprehend the particular nature of the labor process in capitalist production and fails to explain why there are very few firms in a capitalist economy where workers hire capitalists and managers to work for them.

Neoclassical theory fails also to comprehend the nature of worker-capitalist conflict at the workplace.[12] The labor contract differs from other contracts because workers, unlike animals or inanimate objects, can actively seek to change the conditions under which they produce and sell their labor power. The wage bargain is likely to be less flexible in a downward direction than other contracts, and workers will want higher wages when they see that their productivity is being increased. The rigidity of the labor market, though highlighted by Keynes, is generally ignored in the microeconomic analysis of neoclassical theory.

The Neglect of Collective Action in Neoclassical Theory

In both the general equilibrium and the aggregate partial equilibrium variants of neoclassical theory, the center stage is given to the optimizing actions of individual economic agents meeting in markets. Individuals are presumed to maximize their self-interest, allying with others only when mutual net

---

[12] This point is discussed further in this chapter. See also Michael Reich and James Devine, "The Microeconomics of Conflict and Hierarchy in Capitalist Production," *Review of Radical Political Economics* (Winter 1981).

gain thereby occurs. Neoclassical theory, therefore, not only neglects collective behavior by workers or by capitalists but conflict between these classes as well. It also denies that such phenomena could long exist.

The neoclassical paradigm gives short shrift to collective action primarily because it sees individual interest as usually conflicting with collective action. Collective behavior is likely to be short-lived, unless the relevant economic agents number no more than a handful. For example, individual producers in an industry that is organized into a price-setting cartel can increase profits by lowering their prices below the cartel-set level, and thereby expand their sales. Unless the cartel is very small, such violations of the collective norm can be undertaken secretly to avoid sanctions. The cartel will not be able to enforce its collective interest and will dissolve. Similar problems will beset labor unions that cannot control entry into an industry.[13]

Voluntary collective action is also thought to be unlikely because of the so-called prisoner's dilemma and free rider problems. Because of the high costs in setting up a coalition, an initiator will not succeed unless others are also willing to take risks. Since these risks are substantial the likelihood of cooperation must be weighed against pursuing an alternative strategy under a noncooperative situation. It is therefore not rational for risk-averse individuals to take the first step, and the coalition will never be formed. This is the prisoner's dilemma problem.

Even if a coalition is organized, individuals can obtain a free ride and receive the benefits of the collective action without paying a price. If the coalition is large, the participation of any individual makes little difference, so that the price of non-participation is close to zero. Hence, no one participates and the coalition collapses. This free rider analysis leads to such

[13] Mancur Olson, *The Logic of Collective Action* (Cambridge: Harvard University Press, 1964).

184

absurdities as predicting that individuals will never want to vote, join unions, or fight in a war.

But this result follows only if one accepts the neoclassical axiom that individuals seek to maximize only their short-run self-interest. The prisoner's dilemma problem of who will take the first step in forming a coalition forgets that over time a considerable amount of communication and implicit and explicit bargaining can go on among cooperators as well as retaliation against noncooperators in order to insure that the coalition will succeed once it is formed.[14] Moreover, individuals engage in collective behavior because they are social beings imbued with ideologies that motivate their actions as much as self-interest does. Indeed, ideology may play a role in the formation of the concept of self-interest itself. In the United States today, a bewildering variety of individualistic and collectivistic ideologies seem to coexist in the population, not infrequently even within the same individual. Some of these ideologies promote collective action and others do not. Individual participation in collective action can be better understood by seeing individual actions as the outcome of a relation between ideology and self-interest.[15]

Neoclassical economic theory does recognize some situations when collective action will occur. As we have seen, externalities, natural monopolies, public goods, and other market failures provide instances where neoclassical theory indicates that some collective action through the state will occur.

However, this outcome is seen as the result of actions by citizens who are pursuing their collective public interest at the voting booth on election day. This view of the political process

---

[14] See Matthew Edel, "A Note on Collective Action, Marxism, and the Prisoner's Dilemma," *Journal of Economic Issues* (September 1979).

[15] For two recent empirical studies that find ideology to be an important determinant of decision-making, see Douglas Hibbs, "Political Parties and Macroeconomic Policy," *American Political Science Review* (December 1977); James Kau and Paul Rubin, "Self-Interest, Ideology and Logrolling in Congressional Voting." *Journal of Law and Economics* (October 1979).

185

differs considerably from one in which heterogeneous economic classes pursue their opposed collective class interests in
the political arena.[16] Hence, these accounts expand the
individualistic focus of the neoclassical paradigm to incorporate state activity while continuing to neglect collective action.

A Class Conflict Model of the Economic Process

The neoclassical view of the economy poses economic
relations in terms of freedom and equality. Individuals are free
to enter into exchange contracts without interference or
coercion and only when the exchange is beneficial to each
party; equality inheres in the exchange, because buyer and
seller are on the same footing. The neoclassical method erases
the differences between labor and capital, thereby attempting
to construct a general theory of optimal choice that is subject to
constraints applying to all economic agents. Recent neoclassical theory has emphasized that most labor supply
decisions by workers involve elements of investment, thereby
further reducing the analytical distinctions between labor and
capital in the theory.[17]

This approach cannot explain the observed persistence of
class inequalities in capitalist economies nor the prevalence of
conflict and hierarchy in capitalist production.

A theory that accounts for these phenomena must depart
from the neoclassical view of the economy. To explain inequality and collective action, such a theory must contain a
more articulated view of the structural class relations that
individuals bring to the marketplace. To account for the

[16] In recent decades attempts have been made to incorporate group political
activity into neoclassical economic theory. This so-called public choice
literature is surveyed in Norman Frolich and Joe Oppenheimer, *Modern
Political Economy* (Englewood Cliffs, N.J.: Prentice-Hall, 1978). This literature, however, continues to assume that political actors are only self-interest
maximizing individuals.
[17] The capital components of the labor supply decision include the acquisition of skills as well as location decisions.

186

employment relation inside the capitalist firm, the theory must analyze more closely the exchange relation between workers and capitalists. I outline here a class conflict theory with these two characteristics.

The first step involves articulating the structural context in which the principal economic agents carry out their activities. Drawing on the tradition of the classical economists, I indicate at the outset each of the main economic groupings and show how they differ distinctively from one another in their relation to economic life. The analysis here thus emphasizes the differences between labor and capital.

The class conflict theory presented in this section does not do away with all individual decision-making, but shows how economic and political structures form individual decisions. Two dimensions of human activity are recognized: competition among individuals and class struggle between capitalists and workers. While neoclassical theory recognizes only the first of these dimensions, the class conflict analysis integrates the two dimensions into a single analysis.

The Principal Economic Classes

The capitalist class and the working class, the two great classes whose relation Marx persistently examined, now, more than ever, dominate the economic life of advanced capitalist countries. Ownership of capital assets has become increasingly more concentrated than in the nineteenth century, or even in the first third of the twentieth century, while the growth in the proportion of the population whose livelihood depends exclusively or almost exclusively on the sale of labor power has been equally spectacular.[18] In the model of a perfectly competitive market economy, these two classes meet in the marketplace as atomistic individuals with different initial endowments, some holding only labor and others with capital. How does this meeting differ from the neoclassical tale of the equal relations that are inherent in a free market?

[18] See the references cited in note 10.

187

One difference concerns the market outcomes resulting from the initial unequal endowment distribution. The initial lack of assets among workers other than their labor power insures that worker households have no choice but to supply their capacity to labor to the market. Wages are determined by supply of and demand for labor power. For a capitalist-type market economy to exist, labor must be supplied with sufficient elasticity to meet the condition that the market-determined wage rate is significantly less than the average product of labor. This condition is usually met through a variety of mechanisms: periodic economic downturns limit the demand for labor, new groups join the wage-labor population, labor productivity rises, and so forth. The elasticity of the labor supply guarantees that, whatever the demand for labor, capitalists can appropriate a share of the total product.

Competition among firms in the labor market insures that firms pay a wage equal to a worker's marginal product, as neoclassical theory suggests. The difference between the marginal product received by labor and the larger average product produced by labor constitutes the return to capital (profits). With the condition that wages (expressed in money terms using ruling prices) are strictly less than the average product of labor (expressed also in ruling prices), the equilibrium rate of profit will be strictly positive.[19]

Capitalists then reinvest their profits (or at least the proportion they do not expend on consumption), thereby setting in motion on an expanded scale another cycle of production, exchange, distribution, consumption, and investment. Competition among capitalists necessitates the expansion of capital in order to reduce average and marginal costs. Over time the stock of accumulated capital does expand. The supply and the productivity of labor also grow, thereby con-

[19] For a more rigorous statement of this proposition, see Michio Morishima, *Marx's Economics* (New York: Cambridge University Press, 1973); or Donald Harris, *Capital Accumulation and Income Distribution* (Stanford University Press, 1978).

tinuing to insure a positive return to capital. The market meeting between workers and capitalists therefore permits capitalists to expand their capital.

The results for workers are quite different. Although real wages may rise substantially above the socially determined level of subsistence, which also tends to rise over time, most workers' income levels permit a very small amount of personal household savings over their life cycle. Moreover, the greatest part of these savings is reserved for illness, retirement, children's education, and other specific activities. That is, these savings constitute a reallocation of expenditures over the life cycle rather than a sustained accumulation of assets. Since these life-cycle oriented savings do not result in the accumulation of financial assets, they do not change the worker's financial dependence on labor earnings. And it takes a substantial accumulation of financial assets to permit long-term independence from labor market earnings. Consequently, the market reproduces the workers' necessity to sell their labor power, thus reproducing the unequal class relation between workers and capitalists. Perfectly competitive markets are consistent with the reproduction of classes, with immobility, that is, between classes.

This immobility is relative rather than absolute. For example, some workers are able to save sufficiently to start their own small businesses. Such businesses usually depend on large inputs of the owners' labor as well as their capital. Most of these small businesses fail in their first few years of operation. A minority succeed, however, and together with the short-lived failures, they constantly replenish the ranks of small capitalists, one of the middle groupings between the capitalist class and the working class.

A very low percentage of small businesses are much more successful and expand to the point where the owner-enterpreneurs not only employ wageworkers, but also hire managers. Once they no longer need to mix their own labor with their newly accumulated capital in order to make profits, these small capitalists rise in status to capitalists proper. Such

189

Horatio Algers are exceedingly few in number in relation to the size of both the working class and small capitalists, but they may play a significant role in replenishing the ranks of the capitalist class. Moreover, they generate powerful aspirations for upward mobility among the remainder of the population and sustain the hope among many workers that hard work and initiative will result in such economic success.

The small business class always exists in a capitalist economy, although its relative size is much smaller today than in the beginning of the nineteenth century. This intermediate class between workers and capitalists blurs the line that demarcates one class from another. It also makes the capitalist class a heterogeneous category.

A capitalist economy also contains another group whose economic position lies somewhere between workers and capitalists: managers and professionals. Managers themselves form a spectrum from first-line supervisors, who are entirely subordinate to capitalists, to presidents of large corporations. The class position of presidents merges with that of the capitalist owners. Professionals are more difficult to categorize, since they perform a variety of tasks in widely varying conditions of supervision and autonomy. They occupy a contradictory position that incorporates attributes of both workers and capitalists.[20] These groups have grown markedly in size in this century.

Finally, we can also discern significant differences within the working class itself. Three main working-class segments are identifiable. Some wageworkers are artisans, possessing considerable skills in their crafts; this group has much in common with many professionals and low-level managers. A second group works at more routinized jobs requiring little skill; these workers constitute the traditionally identified working class.

---

[20] For more detailed discussions of these intermediate strata, see Erik Wright, *Class, Crisis and the State* (London: New Left Books, 1978), chapter 2; and Richard Edwards, *Contested Terrain: The Transformation of the Workplace in the Twentieth Century* (New York: Basic Books, 1979).

Other workers are employed irregularly; they are rarely unionized and often depend on welfare, unemployment insurance, and other transfer payments for their survival.[21]

The structural class position model presented here more powerfully explains the distribution of earnings than the usual human capital model of neoclassical theory. Both the level of income and the returns to skill investments of individuals are significantly affected by their position in the class structure. A model that highlights these structural relations thus turns out to be superior to a model that obscures them.[22]

The structural conditions that give rise to the contemporary organization of classes and to conflict between classes are better understood with a more articulated analysis of the modern capitalist firm. This analysis of the capitalist firm constitutes the second main characteristic distinguishing the class conflict theory from the neoclassical approach.

A Class Conflict Theory of the Capitalist Firm

Class conflict theory views the worker-capitalist employment relation in the firm as follows. Workers sell their labor time to capitalists in exchange for a wage or salary. The worker gets a specified amount of money, the capitalist gets control over the worker's labor capacities for a specified time period. Capitalists, usually together with their managers, decide what products will be produced and how the work will be organized. Capitalists legally own the product that the workers produce, and they attempt to sell this product at a price that generates profits to them.

By entering the employment relation, workers surrender to capitalists not only authority over the tasks they will perform, but also most of the political and civil rights they enjoy as

[21] This tripartite division of the working class follows recent labor market segmentation analysis. See Michael Reich, Richard Edwards, and David Gordon, *The Segmentation of Labor in U.S. Capitalism* (New York: Cambridge University Press, 1981).

[22] See Erik Wright, *Class Structure and Income Determination* (New York: Academic Press, 1979); Reich, Edwards, and Gordon, *Segmentation of Labor*.

191

citizens of the state. When they walk into the factory or office, they are on the private property of the capitalist, where the guarantees provided by the Bill of Rights do not apply. Freedom of speech and assembly, the presumption of innocence until proven guilty, due process, equality before the law, and other rights protect citizens from action by the state. Except for a limited number of government incursions into the employment relation, workers have no analogous legal protections from the actions of employers at the place of employment.

Some rights have been won by workers and are recorded in collective bargaining agreements or in Federal law. For example, the grievance filing procedures contained in virtually all collective bargaining agreements give unionized workers some due process rights, and Federal legislation gives workers the right to bargain collectively, to "engage in concerted activity for mutual aid and protection," some limited free-speech rights, the right not to be discriminated against because of race, sex, religion, or national origin, and the right to submit without penalty complaints concerning safety and health conditions to the Federal Occupational Safety and Health Administration.[23]

The law leaves most rights in the hands of employers. They can legally fire workers for any reason, except a few that are forbidden by law.[24] Whatever other rights workers have at their jobs must be obtained through the collective bargaining process, and less than a quarter of the United States work force is covered by collective bargaining agreements.

In any case, virtually all collective bargaining agreements leave in management's hands the power to decide what will be produced and how, where plants will be located, and who will

[23] The phrase in quotes comes from the key section of the National Labor Relations Act. The limited free-speech rights provided by the NLRA are discussed in Staughton, Lynd, "Employee Speech in the Private Workplace: Two Doctrines or One?" *Industrial Relations Law Journal* (1977).

[24] The rights protected in the law (not always enforced) are mentioned in the previous paragraph.

be hired. For example, paragraph 8 of the General Motors contract with the United Auto Workers contains a long-standing clause spelling out management prerogatives: "The right to hire, promote, discharge, or discipline for cause; and to maintain discipline and efficiency of employees, is the sole responsibility of the Corporation except that Union members shall not be discriminated against as such. In addition, the products to be manufactured, the location of plants, the schedule of productions, the methods, processes and means of manufacturing are solely and exclusively the responsibility of the Corporation."[25] Similarly, although many collective bargaining agreements contain dozens of pages spelling out work rules, almost all of the important decisions concerning the organization of production remain under the control of management. Employers and unions frequently do clash over such issues as the rate at which work is to be performed. But despite the efforts of unions, few labor-management contracts have treaded significantly on management prerogatives.

What exactly does the capitalist purchase by hiring workers? The purchase and sale of labor power by a capitalist differs fundamentally from the purchase and sale of products, raw materials, capital goods, money, land, buildings, and other exchanges in a market economy. When capitalists purchase a machine or a certain quantity of raw material, they are able to determine with considerable precision the place of these inputs in the production process. Similarly, when capitalists hire an independent contractor, they are exchanging a definite sum of money (the agreed-upon price of the product or service) for a rather definite product or service. Typically, a written or an implied contract specifies in great detail what the purchaser is buying from the seller.

The labor contract is different. By hiring an employee, the capitalist does not purchase a specific and agreed-upon set of services to be performed, but rather disposition over the

---

[25] See Staughton Lynd, "Workers' Control and Workers' Rights," *Radical America* (September–October 1976).

worker's capacity to labor for an agreed-upon amount of time. Why emphasize this point? Because unlike the case with other inputs, how much work the worker actually performs for the capitalist is problematic in a central sense. The amount of work to be performed is not expressed contractually, regardless of whether the pay system is organized according to time or piece rates. Instead, the quantity of work performed and its cost depend on how successfully capitalists are able to elicit work from their workers.[26]

The workers want to obtain the maximum wage for the minimum amount of alienating effort and, insofar as possible, to make the work creative and satisfying rather than alienating. The employers' desire to maximize worker productivity and minimize labor costs is inconsistent with these goals.[27] The United States Supreme Court has on occasion voiced a similar analysis. In *Holden* v. *Hardy* (1898), the Court noted

> that the proprietors of . . . establishments and their operatives do not stand upon an equality, and that their interests are, to a certain extent, conflicting. The former naturally desire to obtain as much labor as possible from their employees, while the latter are often induced by the fear of discharge to conform to regulations which their judgment, fairly exercised, would pronounce to be detrimental. . . . In

[26] Although neoclassical theorists have ignored these aspects of the labor contract, they sometimes do feature extensively in institutional labor economics. For example, in 1940 Sumner Slichter wrote: "It is an important characteristic of the labor contract when payment is by the hour or the day that the amount of work to be done is not specified. This may be regarded as a serious imperfection in the terms of the contract because it leaves the amount of work to be determined by a struggle. The management tries to get as much out of the men as possible and the men try to give as little in return as possible." *Union Policies and Industrial Managment* (Washington, D.C.: Brookings Institution, 1940), p. 200. On p. 282 of this same work Slichter stated: "It is also true that payment by the piece leaves an important item of the labor contract undetermined, namely, how long the worker is expected to take to produce a given amount."

[27] This argument is spelled out more rigorously in Reich and Devine, "Conflict and Hierarchy."

194

other words, the proprietors lay down the rules and the laborers are practically constrained to obey them.[28]

Greater worker productivity and cost minimization requires that capitalists manage the workers to exert greater effort without thereby raising labor costs. The conflict between workers and employers on both the individual and class levels rests ultimately on this antagonistic set of interests.

The central point of this argument can be restated as follows. The workplace is not simply a place of technical production where inputs are combined according to engineering and economic principles in such a fashion as to minimize costs. The workplace also constitutes a social system, where the quantity of work performed and the wage paid for the work are variables determined by the interaction of the different actors in the system.

If the employment relation poses such headaches for employers, why do they not simply substitute sales contracts for services performed, acting as traders or contractors who mediate between direct producers and market for the final assembled product? Why doesn't the firm simply concentrate on marketing its products and refrain from playing a very large role in organizing production itself?

Such a view of the firm and employer indeed resembles that found in neoclassical economic theory. This view of the firm had some relevance to eighteenth- and nineteenth-century factory conditions. For example, during the early stage of the Industrial Revolution, the "putting-out" contractors provided or "put out" raw materials to workers producing in their homes and purchased the manufactured product from them. This description of the firm also fits the reality inside many nineteenth-century United States enterprises, where one found considerable "inside contracting"; skilled workers contracted with capitalists to provide a service for a price rather than for a

---

[28] Holden v. Hardy, 169 U.S. 366 (1898), quoted in Glenn Miller, *Government Policy Toward Labor: An Introduction to Labor Law* (Columbus, Ohio: GRID, 1975), p. 112.

wage. The hiring of unskilled helpers and the organization of tasks was controlled by the skilled crafts contractor, while the raw materials, tools, machinery, and other equipment were provided by the capitalist. By the twentieth century, however, such production relations were becoming increasingly rare.

In modern capitalism, most corporations have elaborate labor management structures constructed primarily to extract greater productivity from the employees while at the same time blocking worker coalitions that would give workers greater power and increased wages. These management systems typically take the form of bureaucratic and hierarchical structures of authority at the workplace, and include direct supervision, the use of machine-paced technologies (assembly lines), elaborate promotion ladders, and performance evaluation techniques. Such organizational forms turn out to be more profitable than the earlier model where capitalists played little direct role in organizing the work process.

It is elementary that the likelihood of solidarity among workers depends on the extent of common interests, the benefits any individual obtains by exiting from the collectivity, and the extent of the sanctions the collectivity can enforce on noncooperative individuals. In order to minimize the threat of collective behavior by employees, employers frequently have moved to fragment work groups in order to reduce the common interests of employees. Many employers have chosen to pay wage rates higher than the "market" level to some of their workers in order to elicit loyalty from these workers and make more forceful the threat of dismissal. They also have used the prospect of employee promotion and advancement to secure their loyalty. And they have attempted to structure the allocation of tasks and decision-making in a vertical hierarchical manner in order to minimize the sanctions that a group of workers can impose upon one of their coworkers.[29] The

---

[29] See Herbert Gintis, "The Nature of the Labor Exchange: Toward a Radical Theory of the Firm," *Review of Radical Political Economics* (Summer 1976); George Akerlof and David Soskice, "The Economics of Sanctions," (University of California, Berkeley, Department of Economics, no date).

creation of incentive schemes and "internal labor markets" therefore involve more than attempts to pay individual workers according to their actual productivity.

At the same time, using informal methods as well as formal organizations, workers have attempted to enhance solidarity-enhancing goals and to maximize the leverage they have over other workers and over managers. Although unionization significantly increases worker power in this regard, it is important to stress that unorganized workers also can make significant efforts to the same end.[30] The model of the firm proposed here therefore presents the firm not as a location controlled exclusively by managers and capitalists, but as a contested terrain in which capitalists and managers have predominant but not total power.[31]

If profitability rather than efficiency determines the organization of work in capitalist firms, it would seem to follow that cooperatively run enterprises could prove more efficient.

Although both industrial relations researchers and game theorists have developed an extensive literature on bargaining theory and coalition formation, much of this work takes as given the variables that are emphasized here. For a representative sample of these approaches, see Richard Walton and Robert McKersie, *A Behavioral Theory of Labor Negotiations* (New York: McGraw-Hill, 1965); Neil Chamberlain, *Collective Bargaining* (New York: McGraw-Hill, 1951); Arnold Weber, "The Craft-Industrial Issue Revisited, A Study of Union Government," *Industrial and Labor Relations Review* (April 1963); Orley Ashenfelter and George Johnson, "Bargaining Theory, Trade Unions, Industrial and Strike Activity," *American Economic Review* (March 1969); E.W. Kelley, "Bargaining in Coalition Situations," in Sven Groennings, E.W. Kelley, and Michael Leiserson, eds., *The Study of Coalition Behavior* (New York: Holt, Rinehart and Winston, 1970).

[30] See for example, Stanley Mathewson, *The Restriction of Output Among Unorganized Workers* (Carbondale, Ill.: Southern Illinois University Press, 1969) (originally published in 1931); Donald Roy, "Quota Restrictions and Goldbricking in a Machine Shop," *American Journal of Sociology* (March 1952); Donald Roy, "Efficiency and the 'Fix': Informal Intergroup Relations in a Piecework Machine Shop," *American Journal of Sociology* (1954–1955).

[31] The Appendix to this chapter presents a series of models that articulate this theory of the firm in greater formality, applying it to the case of racial inequality. See also Reich and Devine, "Conflict and Hierarchy."

197

Workers who could borrow sufficient capital could presumably set up their own firms and outcompete their capitalist counterparts. But greater static efficiency does not by itself imply greater long-run competitiveness. The outcome depends on a number of additional variables: the rate of effort and number of work hours that cooperative members would desire to maintain; the wages these workers would pay themselves; the rate of technical change they could sustain; the rate at which they would choose to reinvest their profits in their own enterprise; their flexibility in adjusting to short-term fluctuations in demand; and their capacity and desire to retool their skills and capital goods as demand for their product changes over the long run. A summation of the comparisons between capitalist and cooperative firms on most of these variables would no doubt yield ambiguous results.

However, on one of these variables the capitalist firm maintains a decisive edge. It can use layoffs to shift the burden of recessions and other sources of economic risk onto workers. Capitalists can spread their risk by investing in a variety of industries, but workers invest all their labor power in a particular firm. Moreover, cooperative members invest much of their capital in a single enterprise. These considerations make cooperatives less likely to be competitive with capitalist firms in the long run, and they explain the difficulties facing individual workers' cooperatives when they operate an environment of mainly capitalist firms.

Worker-Capitalist Relations and the State

The modern worker-capitalist relation inside the workplace is not worked out solely between workers and capitalists. Typically a third party, the state, also plays an important role. Federal statutes have defined the rights of workers to organize into unions and bargain collectively, and an elaborate bureaucratic and judicial structure has been constructed to administer this legislation. Other Federal legislation sets standards for minimum-wage levels, maximum hours, administration of pension funds, and internal governance of unions. Some states have "right-to-work" laws that prohibit the "closed union shop." The conflict between workers and capitalists is therefore not limited to struggles of individual employers with their workers, but also takes place on the political terrain of the state.[32]

The evolution of labor legislation reflects the growth of collective worker power in the 1930s and 1940s, as well as the continuing predominance of capitalist power. Unions per se have not been illegal in the United States since the landmark case of *Commonwealth* v. *Hunt* in 1842. But until the 1930s the power of the state was used almost exclusively against unions and strikers. Courts issued injunctions and other judicial decisions against strikers, while the legitimate violence of the state—Federal troops, the National Guard, and local police—was deployed frequently against striking workers. The passage of the National Labor Relations Act of 1935 (known popularly as "the Wagner Act") required employers to bargain with worker organizations, specified a series of unfair employer labor practices, and established a National Labor Relations Board (NLRB) to administer this legislation. State power now also protects some worker rights.

The reforms of the New Deal era substantially advanced and consolidated the political influence of the organized labor union movement. Workers now advance their interests through economic bargaining with employers and through political activity and influence. As a result, the employment relation today is much less of a private contract than it was before the 1930s, and the collective organization and activity of workers in the political arena significantly affects the terms of the worker-capital relation within the firm.

While these changes tip the scales of state justice in labor's direction, capitalists continue to retain the advantage. The Wagner Act and its successors contain numerous loopholes

[32] See Michael Reich and Richard Edwards, "Political Parties and Class Conflict in the United States," *Socialist Review* (May–June 1978), for a more detailed discussion of the role of the state in the process of class conflict.

and inadequate enforcement provisions.[33] The J. P. Stevens case illustrates how a long lag, often lasting for several years, can separate the initial filing of a complaint with the National Labor Relations Board against an employer's unfair practices and an ultimate NLRB decision. Most individual workers and unions cannot afford to rely on this recourse against employer intimidation. Even if the NLRB rules against an employer, the low penalties that the NLRB can impose frequently do not constitute a sufficient deterrent to employers. The J. P. Stevens case is again illustrative here.

Labor-law developments in the post–New Deal era eroded many of the reforms of the 1930s and regulated industrial conflict in order to limit class-wide action by workers. The most significant legislation of this type, the 1948 Taft-Hartley Act, forbade secondary boycotts and otherwise limited solidaristic activity by one section of labor for another. The 1955 Landrum-Griffin Act forbade Communists from holding union office. These and other details of state involvement in the worker-capitalist relation indicate the limitations of the gains won by workers through state activity and illustrate how capitalists have used the state to divide and weaken workers.

The relation between workers and capitalists is also shaped outside of the workplace, notably in the state and the market itself. The active part each group takes in attempting to influence state activities indicates how collective political struggles influence economic variables. These state activities include the macroeconomic policy determining the overall level of economic activity (and therefore the state of the labor market), the structure and incidence of taxation, the level and

---

[33] Many employers refused to abide by the Wagner Act and did not recognize unions in the years after its passage in 1935. It took massive and sustained strikes and factory occupations, such as the 1936–1937 sit-down strikes in auto, rubber, and other major industries to bring many employers into compliance. These labor actions undoubtedly influenced the Supreme Court to validate the law in April 1937. Nonetheless, many employers continued to withhold compliance. See Sidney Fine, *Sit-Down* (Ann Arbor: University of Michigan Press, 1976).

200

composition of expenditures (both purchases and transfer payments), and pay and working conditions for public employees. Macroeconomic policy is especially significant, since a high rate of unemployment will weaken workers' bargaining position while strengthening the position of employers. Economists traditionally recognize the importance of non-market political variables in the setting of tariffs, agricultural subsidies, and other government policies that affect the composition of final demand and the distribution of income. More recently, there has been some recognition of the important distributive effects of various government expenditures, from schooling and military spending to river valley development and power projects.[34] These activities constitute important centers of conflict between classes, for class power significantly influences the distribution of gains and losses from state action. These conflicts therefore call forth collective behavior by both sides.

Conclusion

The general equilibrium or Walrasian neoclassical approach to economic theory clarifies the conditions under which the market interactions of atomistic individual economic agents result in market-clearing equilibrium prices and quantities of each commodity. The theory specifically articulates the necessary and sufficient conditions for the existence, stability, and uniqueness of such equilibria. While general equilibrium theory illuminates the inter-dependence among producers and consumers in a market economy, it has little to say about causal relations in economic dynamics other than that everything depends on everything else.

The partial equilibrium or Marshallian neoclassical approach to economic theory identifies the accumulation of

---

[34] This trend is evident in the essays collected in Samuel Chase, ed., *Problems in Public Expenditure Analysis* (Washington, D.C.: Brookings Institution, 1968).

capital as the main cause of economic dynamics and indicates the necessity for capitalists to receive profit payments if economic growth is to take place. The theory seems to contain a determinate approach to income distribution that excludes any role for conflict and power. However, the partial equilibrium approach is flawed in its logical structure.

Both approaches to neoclassical economics are logically incomplete and fail to specify the specific features, the endowment distribution, and the noncommodity character of labor that distinguish capitalist economies from a classless society of independent producers exchanging their products on a market. These features profoundly affect the determination of the distribution of the total social product and the conflictual and hierarchical nature of the labor process in capitalist production. Neoclassical theory obscures as well the extent and significance of class conflict within the firm and within the state. These weaknesses of neoclassical economics suggest why its explanations of racial inequality seem so inadequate.

The importance of class conflict and power in the economy becomes clearer with an alternative Marxian conception. The productivity of workers and their wage payments now become variables determined not solely by their skills and the complementary capital goods with which they work, but also by their bargaining power. Worker solidarity tends to retard productivity while advancing wage pressures on capitalists. Class conflict in the political arena both affects workplace relations between workers and capitalists and influences governmental determinants of the distribution of income.

The degree of worker solidarity has been limited to some extent by capitalists. Hiring, pay, and promotion policies that reduce and limit worker solidarity serve the interests of individual capitalists and persist in both perfectly competitive and monopsonistically competitive markets. The internal job structure of the firm results from the interplay of these class forces with technological and market factors.

This theoretical analysis illuminates how racial inequality can divide workers and benefit capitalists in a capitalist economy. As the models presented in the Appendix to this chapter show, the class conflict theory accords with econometric evidence indicating that most white workers are hurt by racism. These results strengthen the advantages of the class conflict theory over the neoclassical theory.

APPENDIX TO CHAPTER FIVE

MODELS OF CLASS CONFLICT AND RACIAL INEQUALITY WITHIN THE FIRM

THE DISCUSSION in this chapter has centered on collective conflict between workers and capitalists within the firm and within the state. In this appendix I show how intrafirm conflict between workers and capitalists can be modeled and related to external conditions of market competition. The models illustrate how capitalists can gain by exploiting racial differences among workers instead of treating them anonymously. The persistence of racial inequality is therefore consistent with employer profit-maximization under conditions of perfect competition.

The basic assumptions of the competitive model presented here are that the capacity of workers to organize and sustain an antiemployer coalition constitutes an important intrafirm externality and that the strength of this coalition depends on the extent of common interests among the workers. Consequently, employers will be willing to pay premia to some workers and to exploit racial divisions in order to minimize worker coalitions. This conclusion is strengthened further when the assumption of perfect competition is relaxed and monopsonistic elements are added to the analysis.

The models presented in this appendix are not intended to explain the actual processes by which racial inequality is produced in the United States today, nor to account for all the determinants of worker bargaining power or inequalities among workers. To provide a more complete explanation, it would be necessary to introduce the effects of technology on the skill composition of employment, the variables determining the relations between craft and industrial workers, and such extrafirm phenomena as macroeconomic conditions (including the state of the labor market), relations between competitive and monopsonistic sectors, discrimination in the housing market, and the effects of government policies (especially in education and training). In Chapter 6 I present a series of historical studies in order to construct the outlines of a more articulated theory. Here, I simply want to illustrate how the construction of interracial coalitions within a firm can be simultaneously pursued by unions and constrained by employer profit-maximizing behavior.

Consider an individual firm with three sets of actors: employers, white workers, and black workers. Three distinct two-party coalitions are possible: (1) Black and white workers ally against employers, with the strength of their alliance constrained by the racial divisions between them. Those divisions are a function of racial economic inequality and relative proportions of black and white workers. (2) White workers ally with employers against black workers. (3) Black workers ally with capitalists against white workers. This case, which is formally symmetrical with the white worker-capitalist alliance, relates to the strategy articulated in a famous speech by Booker T. Washington in 1895. It is not germane, however, for current analysis and will not be considered further here.

The competitive model is elaborated by examining the relation among worker effort, worker bargaining power, and the relative wages of black and white workers in a competitive firm.

If workers did not engage in collective action against employers over the rate of worker effort, the labor done (LD) would be proportional to total employment (L), and the employer would face the standard profit-maximizing function:

$$\Pi = \bar{p}f(LD) - w_B L_B - w_W L_W.$$

where $f' > 0$, $\bar{p}$ is the output price, $LD = \bar{g}L$ ($\bar{g}$ is a constant) and $L = L_B + L_W$. The wage rates w_B and w_W are set in the

205

labor market. Competition among profit-maximizing firms and perfect substitutability between L_B and L_W implies that:

$$w_B = w_W = \bar{p}\,\frac{\partial f}{\partial L_B} = \bar{p}\,\frac{\partial f}{\partial L_W}.$$

This is the traditional neoclassical approach and the usual result.

Suppose, however, that the rate of worker effort depends on workers' collective bargaining power (BP). Total labor done is then:

$$LD = g(L,BP) \text{ and } \frac{\partial g}{\partial BP} < 0$$

The key issues involve the determinants of BP. In the present context the important point is that racial divisions can create barriers between black and white workers, reducing their solidarity and therefore their bargaining power. (The plausibility of this hypothesis emerges from historical material presented in Chapter 6; it is further developed and tested in Chapter 7.) It therefore seems appropriate to hypothesize that the hiring of a racially mixed labor force is necessary to produce racial divisions.

However, such a mixed labor force is not sufficient for racial divisions to occur, since blacks and whites at the same economic level presumably would have only common interests and would ally with each other. But if a racial disparity in wages can be created (and this is possible because the external market sets only a floor on wages), the privileged group and the disadvantaged group will not be able to sustain so strong a coalition as previously. To achieve this outcome, an employer will therefore be prepared to offer an above-market premium to white workers. (In principle, the same effect could be attained by paying a premium to black workers, but that is not the historical case at hand.) By paying the white workers more than their marginal product, the employer captures the externality of potential coalition-formation that exists among

206

the workers in the firm. (The wage discrimination could take the legal form of racial assignments to jobs with different titles.)

This discussion suggests that BP is a function of both relative wages and relative quantities of white and black workers:

$$BP = h(R_W, R_q)$$

$$\text{where } R_W = \frac{w_W}{w_B} \text{ and } R_q = \frac{L_W}{L_B}$$

For a given R_q, we can hypothesize that BP will be bow-shaped in R_W (see Figure 5.1). The greater the racial disparity in wages, the lower is overall worker solidarity and bargaining power:

$$\frac{\partial BP}{\partial R_W} = 0 \text{ at } R_W = 1 \text{ and } \frac{\partial BP}{\partial R_W} < 0 \text{ for } R_W > 1$$

For a given R_W, BP will be U-shaped in R_q. Divisions are greater when there are substantial numbers of both white and black workers than when either is barely present.

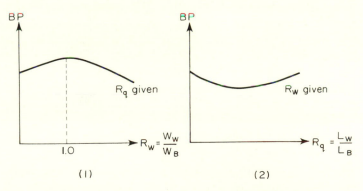

Figure 5.1. Racial Inequality and Worker Bargaining Power

207

The firm's profit function is still:

$$\Pi = \bar{p} f(LD) - w_B L_B - w_W L_W.$$

Substituting the above relations and using the identity $L = L_W + L_B = (R_q + 1)L_B$, we can rewrite the profit function as:

$$\Pi = \bar{p} f[g(L,h(R_W,R_q))] - w_B L_B - R_W w_B R_q L_B$$

$$= \bar{p} f[g(L,h(R_W,R_q))] - (R_W R_q + 1)w_B L_B.$$

The labor market will fix w_B at some level > 0. The three independent instruments available to the employer are R_W, R_q and L_B.

The preceding discussion has suggested that the employer will be willing to pay white workers an above-market premium until the benefits (lower worker bargaining power) are just matched by the increased wage costs. Both the benefits and the costs will depend on the racial composition of employment (R_q). Even though the white workers receive a higher wage, the employer will want to hire both white and black workers. Segregation would only result in greater worker bargaining power. The extent of racial integration will also depend on the associated benefits and costs.

These findings can be obtained rigorously by letting the employer vary all three independent variables simultaneously and solving the associated three first-order conditions for profit-maximization:

(1) $\quad \dfrac{\partial \Pi}{\partial R_W} = \bar{p} \dfrac{\partial f}{\partial g} \dfrac{\partial g}{\partial BP} \dfrac{\partial BP}{\partial R_W} - R_q W_B L_B = 0.$

(2) $\quad \dfrac{\partial \Pi}{\partial R_q} = \bar{p} \dfrac{\partial f}{\partial g} \left(\dfrac{\partial g}{\partial L} \dfrac{\partial L}{\partial R_q} + \dfrac{\partial g}{\partial BP} \cdot \dfrac{\partial BP}{\partial R_q} \right) - R_W W_B L_B = 0.$

(3) $\quad \dfrac{\partial \Pi}{\partial L_B} = \bar{p} \dfrac{\partial f}{\partial g} \dfrac{\partial g}{\partial L} \dfrac{\delta L}{\delta L_B} - (R_W R_q + 1) W_B = 0.$

The convexity assumption on the relation between BP and R_q insures that $L_B > 0$ and $L_W > 0$. Hence, $R_q > 0$. Since $w_B > 0$, we also have $R_q w_B L_B > 0$. We also know that

$\frac{\partial f}{\partial g} > 0$ and $\frac{\partial g}{\partial BP} < 0$. Therefore, (1) tells us that $\frac{\partial BP}{\partial R_W} < 0$. Consequently, $R_W > 1$ and (2) and (3) are consistent with this result.

This analysis indicates that racial inequality can be stable in a competitive economy even in the absence of collusion among employers. This finding, which neoclassical economics has not been able to obtain, is consistent with the empirical evidence presented in Chapter 4, that capitalists benefit from racial inequality while white workers lose. It is also consistent with a direct test of this model, to be presented in Chapter 7.

However, the limitations of this abstract model should be reemphasized. First, worker coalitions may be able to prevent employers from reaching the profit-maximizing point. The three instruments are not entirely under employer control. Second, it is important to consider the case when some workers occupy skilled jobs. Third, the relation between racial inequality generated within firms to that produced outside firms must be specified. Fourth, the microeconomic competitive model must be extended to incorporate macroeconomic variables and imperfect competition. While I do not seek to overcome all of these limitations here, the assumption of perfect competition can be easily relaxed.

Noncompetitive elements comprise an inherent part of modern capitalism. Large modern capitalist firms have developed elaborate bureaucratic structures of internal organization, also known as "internal labor markets."[35] Much worker mobility occurs on job ladders within these firms, rather than by movement between firms. Workers who have seniority and other advancement privileges or firm-specific skills would incur large transfer costs by obtaining alternate employment. These costs give employers an element of monopsony power even when the external labor market is organized competitively.

[35] See Peter Doeringer and Michael Piore, *Internal Labor Markets*, for an elucidation of this concept.

THEORY AND CLASS CONFLICT

Capitalists have a special incentive to prevent worker coalitions, for a labor union could capture the monopsonistic rents without a decline in employment. Moreover, capitalists can increase their monopsonistic rents by engaging in wage discrimination. It is therefore profitable for individual employers not to pay workers according to their productivity, but to encourage distinctions among workers that inhibit worker solidarity. Profit-maximizing behavior by firms in competitive factor markets will not compete away such wage differentials. Since overt wage discrimination is illegal, inequalities may appear through the allocation of different workers to unequal jobs.

This model of monopsonistic competition has been formalized for the case where the labor market is segmented into two (or more) submarkets and the workers in each segment have differing labor supply elasticities. The worker group in the disadvantaged market segment has fewer market opportunities. Consequently, the labor supply of this group will be less elastic with respect to wage rates than the labor supply of the advantaged group. A discriminating monopsonist exploits this situation to increase profits.

This model has interesting properties. It turns out that, compared to the pure monopsony case, labor market segmentation results in lower wages for the disadvantaged workers, higher wages for the advantaged workers, and greater profits for the discriminating monopsonist. Moreover, the formal mechanics of the model do not depend on the traditional assumptions of differing labor supply elasticities, for the analysis can be restated in terms of the divide and conquer theory of the firm presented above. This rescues the monopsony model because its labor supply assumptions are contradicted by empirical studies of the matter.

Consider first the model expressed in terms of labor supply elasticities. The definition of the supply elasticity of labor is:

$$(4) \qquad e_s \equiv \frac{\partial L}{L} \bigg/ \frac{\partial w}{w} = \frac{w}{L} \frac{\partial L}{\partial w}, \ e_s \geq 0.$$

210

where L = quantity of labor supplied and w is the wage rate. The marginal cost to the monopsonist of hiring an additional worker is,

$$(5) \qquad MC = w + L\frac{\partial w}{\partial L} = w\left(1 + \frac{1}{e_s}\right)$$

Suppose the monopsonist employs two types of labor, distinguished by differing labor supply elasticities. The monopsonist maximizes profits by equating the marginal cost of each type of labor:

$$(6) \qquad MC_1 = w_1\left(1 + \frac{1}{e_1}\right) = MC_2 = w_2\left(1 + \frac{1}{e_2}\right).$$

From (6) we get,

$$(7) \qquad \frac{w_1}{w_2} = \frac{(1 + 1/e_2)}{(1 + 1/e_1)}$$

Suppose that $e_1 < e_2$. Then $\left(1 + \dfrac{1}{e_1}\right) > \left(1 + \dfrac{1}{e_2}\right)$, im-
plying:

$$w_1 < w_2.$$

The group with the more inelastic labor supply receives a lower wage.

This model is applied to the case of black and white workers by examining the supply elasticities of black and white labor. If the black labor supply elasticity, e_B, is less than the white labor supply elasticity, e_W, the wage paid to black workers will be less than that paid to white workers: $w_B < w_W$.

This algebraic analysis, which was first developed by Joan Robinson in the 1930s, can also be presented in graphical terms.[36] In Figure 5.2, S refers to the labor supply schedule

---

[36] See Joan Robinson, *The Economics of Imperfect Competition* (London: Macmillan, 1933), pp. 301–304. The graphical analysis of a discriminating monopsonist is also presented by Robinson in these pages. I have followed

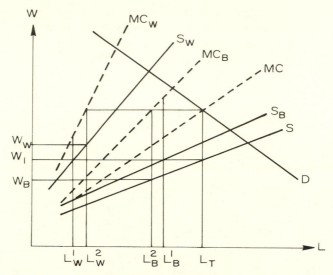

Figure 5.2. Discrimination as Labor Market Segmentation

and MC to the marginal input cost of labor. In the absence of market segmentation the monopsonist chooses a wage $W = W_T$ and employment $L = L_T$. Black employment is then L_B^1 and white employment is L_W^1.

At $L_W = L_W^1$ and $L_B = L_B^1$ the marginal cost of hiring black labor is greater than that of hiring white labor: $MC_B > MC_W$. Consequently, a discriminating monopsonist can expand profits by hiring less black labor and more white labor, bringing $MC_B = MC_W = MC$. At this profit-maximizing situation:

$$L_B = L_B^2 < L_B^1, L_W = L_W^2 > L_W^1$$

and $w_W > w_1 > w_B$.

here the useful presentation by Martin Bronfenbrenner, *Income Distribution Theory* (Chicago: Aldine, 1967), pp. 199–204. For a contemporary restatement of Robinson's analysis for wage differences by sex, see Janice Madden, "Discrimination—A Manifestation of Male Market Power?," in Cynthia Lloyd, ed., *Sex, Discrimination, and the Divison of Labor* (New York: Columbia University Press, 1975), pp. 146–174.

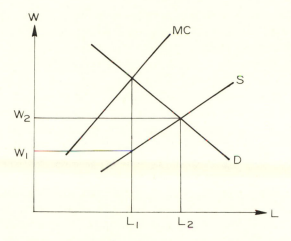

Figure 5.3. Union Gains from the Overthrow of Monopsony

This analysis suggests that both white workers and employers gain from discrimination. Profits and w_W are higher in
comparison to the pure monopsony situation. White workers
would therefore seem to share an interest with employers in
maintaining the racial discrimination that segments the two
labor markets.

This conclusion holds only if the employer's monopsony is
assumed to be unshakable, for both black and white workers
share a common interest against the employer in eliminating
the monopsony. This can be seen in Figure 5.3. A union or
minimum-wage law will raise both employment and the wage
rate above the pure monopsony case. Employment rises from
L_1 to L_2, and the wage rate rises from w_1 to w_2, transferring
monopsonistic profits to workers (and to greater output). The
white workers have more to gain from overthrowing the
monopsony than from supporting racial discrimination.
White workers have less of a stake than employers in maintaining the monopsony.

The main difficulty with this model lies in its assumptions
concerning labor supply elasticities. A wide variety of careful
econometric studies of cross-sectional data indicate that the

213

labor supply of blacks (and women) is more elastic than that of white men, not less elastic, as this model assumes.[37] If these empirical findings are valid, the discriminating monopsony model predicts that the wage rate received by white men would be lower than that of blacks or women.

Do blacks in fact offer their labor with greater elasticity than whites? The availability of alternative income sources, such as government transfer payments to the poor, who are disproportionately black, may explain part of the observed patterns of labor supply. However, it is likely that institutional and demand factors that are ignored by the econometric studies play a larger part in explaining the labor supply configurations. The institutional factors include the prevalence of the forty-hour week as the definition of full-time work, and the importance of seniority in determining layoffs. If employers array their workers in a queue, and black workers are concentrated at the end of the queue, the greater variation observed in black workers' labor time that is supplied may reflect their concentration in part-time employment and in the reserve army of labor. In this institutional context labor-demand effects can thus produce empirical results that have been wrongly attributed to labor supply variables.

With these considerations in mind, we can revise the discriminating monopsonist model of the firm in a more plausible framework that is consistent with observed patterns of racial wage differentials and patterns of white gains from racism. Worker segmentation is attributed not to external labor-supply elasticity conditions, but to internal features of the organization of the firm. Workers are segmented either by

[37] See, for example, Glen Cain and Harold Watts, eds., *Income Maintenance and Labor Supply: Econometric Studies* (New York; Academic Press, 1973), especially chapter 9, "Toward a Summary and Synthesis of the Evidence," pp. 328–367. While the studies in this volume contain considerable variance in the estimates of income and wage changes in labor supply, most find significantly greater elasticities for women and black males than for prime age white males.

214

overt racial discrimination or by bureaucratic techniques that divide them, creating racial inequality as a byproduct.

These divisive strategies constrain the capacity of workers to bargain with employers, give employers an element of monopsonistic power, and further increase their profits. Notice that capitalists need not be the actual agents of racial discrimination to benefit from it. However racial inequality is produced, it will result in gains to individual capitalists. Market competition will not by itself eliminate racial inequality. We thus see theoretically why white capitalists benefit and white workers lose from racial inequality.

CHAPTER SIX

Racism and Class Conflict,
1865 to 1975

IN THE PAST SEVERAL DECADES historians and historical economists have significantly advanced our understanding of the complexity of race relations in the United States since 1865. Two areas of recent research are especially germane for the present study. First, scholars of the postbellum South have recently investigated the structure and dynamics of the relations between the black ex-slaves and the white ex-slaveholders in the decades following Emancipation. Second, labor historians have examined the evolution of race relations in Southern and Northern industry.[1]

Although these scholarly works provide us with new factual material, the conceptual framework in which the history of race relations can best be understood remains the subject of considerable debate among historical economists. It turns out that the main opposing positions thus far have mirrored the positions of conservative and liberal economic theory described in Chapter 5. Consequently, the dynamics of interracial class coalition formation and class differences among whites have not been studied in most historical economists' treatments.

The recent discussion of Ransom and Sutch's important volume, *One Kind of Freedom*, exemplifies this process. In their book Ransom and Sutch document the high interest rates

---

[1] Examples include Roger Ransom and Richard Sutch, *One Kind of Freedom, The Economic Consequences of Emancipation* (New York: Cambridge University Press, 1977); Gavin Wright, *The Political Economy of the Cotton South* (New York: Norton, 1978); Phillip Foner, *Organized Labor and the Black Worker, 1619–1973* (New York: Praeger, 1974).

that were charged to sharecroppers in the postbellum agrarian South and the associated unfortunate specialization in cotton. The authors argue that Southern economic development and the consequences of racism can best be understood in terms of monopoly and signaling discrimination models. But not all historical economists have accepted Ransom and Sutch's conceptual framework. Some of the critics have preferred competitive models to Ransom and Sutch's monopoly theory. Other critics have conceptualized government action rather than the market process as the main cause of the reproduction of racial inequality, whereas Ransom and Sutch locate the reproduction of racial inequality primarily in the South's economic institutions.[2]

Although differences in theoretical explanations rather than in the facts dominate the debate, certain theoretical elements are common to both sides. Competitive markets provide the norm of comparison, class differences among whites and class conflict variables are omitted (except where geography happens to collapse race and class into a single category), and the relation between governmental activity and economic forces is not investigated in any sustained manner. These omissions suggest a need to examine the historical experience with these variables more clearly in focus.

In this chapter I undertake such an examination by bringing the interaction of race and class to the forefront of the historical material. Instead of amalgamating all whites into a single category, I examine separately the effects of racism on whites in subordinate and dominant classes. And in order to understand better the relation between racism and class conflict in the United States, I focus on the determinants of inter-

---

[2] For the debate, see Claudia Goldin, " 'N' Kinds of Freedom," *Explorations in Economic History* (January 1979); Gavin Wright, "Freedom and the Southern Economy," *Explorations in Economic History* (January 1979); and other essays in the same issue of this journal. See also Robert Higgs, *Competition and Coercion, Blacks in the American Economy, 1865–1914* (New York: Cambridge University Press, 1977).

racial coalition formation. The development of a class conflict interpretation of the history of race relations thus distinguishes this chapter from the standard literature.

In the years since 1865 the segregation of blacks in the cotton plantation belt of the South has been replaced by the incorporation of blacks into urban areas and industries throughout the nation. In order to comprehend this major structural change I examine the interaction of race and class in four major periods of United States history since 1865. Proceeding chronologically, I look at: the South during the critical Reconstruction years 1865 to 1877; Southern agriculture after 1877; Southern industry from the 1880s to 1914; and finally, Northern and Southern industry since 1914.

Two comments should clarify the methodology and form of presentation used in this chapter. First, since the objective is to obtain significant generalizations from a broad historical perspective, I eschew here statistical testing of formal hypotheses with detailed data. Given the current paucity of a relevant institutional literature on race and class formation, it seems more important to construct first of all a theory inductively from case studies. In Chapter 7 I go on to derive some testable hypotheses from the theory, and I examine there the empirical validity of these hypotheses with available data. Second, in this chapter I attempt to order and make sense of an enormously complicated set of historical events. In order to streamline the text I consequently provide historiographic comparisons with the work of other historical economists only when such comparisons contribute to the present purpose.

The historical inquiry does generate interesting findings. I find that the determinants of interracial cooperation among farmers and workers include: the degree of commonality in black and white economic positions; the permissive or hostile character of the state; and the macroeconomic conditions governing the labor market. The first two variables help to explain the greater success of interracial coalitions among industrial workers in the 1930s as compared to those among Southern farmers in the 1890s. I also find that racial divisions inhibited interracial coalitions in each period and locale and that most white farmers and workers were thereby made worse off, as compared to the outcome that would have prevailed without racism. The historical materials presented here thus motivate the theoretical hypothesis that racism hurts most whites by weakening the power of subordinate classes.

RACISM AND CLASS CONFLICT IN THE SOUTH, 1865–1877

Here and in the following two sections of this chapter, I present a new interpretation of the postbellum South, emphasizing particularly the effects of racism on Southern white farmers and workers and the class differences among Southern whites. My account not only fills a gap left by Ransom and Sutch; it also differs substantially from traditional historians, such as C. Vann Woodward, who were attuned to these class relations. Woodward has argued that poor Southern whites constituted blacks' greatest antagonists, and that the development of political power among poor whites correlated precisely with the loss of political power among blacks. In short, racism benefited Southern white farmers and workers.[3] I show here, by contrast, that racism did hurt poor whites and benefited only white planters and industrialists. Racial divisions helped produce the debt peonage system, the disfranchisement of blacks and the emergence of Jim Crow segregation laws, and the patterns of race relations in Southern industry. Each of these institutions worked to the detriment of most white farmers and workers.

Racism and the Class Structure of the Slave South in 1860

The class structure of the South in 1860 was formed by a dual economy, consisting of a cotton plantation center, and a

---

[3] References to Woodward's work are supplied later in these sections. It should be noted that Woodward's early writings do contain considerable evidence suggesting that racism hurt poor white farmers and workers in the postbellum South.

subsistence farming periphery. This dual economy itself was framed by the South's geography. The plantations were concentrated in the lowlands. Here the 2 million (in 1860) white slaveholders formed one major class, the 4 million black slaves, the other major class; 800,000 of the slaveholders owned nearly 3 million of the slaves. Between these two classes stood a small group of white overseers, artisans, professionals, and merchants, as well as a larger group of nonslaveholding yeoman white farmers. The majority of whites resided in the hilly uplands, outside the plantation belt, and were engaged in subsistence farming on small plots of land; the yeoman farmers of the up-country were considerably poorer than their plantation belt counterparts. Nonslaveholding whites as a whole numbered about 5 million in 1860.[4]

Racism comprised an inextricable component of the consciousness and behavior of the nonslaveholding whites. The hegemony among the entire white population of a racist ideology that affirmed the subhuman status of blacks and the inherent superiority of whites helps to explain this deep-rooted racism. But the class position of these whites in the Slave South also played a large part in forming their relations with blacks. Many of the plantation-belt yeomen were threatened by competition with slave labor and aspired to become small slaveholders in their own right. Frequently, familial ties also bound them to the planters, furthering their commitment to racism and slavery. The poorer up-country yeomen, more removed from the plantation areas, desired tight racial controls to keep blacks out of their areas. Sympathy for the states'-rights position of the slaveholders in opposition to the Northern antislavery movement also contributed to their loyalty to the dominant slaveholders.[5] The loyalty of the non-

[4] W.E.B. DuBois, *Black Reconstruction in America, 1860–1880* (New York: Harcourt, Brace and World 1935), p. 32; Gavin Wright, *Political Economy of the Cotton South*, chapter 2.

[5] Eugene Genovese, "Yeoman Farmers in a Slaveholder's Democracy," *Agricultural History* (April 1975); W.E.B. DuBois, *Black Reconstruction*, chapter 2.

slaveholding whites was expressed in the most profound form possible with their participation in the Confederate army.

Still, class conflict between slaveholding and nonslave-holding whites did occur during the antebellum period. During the Jacksonian era, the yeoman whites won voting and other political rights in many Southern states. But democratization never extended to the question of slavery itself; here the power of the large planters stood firm.[6]

The cotton boom of the 1840s and 1850s opened a greater economic gulf between the slaveholders and the nonslave-holding whites. The price of slaves rose, making it more difficult for yeoman whites to purchase slaves; the proportion of whites who owned slaves consequently decreased markedly in these decades. At the same time, the cotton boom created further expansionistic pressures from the plantations, swelling the ranks of poor whites and pushing many independent small white farmers into the mountains and other less fertile regions of the South and into the western frontiers.[7] Slavery thus did not enrich most Southern white farmers.

Nor did slavery benefit nonagricultural white workers. Cheap black labor kept down white workers' wages, and slaves frequently were used to impede labor-organizing by white workers. Southern employers argued that slave mechanics provided "our safeguard against the turbulence of white mechanics, as seen in the great strikes, both in England and in the North, and [was] the only protection we [had] in any possible struggle between capital and white labor."[8] In 1847 the important Tredegar Iron Company of Richmond broke a strike of its white workers by substituting slaves for the strikers; thereafter slaves were used for most nonsupervisory jobs.[9] These conditions led Frederick Douglass to

[6] Genovese, "Yeoman Farmers in a Slaveholder's Democracy."

[7] Wright, *Political Economy of the Cotton South*, pp. 31–37.

[8] Quoted in Kenneth Stampp, *The Peculiar Institution* (New York: Random House, 1956), p. 427.

[9] See Ray Marshall, *The Negro Worker* (New York: Random House, 1967), p. 7.

express the position of the nonslaveholding whites as follows:

> The slaveholders . . . by encouraging the enmity of the poor, laboring white man against the blacks, succeeded in making the said white man almost as much a slave as the black man himself. . . . The slave is robbed by his master . . . and the white man is robbed by the slave system . . . because he is flung into competition with a class of laborers who work without wages. At present, the slaveholders blind them to this competition, by keeping alive their prejudices against the slaves as *men*—not against them as *slaves*. They appeal to their pride, often denouncing emancipation, as tending to place the white man on an equality with Negroes, and, by this means, they succeed in drawing off the minds of the poor whites from the real fact, that by the rich slave-master, they are already regarded as but a single remove from equality with the slave.[10]

Some of these poor whites actively opposed Southern secession and deserted the Confederate army during the Civil War. But most accepted the hegemony of the slaveholders. Slavery degraded black people to a subhuman status; they were merely pieces of property without basic human rights. In these conditions most nonslaveholding whites could not imagine allying with black slaves against the slaveholding class.

While these class differences between blacks and nonslaveholding whites continued to play a formidable role in the crucial years following 1865, new forces were set into motion after the Civil War. These forces would open some possibilities for black-white class unity in subsequent decades.

The Reconstruction Era: 1865–1877

The antislavery movement finally achieved its victory during the Civil War. As the war drew to a close, it was widely recognized that the abolition of slavery advanced an essential free-

[10] *The Life and Times of Frederick Douglass* Hartford, 1883; reprint ed., New York: Collier-Macmillan, 1962), p. 284.

dom to blacks, but it did not by itself provide the political and economic basis for the elimination of racism and the end of racial inequality. Voting rights for blacks and equal protection before the law were necessary, and literacy and schooling were essential if blacks were to be able to exercise their rights fully. Equally important, the freed ex-slaves needed some economic assets—land, tools, animals, credit, and so on—to engage in agricultural production.[11]

The years from 1865 to 1877 mark an era of an intense political struggle in both the South and the North over the contours of the new institutions to be constructed in the South. Suffrage, civil rights, schooling, redistribution of the planter-owned land, and the organization of labor were among the key issues. Many initial advances occurred during the Reconstruction era, especially in suffrage and schooling, only to be negated by the Compromise of 1877. After enjoying a brief period of political power, blacks again became subject to unequal legal protection, unequal schooling, and other forms of discrimination.

The struggle to reconstruct and democratize the South by extending political rights, education, and land reform for blacks was fought in the South by an interracial coalition. This coalition consisted of the freed blacks, Northern whites who had moved to the South, and a minority of Southern whites. The latter group included some planters and business-

---

[11] For general historical accounts of the Reconstruction period and its aftermath, see W.E.B. DuBois, *Black Reconstruction;* Barrington Moore, *Social Origins of Dictatorship and Democracy* (Boston: Beacon Press, 1967), chapter 4; "The American Civil War"; Kenneth Stampp, *The Era of Reconstruction, 1865–1877* (New York: Knopf, 1965); Jonathan Wiener, *Social Origins of the New South, Alabama 1860–1885* (Baton Rouge: Louisiana State University Press, 1978); C. Vann Woodward, *Origins of the New South, 1877–1913* (Baton Rouge: Louisiana State University Press, 1951).

Econometric historians have recently paid renewed attention to the postbellum South. The most useful works are: Jay Mandle, *The Roots of Southern Black Poverty* (Durham: Duke University Press, 1978); Roger Ransom and Richard Sutch, *One Kind of Freedom;* Wright, *Political Economy of the Cotton South;* see also Robert Higgs, *Competition and Coercion.*

223

men but was made up primarily of yeomen and up-country poor whites who hoped to obtain the planters' lands.[12] Each of these groups elected members to the Reconstruction legislatures and participated in local movements to reorganize Southern society.

This alliance was opposed fiercely by the old planter class and its loyal allies. Branding the white Northerners as "carpetbaggers," and the progressive white Southerners as "scalawags," they mobilized the Ku Klux Klan and similar terrorist organizations against opponents of the old regime.

Both the Northern carpetbaggers and the Southern scalawags proved to be unreliable partners in this alliance. Northern business and labor each had mixed interests in Reconstruction. Radical Republicans in the Congress had hoped to institute a land reform plan, giving "forty acres and a mule" to every black Southern family, in order to break up the large plantations and destroy the power of the old planter class. Northern business interests found this radical attack on property too much for a propertied group to support. Once these business interests had achieved many of their goals after the war—protective tariffs for manufactures, internal improvements and railroad construction—further remaking of the South seemed less urgent. The economic crash of 1873 and the subsequent upsurge of Northern labor militancy increased capitalists' own problems, and prompted conservative Northerners to seek a peace with Southern planters in order to obtain their support in restoring order in the North.[13]

Northern labor expressed greater support for the Radical Reconstruction program. Although many workers feared

---

[12] Stampp, *Era of Reconstruction*, pp. 163–165; Allen Trelease, "Who Were the Scalawags," *Journal of Southern History* (November 1963); Peter Kolchin, "Scalawags, Carpetbaggers and Reconstruction: A Quantitative Look at Southern Politics, 1868–1872," *Journal of Southern History* (February 1979).

[13] See Moore, "American Civil War."

competition in Northern labor markets from the freed slaves, Northern labor supported many elements of the radicals' program. Land reform would eliminate the movement of black workers into direct competition with white workers. Moreover, land reform constituted a model for the redistribution of wealth that labor desired from Northern capital. The example of Reconstruction doubtless fueled the growth of labor militancy in the North during the post–Civil War years; this militancy reached a peak in 1877, not coincidentally the same year that the North reneged on Reconstruction.[14]

Within the South the interracial coalition of planter opponents did not long survive. This coalition had two crucial weaknesses. First, most of the scalawags were hill-country whites, spatially separated from both the blacks and the planters, and interested primarily in protecting their own localities. Second, the Radical Reconstruction program offered little to whites in the plantation belt itself. Consequently, the organized efforts of the planters easily exploited fears of "Negro domination" among these whites and incited terrorism against whites who did cooperate with blacks.

The active role played by poor whites in the racist terror of the immediate postbellum era can lead one to the conclusion that these whites were primarily responsible for the events. Indeed, a standard view of the Klan and other terrorist groups attributes the extremes of mob violence and lynchings to the poor whites and suggests that the planters and professionals abhorred such violence or at least dissociated themselves from it. However, a recent major study by Allen Trelease develops different findings. Trelease notes that vigilantism, including lynchings, had played an essential role in the Old South's defense of slavery and that the planters themselves had sanctioned lynchings and vigilantism. Such violence was already institutionalized before the Civil War. On the basis

[14] David Montgomery, *Beyond Equality, Labor and the Radical Republicans, 1862–1872* (New York: Knopf, 1967).

of a state-by-state review of available records, Trelease finds that while the Klan's memberships were broadly-based, the leaders invariably belonged to the planter class. Indeed, it was the Klan's espousal of political opposition to the radical program that made it more significant than other similar early terrorist organizations, for upper-class Southerners assumed leadership within the Klan to pursue this political role.[15]

The victory and continuing power of the planters meant not only that the South would remain racist, with the ex-slaves the main victims. It also led to a new system of debt peonage that would work to impoverish poor and middle-income whites. Within a few decades the economic class interests of many whites would increasingly coincide with those of blacks, permitting a new interracial alliance to develop on a scale that was unthinkable during the slavery era.

The Development of Debt Peonage

After the Civil War the best land in the South remained in the hands of the large planters. Some freed blacks were able to purchase land for farming, but most of this land was located in the least fertile areas, and in most cases did not amount to very much. In 1880 blacks owned only 1.6 percent (compared to 1.0 percent in 1864) of the land in Georgia, although they numbered 40 percent of the population.[16] Both extreme poverty and the hostility of whites to black land ownership kept blacks from acquiring much land in the decades following Emancipation.

Most blacks remained without resources on the land in the same states and counties they had inhabited in the slavery era. Some freed blacks moved, either to the cities, to obtain land in the western parts of the South, or to reunite their families.

---

[15] Stampp, *Era of Reconstruction*, p. 196; Allen Trelease, *White Terror: The KKK Conspiracy and Southern Reconstruction* (New York: Harper and Row, 1971), pp. xlvii, 296, 354, 363.

[16] Ransom and Sutch, *One Kind of Freedom*, p. 85.

But the total amount of migration was very small, especially in comparison to the potential economic returns.[17]

While the ex-slaves lacked access to the means of subsistence, the planters still needed labor to plant and harvest their crops. Slavery as an institution had been abolished, but both classes, the ex-slaves and the ex-slaveholders, still needed each other. The question was what set of social and economic relations would replace the slave plantation system. The outcome reflected both black gains from Emancipation and the continued dominance of the planter class.

The planters wanted to retain centrally supervised gang labor in order to preserve economies of scale in cotton agriculture. For a time they experimented with using wage-labor. Many observers have commented on the unsatisfactory results.

Gavin Wright and others have argued that the wage-labor experiments failed largely because of the collapse of cotton prices in the years immediately following the Civil War. Low prices undoubtedly created a major profitability problem for the planters. But the difficulties seem deeper.

A labor system based on direct supervision and management of black labor by white planters or their agents provoked widespread resistance from the former slaves. Planters complained that black wageworkers were too unreliable, since they could not be counted on to show up for work when needed. And major motivational problems lowered the wageworkers' productivity while raising supervisory costs. The ex-slaves preferred to own or rent land than to work for wages. They remembered the oppressive gang supervision under slavery and felt the planters and their white supervisors were not capable of carrying out a free and equal wage-labor relation with black workers. They also understood that wage

---

[17] Gunnar Myrdal, *An American Dilemma*. Higgs, *Competition and Coercion*, chapter 2, presents the most positive view of the extent of black mobility, but even he concludes (p. 28): "The most outstanding feature of the regional distribution of the black population during the period 1865–1914 was its stability. In 1910, the blacks lived by and large, in the same areas they had inhabited in 1860."

payments would not include the surplus income that they might obtain, and they preferred economic independence to wage-labor status.[18]

The planters used their influence in the state legislatures, the Union army, the Freedmen's Bureau, and the Ku Klux Klan to impose gang labor upon the freed blacks. But these attempts failed as well.[19] The economic interest of the planters to use wage-labor was thus thwarted by black resistance.

The planters also attempted to recruit other, potentially more manageable, labor supplies. When white immigrants proved to be difficult to attract, they turned to the importation of Chinese workers, from Cuba and the Philippines. It was hoped that competition from these new groups would make the blacks more tractable. This attempt also failed; the Chinese soon left the plantations for the cities of the South.[20]

In response to this predicament, the planters ultimately began to subdivide their plantations into small farms, each for rent to a single family. Robert Higgs and other neoclassical historical economists have argued that this family tenancy or sharecropping system developed because it was more efficient than gang labor, with all parties benefiting from the change. But blacks preferred to own land while the planters preferred the gang-labor system. The power of the planters and their hostility to black landownership precluded one outcome— the resistance of the freed blacks precluded the other. Tenancy was not a product of efficiency-generating market forces, but of conflict between two classes, mediated by continuing racial subordination.

[18] Wage-labor did not supplant plantation labor in most post-Emancipation societies in the Western Hemisphere. Emancipation resulted in a free labor system only in Antigua and Barbados, small and isolated islands where labor had nowhere else to go. See Jay Mandle, "The Economic Underdevelopment of the Post-Bellum South," *Marxist Perspectives* (Winter 1978).

[19] Wiener, *Social Origins of the New South*, chapter 2.

[20] Roger Shugg, *The Origins of Class Struggle in Louisiana* (Baton Rouge: Louisiana State University Press, 1939), p. 320. This strategy proved more successful in Guyana and Cuba.

228

Because the planters were still the dominant class, they were able to use their power to create a tenancy system on terms favorable to them. Above all, they cooperated in order to limit the mobility of black labor and inhibit competition among landlords. According to Wiener, "Planters organized in every county of the black belt in 1866 and 1867 and agreed that none would hire freedmen who had left other planters, and that they would enforce these agreements on other planters." These practices were formalized into state law and imposed on any noncooperating landlord through a series of harsh vagrancy laws and antienticement acts.[21]

The development of tenancy provided a decentralized means of continuing cotton agriculture under planter supremacy. But blacks did not now work in gang labor under the direct supervision of white overseers. Instead, the ex-slaves had more control over the labor time they put into production, and they were freed of the oppressive management they experienced as slaves. Not surprisingly, the labor input of blacks was not as high as under slavery. Black women particularly left cultivation of cotton in the largest numbers for "house and gardening."[22]

While there were several variations of the sharecropping system, they shared the same essential characteristics: planters or country merchants advanced credit and supplied land, and often provisions, seed, tools, and animals to the farmers in return for a lien on their crops. Merchants were essentially local monopolists who charged interest rates of up to 40 or 50 percent, appropriating whatever surplus was produced in

[21] Wiener, *Social Origins of the New South*, chapter 2. This extralegal coercion and the inability of tenants to accumulate sufficient cash to leave the plantation belt contradicts Higgs's claim that a reasonably free labor market developed in the South.

[22] In *One Kind of Freedom*, Ransom and Sutch estimate that labor effort by ex-slaves decreased about 30 percent, accounting thereby for much of the immediate postbellum drop in cotton production. Much of the cost of reduced input was borne by the landowners; see Mark Aldrich, "A Response to Ransom and Sutch," *Review of Black Political Economy* (Summer 1979).

agricultural production and removing thereby an incentive to capital investment in agriculture.[23] Facing very high interest rates, the farmers' returns usually sufficed only to maintain the same state of indebtedness the following year, or to increase the indebtedness even further. Planters and merchants frequently took advantage of the illiterate farmers by cheating them out of returns due to them. The need to pay off their debt locked the farmers into the system, restricting their mobility and forcing them to grow cash crops, notably cotton, rather than crops for their own subsistence. The term "debt peonage" fits this system quite well.

Debt peonage not only perpetuated black poverty, it also held back the economic development of the South and impoverished many white farmers. Racism, which had led to the creation of the debt peonage system, did not work to the benefit of most Southern whites.

The econometric investigations of Ransom and Sutch and others have shown how debt peonage impoverished black and white farmers. Debt was incurred with an annual contract, making it difficult to engage in improvements that might and did involve short-run costs and long-run benefits. The credit monopoly of the planter-merchants meant that they could and would appropriate any increased surplus, thereby removing the incentive for farmers to increase productivity on their farms. Since agricultural work did not require literacy or skills, there were few incentives for schooling among the rural population or the acquisition of skills. The effect of

---

[23] Ransom and Sutch, *One Kind of Freedom*. Some of the local rural merchants had ties to the North and to Northern financial institutions. With their key monopoly over credit they threatened to displace the dominant position of the old planter class, and many merchants purchased real estate with their incomes and became landlords themselves. According to Wiener, the planters used their political power in the state legislatures to deprive black-belt merchants of their prior crop liens. The planters thereby also became merchants rather than the merchants becoming the dominant landlords, and the old planter class remained in power in the South.

debt locking farmers into the cash crop of cotton prevented diversification and impeded interregional labor mobility.[24]

Debt peonage, in effect, provided a ready supply of cheap labor to the planters and allowed them to increase their income by squeezing farmers harder, rather than by increasing productivity in agriculture. Indeed, cotton turned out to be the last major staple crop to be mechanized in the United States. Southern agricultural incomes stagnated under this system, the economy remained largely rural, and it did not develop a major alternative economic base.

The planter class impeded for decades the capitalist development of Southern agriculture; the consequent low productivity base of the South surely contributed to the Southern and black poverty of the twentieth century. But the planters also resisted and impeded the industrialization of the South. Wanting to restrict alternative sources of employment for their labor force, and concerned about preventing new bases of power in the Southern states, the planters used the political power at their disposal to retard the development of industry in both rural and urban areas.[25] This, too, contributed to Southern poverty for whites and blacks.

Although debt peonage began as a racial system in the plantation belt, it soon became a class system, incorporating many whites and extending far beyond the plantation belt. Low cotton prices in the period 1866 to 1879 impoverished white farming families, impelling them to have more children who could help work the land. Since farms were broken up at death to be passed on to descendants, the high rate of population growth led to a decrease in farm size after 1860.

---

[24] This paragraph presents the main theses of Ransom and Sutch. *One Kind of Freedom*. As already noted, much of the criticism of this volume has focused on whether the merchants really were monopolists or whether their credit charges were justified by risk, as in a competitive neoclassical model. However, this criticism is irrelevant; whatever the reasons, debt did force farmers to specialize in a single cash crop, cotton. See the references in note 2.

[25] Wiener, *Social Origins of the New South*, part 3.

Consequently, many formerly self-sufficient white farming families no longer could produce their own subsistence. They were forced increasingly to grow cash crops and to borrow from merchants.[26] The white farmers could secure such loans only by mortgaging their land; many then lost their land to foreclosures when they could not meet their mortgage payments.

Whites thus experienced a rise of tenancy. By 1880 one-third of white farm operators and four-fifths of black farm operators in the cotton South were tenants. The movement of white farmers into debt peonage continued as tenancy spread further in the ensuing decades. In 1880 40 percent of the tenants were white; by 1900 a majority of the tenants were white. By 1930 only 44 percent of Southern farms were operated by owners, as compared to 53 percent in 1900 and 64 percent in 1880.[27] By contrast, in other agricultural areas in the nation during this period the family-owned farm prospered and grew in size.

While blacks advanced from slavery to sharecropping, both white yeoman farmers of the plantation belt and poorer up-country whites experienced a significant loss in economic independence. These two groups entered cotton production and tenancy in large numbers during this period, bringing the white farmers into a class position much more parallel to that of blacks. Although blacks were poorer and more likely to be tenants than whites, the difference became one of degree rather than of kind, as in the slavery era. Both groups now faced similar problems and experienced common

[26] Wright, *Political Economy of the Cotton South*, p. 178.

[27] Ransom and Sutch, *One Kind of Freedom*, p. 84; Myrdal, *American Dilemma*, p. 242. This experience of white farmers indicates limitations of the land reform program of the Radical Republicans. Had land reform been enacted, many black farmers would still have lost their land in the ensuing decades. The difference would have been that Northern capitalists rather than Southern planters would have become the landowners. The real significance of land reform would have been to break the political power of the old planter class.

grievances. The basis was being laid for unity rather than division between exploited blacks and whites. Such an interracial alliance developed in the 1880s and 1890s with the Populist movement.

SOUTHERN POPULISM AND CLASS CONFLICT IN THE AGRARIAN SOUTH

In the 1880s and 1890s, a time of declining cotton prices and falling incomes for Southern farmers, a mass agrarian movement, the Southern Populists, arose to protest exploitative railroad rates, the "trusts" and banks, and above all the oppressive credit and marketing monopolies of the large planters. Populism quickly became a mass movement, with millions of enrolled members.[28]

Although Populists organized at first in separate racial organizations, the Farmers' Alliance and the Colored Farmers' Alliance, a biracial class alliance soon developed between the two groups. Throughout the South, as white and black Populists worked together actively in electoral campaigns for Populist candidates, they sought higher agricultural prices and lower freight rates and interest charges.

White Populists also openly opposed lynchings, advocated the political rights of blacks, and otherwise struggled against racism. In one dramatic incident, Tom Watson, the most important of the white Southern Populist leaders, mobilized 2,000 white farmers to prevent the lynching of a black clergyman who was a Populist activist.[29] Despite generations of white supremacy ideology, the poor white Southern farmers of the alliance recognized that their economic positions contained many commonalities with those of black farmers; the

---

[28] On the Populist movement, see Lawrence Goodwyn, *Democratic Promise, The Populist Movement in America* (New York: Oxford University Press, 1976); as well as C. Vann Woodward, *Tom Watson: Agrarian Rebel* (New York, 1938); Woodward, *Origins of the New South.*

[29] Woodward, *Tom Watson*, pp. 239, 271.

self-interest of each group indicated gains from alliance with the other.

This awareness was already apparent in 1892, the year of the formal creation of the People's Alliance. For example, while speaking in Georgia in 1892, Tom Watson appealed to black and white farmers to form a united front: "Now the People's Party says to these two men, 'You are kept apart that you may be separately fleeced of your earnings. You are made to hate each other because upon that hatred is rested the keystone of the arch of financial despotism which enslaves you both. You are deceived and blinded that you may not see how this race antagonism perpetuates a monetary system which beggars both.'"[30]

Through Populism, many white Southerners discovered the importance of interracial solidarity to the pursuit of their own self-interests. The Populist movement provided a concrete context, without precedent in Southern history, for white farmers to transcend their racial prejudices and to begin to reject the race-baiting of their opponents.[31]

Populists made their greatest gains in the electoral arena. White Populists had left the Democratic party because upper-class Redeemers had prevented up-country whites from electing their own officials and had cut back government expenditures in poor white areas. By the early 1890s the bi-racial alliance threatened Democratic party power in many Southern states.[32]

[30] Quoted in ibid., p. 220.

[31] Populists also forged alliances with sections of the industrial labor movement, such as the Knights of Labor in 1890 and parts of the Birmingham work force. For a time, they allied also with reform-minded small business progressives who also opposed high railroad rates. See Judith Stein, "'Of Mr. Booker T. Washington and Others': The Political Economy of Racism in the United States," *Science and Society* (Winter 1974–1975), p. 439; Sheldon Hackney, *Populism to Progressivism in Alabama* (Princeton: Princeton University Press, 1969).

[32] J. Morgan Kousser, *The Shaping of Southern Politics, Suffrage Restriction and the Establishment of the One-Party South, 1880–1910* (New Haven: Yale University Press, 1974), pass.

The Populist challengers were defeated primarily by electoral fraud practiced openly by the Democrats. This fraud was facilitated by repressive violence and racist appeals to white Populists. As Woodward puts it, the Southern planter and industrial elite responded to the Populist challenge by heightening racial tensions. They used "fraud, intimidation, bribery, violence, and terror, . . . stirring up fears of Negro domination . . ." and ". . . stopping at nothing."[33] White Populists were accused of undermining white supremacy because the People's party challenged the position of the Democratic party, even though the Redeemer Democrats had offered so little to poor white farmers.

In 1896 the Democratic party co-opted the Populists' currency issue. This shift led to the final collapse of the People's party and the demise of the biracial agrarian coalition.

What happened after Populism? The traditional historical explanation of the defeat of the Populists focuses on the fragility of the biracial coalition and the racism of poor whites in particular. In this view, the poor white farmers turned on their black allies when the going got rough. They decided that the black vote was so controlled by conservatives that the only way to eliminate conservative influence was to disfranchise blacks. C. Vann Woodward writes that "it is one of the paradoxes of Southern history that political democracy for the white man and racial discrimination for the black were often products of the same dynamics."[34] Once in power, and lacking the gentle paternalism of upper-class whites, the poor whites instituted a much harsher system of racial oppression than existed under the old Redeemer planters.

This analysis seems to explain the shift that occurred throughout the South between 1890 and 1910. Paternalism gave way to disfranchisement, Jim Crow laws, beatings and lynchings, and many poor whites participated in these racist

[33] C. Vann Woodward, *The Strange Career of Jim Crow* (New York: Galaxy, 1966), pp. 74, 82.
[34] Woodward, *Origins of the New South*, p. 211.

practices. The new racist careers of former Populists, such as Tom Watson, who reemerged as one of the most virulent proponents of white supremacy in Southern politics, also seem to illustrate the traditional view.

Thus, discussing the abandonment of the racial Reconstruction goal of racial equality in 1877, Woodward writes,

> The freedmen were not yet wholly abandoned to their worst enemies nor entirely without friends of a kind. Harder times were to come, but meanwhile they fell under the paternalistic regimes of the Southern Conservatives. . . . They did not feel the need for humiliating and persecuting the Negro, as did the men who were to gain control of race relations in the future. The Conservatives professed to feel a paternalistic response for the underprivileged freedmen.
>
> For a time this balance of forces restrained extremists who advocated systematic disfranchisement and rigid segregation of the blacks.

Woodward then goes on to explain how Redeemer paternalists were displaced by the freedmen's "worst enemies." "The Conservatives themselves were to blame for opening the way to segregation and disfranchisement. In order to defeat the Populists, a radical movement of the early nineties that sought black support, they once again lifted the cry of white supremacy as they had in their struggle to overthrow the carpetbaggers. But this time they could not tame the passions they aroused, and the extremists took over."[35]

This traditional explanation has two main weaknesses. First, it understates the role of conservatives and other powerful upper-class whites in the evolution of the harshest elements of post-Reconstruction racism. The planters may have appeared benevolent to blacks because they needed their labor on the plantations and wanted influence over their

[35] John M. Blum et al., *The National Experience* 3d ed. (New York: Harcourt Brace Jovanovich, 1973), pp. 385–386. On p. vi of the preface, C. Vann Woodward is given credit for writing the chapter from which these excerpts are taken.

vote. However, these same planters organized the repressive legislation that impeded mobility out of the plantation belt. Prominent conservative Southerners, for example, instituted the brutal convict lease system, often openly receiving kickbacks. These same white Southerners made speeches year after year extolling white supremacy.[36]

Moreover, established national power in Washington had capitulated to and legitimated harsh racist practices in the South. Thus, in the 1890s the Senate refused to pass the Lodge Bill, which would have sent Federal marshals into the South to oversee elections and insure voting rights for blacks. In 1896 the Supreme Court ruling in *Plessy* v. *Ferguson* sanctioned Southern segregation laws; in 1898, in *Williams* v. *Mississippi*, the Supreme Court declared constitutional a Mississippi plan to disfranchise blacks. Across the nation racist hysteria was whipped up in conjunction with United States imperialist actions in the Philippines and in Cuba. In the Philippines, in particular, racist massacres carried out by the U.S. Army rivaled in their brutality the lynchings that were taking place illegally in the South.[37] The racism of poor Southern whites thus must be understood in the context of the examples set by the politically powerful whites who molded the Southern racial order.

Second, the traditional explanation misstates the class basis of the disfranchisement movement, attributing a racist zeal to poor white Southerners who in fact were opposed to disfranchisement. Careful statistical analysis of Southern voting patterns by Morgan Kousser has shown that the extremism of the post-Populist era is attributable more to attempts from above by the upper class to prevent another Populist-like movement from arising than from a mass racist movement from below.

[36] These points are documented in Woodward's earlier work, *Origins of the New South*.

[37] On the Philippine war, see Daniel Schirmer, *Republic or Empire* (Cambridge, Mass.: Schenkman, 1972).

Populists opposed the disfranchisement movement that began in the 1890s, recognizing that the voting exclusion measures would effectively disfranchise many poor whites as well as blacks. Indeed, in almost every state disfranchisement occurred *after* the defeat of the Populist challenge, indicating that the disfranchisers were not acting to exclude blacks solely because of racism. Kousser's evidence concerning the political forces behind disfranchisement is thus consistent with the hypothesis that planters and industrialists, working through the Democratic party, organized to prevent an interracial class coalition from arising again in the South.[38]

The one-party system of the South which followed, led often by racist demagogic politicians, such as Watson, Tilman, and Vardaman, has often been seen, as by Woodward, as an expression of the racism of poor Southern whites. But Kousser has shown, through a regression analysis of local Southern voting patterns, that the Southern demagogues received most of their support from affluent whites, and *not* from poor whites. He demonstrates from an analysis of political outputs that the one-party system worked to the advantage of the already privileged, and resulted in fewer services for blacks and poor whites.[39]

Disfranchisement was soon followed by apartheidlike Jim Crow legislation, marking a new and ugly chapter in the history of American racism. The new climate made any interracial organizing and action among the poor people of the South extremely difficult, if not impossible. Cut off from the possibility of alliances with blacks, poor Southern whites acquiesced in policies of racism and white supremacy. Not until the creation of the biracial Southern Tenant Farmers Union in 1934 would there again arise a significant political movement among Southern farmers.[40]

[38] Kousser, *Shaping of Southern Politics*, pass.

[39] Ibid, pp. 232–237, 247–251. See also the similar analysis by Horace Mann Bond, *Negro Education in Alabama* (New York, 1939), pp. 148–163.

[40] Mark Naison, "The Southern Tenant Farmers Union and the C.I.O.," *Radical America* (September–October 1968).

RACE RELATIONS IN SOUTHERN INDUSTRY, 1877–1914

At about the same time that interracial struggles were shaking the agrarian South, industrial development was beginning in the region. Interracial class struggles shook some of these new industries as well. The "New South" began to industrialize in about 1880, chiefly in cotton textiles and in iron and steel. Textile mills were located near water supplies in the Piedmont area, and iron and steel mills were located in Birmingham, in the middle of the plantation belt. Developments in these two industries, together with those in coal mining and on the docks in New Orleans, indicate the major dynamics in race relations in Southern industry during this period.

While each of these industries exhibits a somewhat different pattern, some common themes and a common outcome can be observed. The repressive role of Southern states, occupational differences between blacks and whites, and the onset of hard economic times each made interracial alliances difficult to sustain. Whatever class solidarity existed among black and white workers in the beginning of this period was eliminated by repression and by the Jim Crow system that had been created in response to the Populist challenge. Racism was now working in an industrial setting, to the detriment of both black and white workers.

Bituminous Coal Mining

Racial developments among bituminous coal miners indicates both how industrial conditions would give rise to interracial solidarity in spite of overwhelming social pressures to the contrary, and how racism ultimately persevered.

The United Mine Workers, founded in 1890 as one of the first industrial unions in the nation, counted more than 91,000 members by 1900.[41] While the UMW exhibited some racism

[41] See Herbert Gutman, "The Negro and the United Mine Workers," in Julius Jacobson, ed., *The Negro and the American Labor Movement* (New York: Anchor Books, 1968).

and segregation, the mine workers also acted with a substantial level of interracial egalitarianism and solidarity in this period. Over 20,000 of the UMW's members were black, most of them working in the bituminous coalfields in Alabama and West Virginia.[42] By and large, blacks and whites belonged to the same locals. A significant number of blacks were elected to leadership positions in integrated locals and helped organize both black and white miners.

Like the Knights of Labor, who had organized coal miners successfully in West Virginia in the 1880s, the UMW also found a policy of racial equality to be essential for their success. Mining required very little skill, and blacks had worked as miners during slavery.[43] A craft-oriented all-white union would never have gotten off the ground. With the participation of black workers, the UMW gained ground from 1890 to 1902; in the latter year 65 percent of Alabama coal miners were UMW members.

The UMW, possibly the most integrated voluntary association in the United States of 1900, exhibited more egalitarian race relations than most Northern labor unions. For example, district 20 of the UMW in Alabama succeeded in forcing coal operators to eliminate racial wage differentials as well as the use of race to allocate workplaces. The same union forced Birmingham merchants to reverse their refusal to allow integrated union meetings in their halls.[44] As one black miner wrote in 1899, "I believe that the United Mine Workers has done more to erase the word white from the Constitution than the Fourteenth Amendment."[45]

The UMW record seems particularly impressive because it occurred in an era of increasing racial tension, rigid Jim

[42] Ibid; Sterling Spero and Abram Harris, *The Black Worker* (New York, 1931), chapters 10, 17.

[43] Foner, *Organized Labor and the Black Worker*, pp. 82–88.

[44] Paul Worthman and James Green, "Black Workers in the New South, 1865–1915," in Nathan Huggins et al., eds., *Key Issues in the Afro-American Experience*, (New York: Harcourt Brace Jovanovich, 1971), 2: 65.

[45] Quoted in Gutman, "Negro and the United Mine Workers," p. 115.

Crow legislation, disfranchisement, and racial chauvinism brought about to defeat Populism. "With all these differences," a Senate-created Industrial Commission study of the mining industry concluded in 1901,[46] "it is an easy matter for employers and foremen to play race, religion, and faction one against the other." Indeed, racism played no small part in the destruction of the union.[47]

In 1904 the mining companies mounted a major offensive against the union in Alabama, refusing to renew union contracts and using black strikebreakers with greater frequency than in any other industry. The union countered with a two-month strike in 1908. Despite interracial solidarity among the miners, this key strike was broken after the governor and many whites protested the organization of blacks in the same union as whites.

Upholding Jim Crow segregation, the governor had the tents in which the black and white strikers lived cut down, and forced the union to abandon the coalfields.[48] The union did not survive such pressure; by 1908 industrial unionism in bituminous coal was crushed in Alabama and also in West Virginia. It would not rise again until the late 1930s.[49] The Jim Crow system had made interracial organizing next to impossible, and the South had lost its most effective institution for combating racial hostility.

New Orleans Dock Workers

The experience of dock workers in New Orleans indicates that white workers could engage in interracial cooperation with black workers, yet succumb to racist appeals during hard economic times. In 1865 shipowners brought blacks into the previously all-white industry, attempting to drive down

[46] Quoted in ibid., p. 52.

[47] Foner, *Organized Labor and the Black Worker*, p. 99.

[48] Spero and Harris, *Black Worker*, p. 358.

[49] Gutman, "Negro and the United Mine Workers," p. 114 and pass. The UMW continued to grow in anthracite coal mining, but few blacks were employed in this geographically distinct segment of the industry.

241

prevailing wage rates. An interracial strike of dock workers followed, but was defeated after police arrested black longshoremen.[50] However, large numbers of blacks continued to work on the docks.

White dock workers, most of them Irish, decided it would be better to ally with blacks than to face them as strikebreakers. Separate black and white unions were formed and they cooperated closely. Thus, in 1872 white dock workers helped organize a union for black screwmen, the most skilled occupation on the docks.[51] This solidarity collapsed, however, during the depression that began in 1873, when employers and politicians openly exploited competition for jobs on the waterfront in order to heighten racial antagonisms. "The competition," Roger Shugg writes, "was not unwelcome to merchants, shipmasters and employers in general, because it tended to reduce the wages of the unskilled, white or black, to the level at which freedmen could subsist."[52]

In order to gain political support for their efforts to oust the Republican carpetbag government, planters and merchants urged employers to fire their black workers and hire white workers instead. Many employers heeded this advice, but they paid whites the prevailing black wage. How ironic, Shugg remarks, to raise "the cry of 'white supremacy' in politics, and at the same time reducing this race to colored wage levels."[53]

Solidarity between black and white workers was rebuilt throughout the economic expansion of the 1880s. A refusal by employers to negotiate with a black draymen's union was met by a city-wide sympathy strike in which every craft struck until the union was recognized.[54] The efforts were

[50] Dave Wells and Jim Stodder, "A Short History of New Orleans Dockworkers," *Radical America* (January–February 1976), pp. 45–46.

[51] Spero and Harris, *Black Worker*, pp. 183–186.

[52] Wells and Stodder, "Short History of New Orleans Dockworkers," p. 46; Shugg, *Origins of Class Struggle in Louisiana*, p. 302.

[53] Ibid., p. 303.

[54] Spero and Harris, *Black Worker*, pp. 44, 184.

coordinated by the Central Trades and Labor Assembly in New Orleans, which was credited by one contemporary observer as having "done more to break the color line in New Orleans than any other thing . . . since emancipation of the slaves."[55]

In this period a joint committee coordinated the black and white unions, assigning work on the docks equally between the two races and establishing a uniform wage scale. But since many more blacks than whites sought jobs on the waterfront, an equal racial allocation maintained a relative advantage for whites. Many black longshoremen could obtain work only intermittently, while white longshoremen were able to maintain steadier employment.

When a group of teamsters, scalesmen, and packers struck their employers in 1892, an interracial alliance among New Orleans workers successfully carried out a general strike involving 25,000 workers and forty-nine unions affiliated with the American Federation of Labor (AFL). White strikers did not heed appeals to racial prejudice in the press. The employers offered to sign an agreement with only the predominantly white unions. But this attempt to split the strike also failed. The employers were forced to agree to arbitration, and the strikers won most of their demands (but not recognition of the union).[56] A German economist, Sartorius von Waltershausen, was moved to write, "In New Orleans the unions were able, despite the occasional outbreak of racial antipathy, to harmonize the opposing factors, and have undertaken, through the recognition of black labor, a problem in civilization whose solution they will probably not live to see."[57]

Interracial solidarity again weakened in the hard times following the Great Depression of 1893, culminating in a riot by white racists in 1894. Sharp wage cuts and massive layoffs

[55] George McNeil, *The Labor Movement* (1887), p. 168, cited in Spero and Harris, *Black Worker*, p. 44.

[56] Foner, *Organized Labor and the Black Worker*, pp. 66–68.

[57] Quoted in Spero and Harris, *Black Worker*, p. 184.

243

had once again heightened job competition. Labor solidarity returned after the economic recovery in 1901, and in 1907 an interracial coalition conducted an impressive general strike in New Orleans.[58]

The New Orleans example indicates that white workers would ally with black workers when the similarity of their class positions made such coalitions advantageous. In particular, interracial solidarity was more likely when unemployment was low. Throughout this period, however, the white workers maintained a relative advantage in wages and employment. The threat of wage and employment cuts during economic downturns frequently led white workers to seek to protect their interests by attempting to shift the burden of recessions onto blacks instead of maintaining their interracial alliance. While this narrow response benefited the shipowners, it did not lead to lasting gains for white workers.

Alabama Iron and Steel Workers

The New Orleans dock workers showed, especially by the 1892 General Strike, the possibility of interracial cooperation among industrial workers in the Deep South. The New Orleans example was not unique. We have already seen a similar pattern in Alabama coal miners. In the 1880s interracial solidarity could also be found in the Knights of Labor, especially in the earlier years of that organization. In their survey of black workers in the New South, Worthman and Green cite similar incidents of racial cooperation in Georgia, Alabama, and Florida.[59] Perhaps the most important instance of racial cooperation occurred among iron and steel workers in and around Birmingham, Alabama, in the 1890s. Here, as in the other examples, interracial solidarity among workers was eventually broken up by racism, leading to losses for white as well as black workers.

The Alabama iron and steel story concerns the deteriora-

[58] Stodder and Wells, "Short History of New Orleans Dockworkers."
[59] Worthman and Green, "Black Workers in the New South," p. 67.

244

tion of relations between black and white workers that resulted, in large part, from the inflammation of white segregation and supremacist policies initiated to undo the Populist uprisings of the 1890s. Industrial capitalists had long used black labor, but in the 1890s they increasingly substituted black workers for white ones. The hiring of blacks often followed strikes by white workers. Black workers in Birmingham were frequently urged by Booker T. Washington not to cooperate with labor organizers or white workers, but to act as strikebreakers and maintain their friendliest relations with employers.[60]

Despite these hostile conditions, Birmingham AFL locals were able from 1897 to 1904 to achieve significant successes in countering racial prejudice. They organized black and white workers into unions and obtained considerable support among white unionists for black labor.

After 1904 union successes and an economic recession impelled employers to counterattack and destroy unionism in Birmingham. Coal operators in that year refused to bargain a new contract with the UMW. In the resultant strike, "the companies resorted to their usual policies of importing Negro strikebreakers, . . . and trying to split the white and black miners by offering Negroes the best places in the mines, if they would return to work."[61] Black workers stayed out, however, and convinced many black strikebreakers to leave. Only the importation of new labor allowed coal operators to maintain production, and after sixteen months, the 9,000 strikers were defeated.

Another 1904 incident reflects both the support that unskilled white unionists gave to black workers and the different response of skilled white unionists. Skilled white steelworkers who had helped break a strike by unskilled black workers at the Republic Iron and Steel Company were condemned by a

[60] Paul Worthman, "Black Workers and Labor Unions in Birmingham, Alabama, 1897–1904," in Milton Cantor, ed., *Black Labor in America* (Westport: Negro Universities Press, 1970), p. 60.

[61] Ibid., p. 81.

predominantly white convention of unskilled steelworkers. The skilled workers' union refused to cooperate with the organization of the unskilled, not only in Birmingham but throughout the nation.[62] Their position led them to oppose unskilled immigrants as well as blacks.

By 1904 the AFL had retreated from its earlier position of helping to organize unskilled workers into affiliated locals, or Federal labor unions. A national employers' offensive against the unions, begun in 1903, had depleted its treasury and forced the AFL to take a narrower stand on behalf of its own craft members. As a result, unionism collapsed in Alabama iron and steel after 1904. Federal labor unions disappeared throughout the country, and racial hostility among white workers became more rampant than before. Except for a brief but significant episode of interracial unity among IWW-affiliated lumber workers in 1912–1913, racial cooperation among Southern workers was disappearing.[63] At the same time, the disfranchisement of black voters, the institution of Jim Crow segregation, and the violent terrorism against black Southerners made further cooperation among black and whites virtually inconceivable in the South. Racial developments in the cotton textile industry illustrate the consequences.

Cotton Textiles

Cotton textile mills furnished the chief base on which the "New South" began to industrialize after 1880. While black workers were employed in significant numbers in menial occupations on the docks of New Orleans, in Alabama and West Virginia coal mines, and in the Birmingham iron and steel mills, they were excluded almost completely from the textile industry. This exclusion resulted in part from the location of the mills—near water power in the up-country, where few blacks resided. But the pre-Civil War Southern

---

[62] Ibid., p. 83.

[63] Phillip Foner. *The Policies and Practices of the American Federation of Labor 1900–1909* (New York: International Publishers, 1964), pp. 32–33.

textile industry had employed predominantly black labor.[64] In the New South the conscious use of racism by textile employers played an important part in racial hiring patterns.

Cotton textile mills had moved from New England to take advantage of cheaper labor in the South. For example, in the 1880s mill wages for adult males averaged between $2.50 and $4.00 a week in the Carolinas, as compared to $6 and $7 in New York clothing sweatshops in 1885. Profit rates on investment in well-managed Southern mills ranged from 30 to 75 percent.[65] Falling cotton prices were driving many small white farmers to bankruptcy. Hence, these farmers became eager to work in the new mills, even though wages were low and falling, and the work week averaged seventy hours.[66] The millowners thus could draw on a desperate labor supply.

Nonetheless, textile owners were concerned that their workers not engage in union activity and struggle for higher wages and improvements in working conditions, as had happened in the North. As a general policy, employers excluded blacks from employment in the mills, offering up mill employment as a place for white solidarity between employers and workers against blacks. Many of the white workers were women, and sexual fears heightened the emotional bases of racism. By encouraging racism and feelings of white supremacy, employers successfully defeated unionizing efforts and elicited more work at less pay from their white workers.

The millowners seemed to be aware of what they were doing. In a monograph on Southern mill workers, Melton McLaurin writes: "Mill officials skillfully encouraged the mill hands' hatred of the Negroes and manipulated that hatred to their own ends."[67] Writing in 1903, John Graham Brooks captured the prevailing viewpoint in the South: "I asked one

---

[64] Spero and Harris, *Black Worker*, pp. 348–349.

[65] Woodward, *Origins of the New South*, pp. 133–134; Foner, *Policies and Practices of the AFL*, p. 23.

[66] Woodward, *Origins of the New South*, pp. 224–225.

[67] Melton McLaurin, *Paternalism and Protest: Southern Mill Workers and Organized Labor, 1897–1905* (Westport: Greenwood Press, 1971), p. 65.

247

of the largest employers of labor in the South if he feared the coming of the trade union. 'No,' he said, 'it is one good result of race prejudice that the Negro will enable us in the long run to weaken the trade union so that it cannot harm us. We can keep wages down with the Negro, and we can prevent too much organization.' "[68]

Numerous incidents cited by contemporaries and several careful historical studies indicate that the exclusion of black labor from the mills did not provide economic gains for the white work force. Woodward concludes his discussion of how the exclusion of blacks from the cotton mills affected white workers: "If white solidarity between employees and employer was to save the white worker from the living standard of the Negro, the results in the cotton mills were not very reassuring."[69] For example, in 1897 white workers struck an Atlanta millowner who had just hired twenty black women to work in his mill. The company agreed to fire the newly hired black women, but only after it obtained the agreement of white workers to work overtime without premium pay.[70]

Such incidents led Philip Bruce, the distinguished Southern historian whose contemporary account, *The Rise of the New South* (1905), constituted the first major study of the period, to conclude: "The Southern employer's ability to hold the great mass of Negro mechanics *in terrorem* over the heads of the whites" prevented many white workers from joining unions or participating in strikes and, more generally, "in nearly all the trades, the rate of compensation for the whites [was] governed more or less by the rates at which the blacks [could] be hired."[71]

[68] John Graham Brooks, *The Social Unrest* (New York, 1903), p. 102.

[69] Woodward, *Origins of the New South*, p. 225

[70] Foner, *Organized Labor and the Black Worker*, pp. 66–67.

[71] Quoted in Woodward, *Origins of the New South*, pp. 228–229. Numerous witnesses testified to the Industrial Commission of 1900 that the black worker was "a drag on the white laboring class in the Sough, and tends to cut down their wages." See Foner, *Policies and Practices of the AFL*, pp. 240–241. Regional wage differentials persisted; in 1912 and 1913 hourly wages of New England workers exceeded those of Southern workers by 37 percent. See Woodward, *Origins of the New South*, p. 421.

The exclusion of black labor from Southern textiles continued until the 1960s. The 1940 census showed that blacks comprised only about 25,000 of the 635,000 workers in Southern textile mills. Virtually all were employed as sweepers and scrubbers, laborers in the packing and shipping departments, assistants in the dyeing works, or employees doing the dirty work in the picking rooms.[72]

Racial dynamics in these four nineteenth-century Southern industries—bituminous coal mining, dock work, iron and steel, and cotton textile mills—suggest three conclusions regarding the relation between racial inequality and class conflict. First, developments within these industries were affected strongly by the political and cultural practices that organized racism generally in the South. In particular, the machinery set up by the state made successful biracial class organizing extremely difficult in this era. These conditions were common to each of the important industries discussed here, and they frame the patterns of racial inequality that were prevalent in each.

Second, interracial coalitions tended to unravel during economic downturns. This pattern was evident both on the New Orleans docks and in the iron and steel industry. However, the experience of the 1930s would show that this outcome was not inevitable.

Third, the considerable variation in the relations between black and white workers among these different industries was associated with occupational differences, prefiguring future industrial patterns. On the docks and in coal mining, an industrial union model prevailed. With few skilled craft occupations and very limited barriers to entry in these industries, unskilled white workers allied frequently if not consistently with their black counterparts. Developments in these industries thus prefigured the evolution of 1930s-type industrial unionism, showing the advantages to white workers of overcoming the racism of the wider society of which they were a part.

[72] Myrdal, *American Dilemma*, p. 289; Spero and Harris, *Black Worker*, p. 349.

However, the industrial union model was marginal to labor movement activity during most of this period. The racial dynamics in the iron and steel industry exemplify the victory of an exclusionary craft model of unionism over an initially more inclusive model. In some companies, such as the Tennessee Coal and Iron Company, later to become a subsidiary of the U.S. Steel Company, explicit racial quotas and other devices organized by employers achieved this result. But this dynamic also mirrored a more general craft-oriented movement in the iron and steel industry nationally as well as in the American Federation of Labor. Despite this defeat black workers continued to be employed in greater numbers in iron and steel. The growth in the importance of black labor in the industry under conditions of racial inequality would later prove critical for the failure of the 1919 attempt to organize an industrial union in steel.

Racial patterns in the cotton textile mills provided an extreme example of the job segregation that was to develop in both Southern and Northern industry. But here, as in the other industry examples, racism did not provide economic benefits to the white workers. Instead, white racism led to lower wages for white workers in Southern textiles than in comparable industries. Low wages and hostility to unions continue in Southern textiles to the present day. However, subsequent developments in other industries followed a different course.

RACIAL AND CLASS DYNAMICS IN INDUSTRY: 1914–1975

In the decades following the Civil War, industrial development occurred at an impressive rate in the North. This industrial growth was expressed not just in quantitative terms of expansion, but in qualitative change as well. More and more industrial activity was concentrated in large factories, and mass-production workers doing easily learned tasks increasingly supplanted artisans and their helpers as the main ingredient of the factory labor force. In short, an industrial working class was being created in the United States.[73]

With capitalist development the workplace became more of an arena of conflict. In the latter third of the nineteenth century, strife between employers and workers became more frequent and involved more and more workers. As national competition among firms grew and prices fell, many employers attempted to institute wage cuts among their employees and to systematize the organization of work in greater detail. But, as the job conditions of the factory work forces became increasingly homogeneous, it became easier for workers to organize plant-wide and industry-wide collective actions to counter their employers. The result was an upsurge of what can only be called "class warfare."

In this context many employers began to experiment with different techniques to control their "labor problem," as they called it. In particular, employers sought consciously to organize work hierarchically and to institute divisions in their work force in order to preclude united organization among their workers. It took many years for employers to develop sophisticated bureaucratic personnel techniques to achieve these ends. In the interim, simpler methods were applied. These involved introducing moving assembly lines and other technologies to machine-pace workers, as well as cruder divide-and-conquer methods.

Many Northern employers adopted a technique that Southern industrialists had already worked out: the importation of black strikebreakers into an industry and the exploitation of the racism of white workers to help break strikes. Many Northern industries began to employ blacks for the first time in such circumstances. As in Southern industries, the most

[73] The analysis in the next several pages is based on Michael Reich, Richard Edwards, and David Gordon, *The Segmentation of Labor in U. S. Capitalism* (New York: Cambridge University Press, 1981), and Richard Edwards, *Contested Terrain: The Transformation of the Workplace in the Twentieth Century* (New York: Basic Books, 1979).

251

unskilled and demanding jobs would be assigned to black workers. The demand for black labor during the labor shortages of World War I and the subsequent reduction in foreign immigration in the 1920s would lead to further increases in black employment in manufacturing, but the already-developed patterns of racial inequality in industry would continue.

Racial discrimination by Northern employers and employees played only a partial role in excluding blacks from industry before 1914. Conditions in Southern agriculture also played a part. The tremendous demand for labor that came with the industrial expansion of the North after the Civil War was filled primarily by European immigrants and not by Southerners. Before 1915 very few Southern whites or blacks moved to the North to obtain jobs in the burgeoning industries. The low rate of migration out of the South seems remarkable when one considers the widening economic conditions between regions in this period. Certainly there were economic payoffs to migration.[74]

It might be thought that white or black Southerners, with their knowledge of the English language and familiarity with the American culture, would have been preferred by employers to the European immigrants. Indeed, much racial prejudice was expressed among Northerners after 1890, as the European immigration consisted increasingly of dark-complexioned peoples from southern and eastern Europe. But racial prejudice did not hinder the hiring of these workers.

Southern out-migration was low precisely because Southern farmers were kept in debt and could not accumulate the assets needed for a move out of the South.[75] In 1900 three-fourths of all blacks in the United States remained share-cropping farmers in the South. Blacks accounted for only 2.2 percent of nonagricultural employment outside the South in

[74] For a good discussion, see Myrdal, *American Dilemma*, chapter 13, "Seeking Jobs Outside Agriculture."

[75] Ransom and Sutch, *One Kind of Freedom*.

1910, and the majority of these jobs were in household service. In 1910 over 70 percent of the black population still resided in the rural South.[76] The Southern sharecropping system thus kept most blacks out of the growing factory system of the North during this period.

Since World War I and the 1920s, but more especially since World War II, the Southern sharecropping system disintegrated, while the demand for labor in Northern industry continued to expand. Consequently large numbers of blacks have become incorporated in Northern industry. This dramatic shift has provided absolute economic and political gains for blacks as well as some advances relative to whites. But this incorporation, as we have seen in Chapter 2, has occurred in a manner that has reproduced many racial inequalities in the urban and industrial setting. We can understand these twentieth-century developments in relation to the changing demands for black labor and the changing dynamics of worker-capitalist class relations during this period.

The 1919 Steel Strike

Between 1910 and 1920 the number of black industrial workers almost doubled. By 1930 over 100,000 black workers were employed in Northern industry, most in blast furnaces, steel rolling mills, automobile factories, clothing industries, and slaughter and meat-packing houses.[77] Blacks entered most of these industries during strikes and were sometimes kept on after the strikes had ended. Myrdal concludes his detailed discussion of this period as follows: "Many of them wanted to keep their labor force heterogeneous so as to prevent unionization. Some of them even used Negroes as strikebreakers. This had happened several times before the

[76] Myrdal, *American Dilemma*, p. 285; see also Chapter 2 of this study. In 1910 only one major Northern manufacturer, the McCormick Harvesting Company in Chicago, employed blacks in substantial numbers.

[77] Ibid., p. 294. But blacks continued to be excluded from many Northern industries including textiles, sawmills, electrical machinery, bakeries, shoemaking, furniture, and utilities.

first World War. In many of these cases Negro workers were dismissed when the labor conflict was ended. But sometimes, particularly between 1910 and 1930, they actually managed to gain a foothold in this way."[78]

A typical and significant example of this process occurred in 1904, during a midwestern meat-packing strike. Black strikebreakers were brought in by the employers and helped defeat the strike. Blacks stayed on afterward and became the largest group in the Chicago meat-packing industry by 1920.

Most blacks working in Northern industry were employed in the least-skilled occupations, a policy often formalized consciously by employers in racial terms. After World War I racial quotas were instituted deliberately in the Chicago meat-packing industry, in the steel industry, and in the farm equipment and automobile industries.[79] An employment manager of Calumet Steel explained the importance of quotas: "It isn't good to have all of one nationality; they will gang up on you. . . . We have Negroes and Mexicans in a sort of competition with each other."[80] In adopting racial quotas and deliberately inciting racial antagonisms, employers were following the examples set in Southern coal mining, iron and steel, and other industries. U.S. Steel, for example, adopted in Gary the policies of its Southern subsidiaries.

The incorporation of blacks into industry thus occurred with preexisting racial divisions continuing unabated. In this period these racial divisions proved costly to many union-organizing efforts. Nowhere were these effects more visible

[78] Myrdal. *American Dilemma*, p. 293.

[79] Alma Herbst, *The Negro in the Slaughtering and Meat-packing Industry in Chicago* (Boston: Houghton Mifflin, 1932), pp. 103–108; B.J. Widick, *Detroit: City of Class and Race Violence* (Chicago: Quadrangle, 1972), p. ix; Robert Ozanne, *A Century of Labor-Management Relations at McCormick and International Harvester* (Madison: University of Wisconsin Press, 1967), pp. 184–185.

[80] Quoted in the excellent case study of Edward Greer, "Racial Employment Discrimination in the Gary Works, 1906–1974" (unpublished paper, Department of History, Roosevelt University, 1976), p. 12.

and more numerous than during the giant steel strike of 1919.

In 1919, a year of unprecedented strike activity throughout the United States (twenty-five urban race riots also occurred), over 360,000 workers went on strike throughout the iron and steel industry.[81] The strike, organized by a broad coalition of unions representing both skilled and unskilled workers, became a crucial test of an important idea in the labor movement: to organize unions in factory-based industries on an industry-wide rather than occupational basis.

David Brody has chronicled in detail how the steel companies attempted to break the strike. Their main strategy was to exploit the divisions that separated native-born and English-speaking steelworkers, many of them skilled workers, from the thirty or more Eastern European immigrant groups among the steelworkers, most of them unskilled and not English-speaking. The steel companies deliberately hired "foreigners of different nationalities, in order that there would not be free-speaking discourse between them."[82] To the surprise of the companies as well as some labor leaders, the unskilled immigrant workers proved to be strong supporters of the strike, despite employers' attempts to exploit xenophobia among the "Americans."[83]

The weakest link in the workers' chain of solidarity appeared to be race. Although black employment in the steel mills had increased during the war, blacks were still excluded from the skilled workers' union, even during the union organizing drives of 1918–1919. Except in Cleveland and Wheeling, black steelworkers were not sympathetic to such discriminatory unions, nor were blacks outside the industry. The steel companies exploited this situation: in the sixth week of the strike, the steel companies imported over 30,000 black strikebreakers in a short period of time, to keep their plants operat-

---

[81] For detailed accounts, see David Brody, *Steelworkers in America: the Nonunion Era* (Cambridge: Harvard University Press, 1960); David Brody, *Labor in Crisis: the Steel Strike of 1919* (Philadelphia: Lippincott, 1965).

[82] Brody, *Steelworkers in America*, p. 136.

[83] Brody, *Labor in Crisis*, p. 157.

ing. This key move turned the tide, and the strike was soon defeated.

The racism of the unions had broken the strike, and white as well as black workers paid a price: industrial unions did not arrive in the steel industry until the late 1930s. William Z. Foster, a leader of the strike, concluded that the mass production industries would not be unionized until white union leaders made campaigning against racism a central and special priority of organizing efforts. This assessment proved to be correct, as both the employer offensives in the 1920s and labor's response in the turning point of the 1930s would demonstrate.

Turning Point: The CIO in the 1930s and 1940s

The experience of the Southern Populists, bituminous coal miners, New Orleans dock workers, and the steelworkers indicated that attempts were made to build biracial coalitions along class lines and that racism ultimately contributed to the breakup of these coalitions. The conservatism of the AFL, and its attempts to protect skilled craft workers from competition contributed significantly to the perpetuation of racial inequality in industry. But during the Great Depression, the AFL's racial practices were challenged decisively by the new industrial union movement of the 1930s.

Some black union leaders within the AFL had lobbied for decades to change the AFL's policy of countenancing racial exclusion practices among its affiliates. These efforts proved unsuccessful.[84] In 1935 the AFL opposed successfully the incorporation of an antidiscrimination clause in the Wagner Act, preferring to see the bill fail if the antidiscrimination clause were included.[85] The 1935 convention of the AFL not only rejected a proposal to organize industrial unions, but

---

[84] Foner, *Organized Labor and the Black Worker*, chapters 12 and 15.

[85] Ibid., p. 215; Raymond Wolters, "Closed Shop and White Shop: The Negro Response to Collective Bargaining. 1933–35," in Milton Cantor, ed., *Black Labor in America* (Westport: Negro Universities Press, 1970), p. 150.

256

also explicitly rejected a proposal from black unionists to revoke the charters of unions that formally excluded blacks.[86] This action led black union leaders to break with the AFL and to support the formation of the Committee for Industrial Organization (CIO). Industrial unions seemed much more likely to meet the problems of racial discrimination.

By this point, black workers had become an important component of the mass-production work force in many industries, accounting for about 13 percent of workers at Ford's River Rouge Plant in Detroit, 8.5 percent of all steel-workers, and 17 percent of unskilled and semiskilled workers in the slaughter and packinghouse industry.[87] John L. Lewis, probably the most important figure in the early CIO, knew from the mine workers' experience the importance of organizing black workers. It would not be possible to organize industrial unions without the active support of black workers.

Recognizing this reality, the CIO paid special attention to black workers and to opposing racism among white workers. The CIO hired black organizers, built a strong working coalition with the NAACP, and worked actively to educate racist white workers. "Black and white, unite and fight" became one of the CIO's most important slogans in its organizing campaigns. In 1938 the Constitutional Convention of the CIO passed a resolution stating:

> *Whereas*, Employers constantly seek to split one group of workers from another, and thus to deprive them of their full economic strength, by arousing prejudices based on race, creed, color or nationality, and one of the most frequent weapons used by employers to accomplish this end is to create false contests between Negro and white workers; now therefore be it
> *Resolved*, That the C.I.O. hereby pledges itself to uncom-

[86] Foner, *Organized Labor and the Black Worker*, p. 213.

[87] Herbert Northrup, ed., *Negro Employment in Basic Industry: A Study of Racial Policy in Six Industries* (Philadelphia: University of Pennsylvania Press, 1970).

257

promising opposition to any form of discrimination, whether political or economic, based on race, color, creed or nationality.[88]

To carry out its policies, the CIO created a special Committee to Abolish Racial Discrimination; by 1944 eighty-five such committees had been set up at the state and local levels.[89]

In its early years the CIO actively promoted racial equality. In contrast to the AFL, it prohibited constitutional exclusion clauses or segregation of blacks into separate locals. Unlike the AFL, the CIO sought to include black workers on an equal basis.

With this policy the CIO was able to overcome initial black skepticism of the labor movement, which had accumulated over decades of discrimination by white unions. Between 1936 and 1945 the CIO gained endorsements from the NAACP, the Urban League, and the black press.[90] The CIO succeeded in organizing hundreds of thousands of black and white workers in automobiles, electrical equipment, longshoring, meat-packing, the merchant marine, rubber, shipbuilding, steel, warehouses, and many other mass production industries. Consequently, although the black proportion of manufacturing employment declined from 7.3 percent in 1930 to 5.1 percent in 1940, the number of black members of national unions increased from approximately 56,000 members in 1930 (nearly half in the black Brotherhood of Sleeping Car Porters) to 150,000 in 1935 and over 500,000 by 1940. By the end of World War II, black union membership had risen to 1.25 million; black workers comprised over 7 percent of the CIO membership.[91]

CIO organization brought gains to both black and white

[88] Quoted in Foner, *Organized Labor and the Black Worker*, pp. 229–230.

[89] Robert Weaver, *Negro Labor-A National Problem* (New York: Harcourt, Brace and World, 1943), pp. 219–223.

[90] James Olson, "Race, Class, and Progress: Black Leadership and Industrial Unionism, 1936–1945," in Cantor, ed., *Black Labor in America*, p. 164.

[91] Marshall, *Labor in the South*, p. 49; Foner, *Organized Labor and the Black Worker*, p. 173.

258

workers, but especially to black workers. In each industry that the CIO organized, union bargaining committees negotiated contracts with employers that included significant wage gains, particularly for the unskilled segment of the labor force. Large numbers of black workers, concentrated in unskilled occupations, were therefore among the main beneficiaries of these efforts.

By the end of 1937, for example, the Steel Workers Organizing Committee (SWOC, which later became the United Steel Workers of America) included 85,000 blacks among its 550,000 members and had been recognized by the major steel corporations.[92] SWOC had made special efforts to counter discrimination and to organize black steelworkers. When U.S. Steel recognized SWOC in March of 1937, it granted a general wage increase of 10 percent and an increase of 9 percent for unskilled workers. As a result, the earnings of black workers relative to those of whites rose from 79 percent in 1935 to 85 percent in 1938.[93] A similar story was repeated in many industries.

While the CIO brought gains to black workers already employed in mass production industries, it rarely succeeded in significantly changing discriminatory hiring, promotion, and layoff practices in these industries. Many basic industries remained virtually "lily-white" in 1940, and CIO organizing did little for blacks not already included in the industry. As a result, conflicts soon arose between CIO leaders and the black community.

A good example of this conflict occurred in the late 1930s in Harlem, where an estimated 80 percent of the labor force was either unemployed or on Works Progress Administration employment. Several black organizations had criticized the CIO-affiliated Transport Workers Union for not making the elimination of racial job barriers a condition of its negotia-

[92] Ibid., p. 224.

[93] Greer, "Racial Employment Discrimination in the Gary Works," p. 18; Richard Rowan, "The Negro in the Steel Industry," in Northrup, ed., *Negro Employment in Basic Industry*, pp. 260–310.

259

tions. The bus companies had refused to hire blacks as drivers and mechanics, and the subway companies had refused to hire black conductors, motormen, or ticket agents, although many blacks worked as porters and cleaners in these companies. The union leadership was hesitant to take on its more conservative, racist, and largely Irish membership.[94] The episode typified problems that the CIO failed to confront. Later, in the spring of 1941, the TWU cosponsored a bus boycott with Harlem organizations, with the result that the Fifth Avenue Coach Company agreed to employ blacks in 17 percent of its mechanics and driver positions. This, too, typified a smaller number of CIO advances.[95]

The CIO was best able to obtain "equal pay for equal work," thereby eliminating racial differentials paid to workers doing the same job. But black and white workers frequently were assigned to different jobs. Most of the 6,000 black workers at the giant Ford River Rouge plant in 1928 worked in unskilled, dirty, hot, and heavy jobs in the foundry, such as paint departments and rolling mills of the plant. Of about 4,000 black workers at Ford's Highland Park plant, only two were doing skilled work.[96] In the same year, at U.S. Steel's mammoth Gary Works, black and Mexican workers comprised nearly half of the unskilled workers, but only 2 percent of skilled workers; less than 5 percent of black workers held skilled jobs, as compared to nearly half of white workers.[97] Foner reports that in 1940, "General Motors still followed a rigid Jim Crow policy ranging from total exclusion of blacks at Fisher Body to the restriction of blacks to broom-pushers at Chevrolet or to foundry jobs at Buick."[98] "Equal pay for

[94] Mark Naison, "Harlem Communists and the Politics of Black Protest," *Marxist Perspectives* (Fall 1978).

[95] Ibid., p. 42.

[96] Spero and Harris, *Black Worker*, p. 159.

[97] Greer, "Racial Employment Discrimination in the Gary Works," Table 4.

[98] Foner, *Organized Labor and the Black Worker*, p. 232.

equal work" did not address black workers' problems in such situations.

The struggle for racial equality in CIO unions conflicted with another important CIO goal, the establishment of seniority rights. Both black and white workers in the CIO supported and had fought for formal seniority systems in order to curb the arbitrary power of supervisors and management in dictating work assignments, promotions, and layoff decisions. Black workers were the worst victims of the old system, but they continued at a disadvantage under the new one.

In both the South and the North segregated seniority rosters were common.[99] The seniority clause agreements contained in most contracts in effect institutionalized the disadvantages of black workers and maintained the difficulties blacks experienced in advancement into higher-skilled and higher-paid job titles. Often, these seniority rosters were organized on a departmental rather than plant-wide basis, providing a means to discriminate by race that could seem fair and nondiscriminatory in intent.

Moreover, while the CIO had been instrumental in creating integrated union locals throughout the South, an achievement unthinkable a few decades earlier, its principles barring discrimination and segregation were not always followed in practice. And many CIO unions did not confront successfully the racist attitudes and practices of their own members, particularly on issues that involved a community rather than workplace focus, such as segregated housing or schools. Consequently, the gains won by the CIO for black workers remained limited, no matter how much they contrasted with continuing exclusionary policies in the construction craft unions of the AFL.[100]

With notable exceptions, such as in shipyards around

[99] Marshall, *Negro Worker*, p. 271.
[100] Foner, *Organized Labor and the Black Worker*, pp. 233–235.

Baltimore, the racial barriers survived through World War II in most industries. Indeed, blacks began to be employed in significant numbers in war production only after a threatened mass protest march on Washington in 1941 persuaded President Roosevelt to issue a ban on discrimination in war industries and to create a Fair Employment Practices Commission. Black employment, which comprised only 2.5 to 3 percent of war production workers as late as March 1942, grew to over 8 percent by November 1944.[101]

The Postwar Period

After the war the demand for black labor diminished. The CIO initially attempted an organizing drive in the South, where it was still weak, but soon turned its attention to expelling leftists from its own ranks. In so doing it threw out the unions and union leaders that had been most militant in organizing and most committed to the advancement of racial equality.

After 1948 the labor movement failed to make further gains for racial equality; this stagnation paralleled and was directly related to the stagnation of the labor movement itself. By 1950 few CIO unions contained more than a token black among its elected leadership, and only one, the United Packinghouse Workers of America, actively pursued an anti-discrimination program. Throughout the South many CIO affiliates openly practiced Jim Crow segregation in their meeting halls.[102] The CIO's Southern organizing drive, begun in 1946, capitulated to racist practices and collapsed in ignominious defeat by 1952.

By the time of its merger with the AFL in 1955, the CIO no longer was working actively to eliminate racism in employer practices or racism among the AFL unions with which it was confederating.[103] On the eve of the mass protest era of the

[101] Ibid., p. 243.
[102] Ibid., p. 292.
[103] Sumner Rosen, "The C.I.O. Era, 1935–55," in Jacobson, ed., *The Negro and the American Labor Movement*, pp. 190–194.

Southern civil rights movement (the Montgomery bus boycott demanding desegregation took place in 1956), the official House of Labor had given up its place at the cutting edge of the movement for racial equality in the United States.

Accommodation to the racist status quo cost the CIO and white workers dearly. This effect can best be seen by looking not just at individual workplaces, but also at the broadest economic and political results. The failure to organize extensively in the South meant that North-South wage differentials would increase with union wage gains in the North, leading eventually to the relocation of Northern plants in Southern locales. Within the North the influx of blacks into industry in the postwar period would take place under conditions that reproduced enmity between black and white workers and weakened the union movement as a whole. The tensions that produced independent black worker organizations and black caucuses in many industrial unions in the 1960s bear witness to this problem.[104]

Furthermore, the accommodation to the racist status quo hampered labor's political program for liberal welfare-state reforms and for governmental commitments to full-employment policies. In the 1930s it was Southern politicians who blocked Federal relief and other programs that would "disturb the established patterns of segregation" or which would give Washington "the power to tell their states what aid levels they had to provide for Negroes."[105] These same interests

[104] See, for example, Dan Georgakas and Marvin Surkin, *Detroit: I Do Mind Dying, A Study in Urban Revolution* (New York: St. Martin's Press, 1975); James Geschwender, *Class, Race and Worker Insurgency: The League of Revolutionary Black Workers* (New York: Cambridge University Press, 1977).

[105] The quotations are taken from Fred Doolittle's study of the forces that shaped the ADC program in 1935: "Intergovernmental Relations in Federal Grant Programs: The Case of Aid for Families with Dependent Children," (Berkeley: Institute of Business and Economic Research, 1977), pp. 108, 111. For evidence on how Roosevelt was repeatedly forced to defer to Southern Democrats on racial issues, see Harvard Sitkoff, *A New Deal for Blacks* (New York: Oxford University Press, 1978).

opposed any liberal reforms that would have enhanced the mobility of Southern agricultural labor. As a result of the failure to institute the welfare-state agenda, United States workers in the postwar period have experienced higher unemployment rates and lower social welfare benefits than workers in any other advanced capitalist country.

The most highly publicized aspect of postwar race relations concerns affirmative action and desegregation programs set up by governments, corporations, and unions. The effectiveness and magnitude of these programs has been the subject of some controversy. But it seems clear that the stagnation of the economy as a whole has more than offset any gains that blacks have obtained through these programs. Unionization of low-wage employment, especially in the South, and a greater commitment to full employment in government policy would have done more for the advancement of racial equality in the postwar period. Conversely, the incompleteness of welfare-state programs in the United States and the weak commitment to full-employment policies illustrate how racial inequality has held back the political programs of progressive labor-black-Democratic coalitions. Racial inequality has thus continued to hurt a broad spectrum of white workers in the United States.

CONCLUSION

The emancipation of slaves advanced an important freedom to blacks, but it did not eliminate the basis of racism. Blacks remained without independent economic means of support after the Civil War, while the antebellum slaveholding class maintained its dominant position in the South by virtue of its continuing ownership of plantation-belt land. Because of racism most blacks became tenant farmers or sharecroppers; only a few became small landowning farmers. The debt peonage system that developed in Southern agriculture inhibited innovation and the accumulation of capital, thus

264

retarding economic development in the South. This system, together with overt racism, reproduced conditions of poverty for blacks for many decades.

The debt peonage system, which had been created because of racism, soon impoverished white farmers as well as black ones. Racism thus did not benefit most Southern whites in the decades following the Civil War. When poor black and white tenants and small farmers formed a People's Alliance in the 1880s and 1890s, Southern merchants and landowners were able to defeat this coalition, making use of racial divisions to do so. They then instituted state-enforced segregationist measures to prevent further interracial challenges from below. Once again, racism worked to benefit only the most privileged whites.

Southern industry developed after 1880. While blacks were largely excluded from industrial employment, interracial class alliances did develop in the major industries of the New South. Racism ultimately divided and helped defeat these working-class conditions, again to the detriment of most whites. An interracial alliance among bituminous coal miners was broken in 1908 by Jim Crow segregationist forces applied directly by the state of Alabama. This defeat postponed the effective formation of the United Mine Workers Union for decades. Events among the dock workers in New Orleans illustrate the same theme, illustrating as well how racism led white workers to struggle against black workers instead of against employers during economic downturns. The results again did not produce gains for the white workers.

Developments in the iron and steel industry in Alabama in this period illustrate how an exclusionary consciousness among skilled white craft workers resulted only in the ultimate deskilling of the craft occupations. The national iron and steel workers paid a price for this racism in the defeat of the 1919 steel strike, the first major attempt in the United States to organize manufacturing workers into an industrial union. The steel employers' use of overt divide-and-conquer techniques followed examples set in Southern textiles and other Southern industries and was frequently repeated throughout the North.

After the merger wave of 1897 to 1904 and the associated reorganization of much of American industry along oligopolistic lines, employers undertook an antiunion offensive, intensifying the use of divide-and-conquer techniques. Once again, racism worked to hurt white as well as black workers.

In the 1930s and 1940s the formation of interracial industrial unions on a massive and unprecedented scale ushered in a new era for American race relations. Interracial solidarity and the struggle against racism assumed a more central importance for labor organizing strategy than ever before. Industrial unionism and interracial cooperation advanced together as the Congress of Industrial Organizations organized six million white and black workers into unions between 1934 and 1946. The CIO unions countered, to a significant if partial extent, the divide-and-conquer patterns of the past. Both the average worker's wages and the relative wage of black workers came to depend partly on the degree of organization and militancy among black and white workers.

After the late 1940s the CIO no longer played a leading role in the struggle for racial equality, and the labor movement itself stagnated. Consequently, the divisive effects of racism have continued to operate in American industry, but in an institutionalized rather than an overt form.

Significant gains in race relations have occurred, nonetheless. The civil rights movement, allied with liberal forces in the North and in Washington, was able to achieve important advances in the field of political and civil rights for blacks. And the wartime demand for black labor, coupled with the collapse of the Southern debt peonage system, opened up employment opportunities in industry for blacks on a new scale. These advances eliminated major barriers to racial equality and promoted the basis for a renewed interracial alliance.

266

But the shift from excluding blacks from industry to incorporating them into the working class has not by itself resulted in racial equality. Racial inequality is now reproduced by bureaucratic structures in large modern corporations that organize jobs and workers hierarchically and by the farming out of a portion of production to small-scale low-wage employers in competitive market structures. The weaknesses of unions permitted employers to institute these hierarchical structures and to bypass unions with nonunion suppliers.

Racism has weakened the labor movement and hurt most white workers in the postwar period. Unionism remains weakest in the South because of the strength of racism in the region. The resultant low wages in the South have hurt white and black Southern workers directly. Northern workers have also suffered as a result. Wage gains by Northern workers have increased regional wage differentials, impelling many Northern employers to relocate their plants in the South.

The political weakness of progressive forces, due largely to racial divisions and to the continuing power of Southern conservatives in Congress, has also hurt blacks and most whites. These losses are most evident in the failure to achieve the welfare-state agenda that was instituted decades ago in most other developed capitalist countries. In the postwar era United States workers have experienced higher rates of unemployment and economic insecurity and receive a lower level of social-welfare benefits than workers in these other countries. Racism thus continues to hurt most workers, black as well as white.

CHAPTER SEVEN

White Workers are Hurt by Racism: Econometric Evidence

THE ECONOMETRIC FINDINGS, theoretical analysis, and historical evidence presented in the previous three chapters each support a bargaining power theory of income distribution in which racial inequality hurts most white workers. Racial divisions weaken worker solidarity and bargaining power; capitalists gain and most white workers lose.

Racial discrimination may nonetheless benefit skilled workers and professionals in occupations with entry barriers that keep blacks and others out. Most workers in the United States do not belong to such privileged occupations, but it is important to incorporate this qualification into the analysis. Since these beneficiaries have relatively high incomes to begin with, I account for this qualification by restating the main hypothesis as: racial inequality increases inequality among whites by benefiting capitalists and high-income whites and by hurting most white workers.

This hypothesis concerning the effect of racial inequality on the white income distribution does not by itself exclude other effects with possibly quite different distributional implications. For example, racial discrimination in housing may increase the income of ghetto property owners, and racial discrimination in schooling through underfunding of ghetto schools may keep taxes down for all property owners (assuming they bear the burden of school financing). But the econometric results in Chapter 4 indicate the dominance of the bargaining power effects over these others.

Notice that the validity of the bargaining power theory does not depend on the particular mechanisms by which racial

268

inequality is produced. No matter how racial inequality is created, it will have the effect of weakening working-class solidarity. Even if racial inequality resulted entirely from schooling and housing market discrimination, with employers playing no active role, the principal effect would be to produce racial divisions among workers from which employers benefit. This analysis implies that capitalists benefit from racial divisions whether or not they individually or collectively practice racial discrimination.

For these reasons, I have not investigated here the specific mechanisms of discrimination. These reasons also support the use of a racial inequality measure that deliberately does not control for racial differences in individual characteristics nor otherwise attempt to separate the various forms of discrimination from one another.

Nevertheless, it is possible and important to explore further the mechanisms that link racial inequality's effects to diminished worker solidarity and bargaining power. An elaboration of these mechanisms enriches our understanding and further supports the class conflict theory of the effects of racial inequality. In this chapter I explore two mechanisms that connect racial inequality to inequality among whites:

1. The effect of racial inequality on worker solidarity in wage bargaining. Racial inequality exacerbates inequality among whites because racial antagonisms inhibit union bargaining strength and militancy, thereby reducing the total income share of labor.

2. The effect of racial inequality on the solidarity of coalitions of black and low- and middle-income whites in the political arena. Racial inequality exacerbates white inequality because racial antagonisms reduce the redistributive nature of expenditures on local public services. That is, racial antagonisms result in a reduced effective supply of public services, such as public schooling and welfare, that are available to low- and middle-income whites.

269

These mechanisms are testable empirically using the cross-metropolitan area model of income distribution developed in Chapter 4. In this chapter I discuss the unionism and public services mechanisms in relation to these econometric tests. I also discuss in detail the expected relation between unionism and the earnings distribution in a metropolitan area, and present the results of the econometric tests. The findings show that both of these mechanisms do work to hurt most whites. Finally, drawing on detailed industry data on wages, unions, and profit rates, I report the results of a more direct test of the bargaining-power model. These findings also show that greater racial inequality in earnings is associated with lower wages, less unionism, and higher profit rates.

MECHANISMS: UNIONISM AND PUBLIC SERVICES

The first mechanism suggests that the bargaining strength of labor unions is lessened by racial inequality. The fear of a cheaper and underemployed black labor supply in the area affects labor when it presents and negotiates its wage demands. Racial antagonisms on the shop floor deflect attention from labor grievances relating to working conditions, permitting employers to cut costs without a substantial decline in net worker productivity. Racial divisions among labor inhibit the development of united worker organizations both within the workplace and in the labor movement as a whole. As a result, unionization and union militancy will be less, the greater are the extent of racial divisions.

Some economists have pointed to greater racial inequality to explain why the extent of unionization is much lower in the South than elsewhere in the United States. Differences in industrial structure between the regions do not account for this lower extent of unionism.[1] Southern unionization is significantly lower within nearly every industry that has an

[1] F. Ray Marshall, *Labor in the South* (Cambridge: Harvard University Press, 1965), chapter 18.

270

appreciable number of employees in both the South and the rest of the nation. The greater virulence of racism in the South seems to be one of the principal factors responsible for the inability of unions to develop a larger base there.[2]

The hypothesis that unions are hurt by racism may seem surprising to some, given the egregious racism of much of organized labor. Indeed, many students of the labor movement have demonstrated that discriminatory policies have been practiced by organized labor from its earliest history.[3] In their early years, for example, the constitutions of many craft unions expressly prohibited blacks from joining. It is often argued that union pressure comprises one of the primary forces compelling otherwise profit-seeking employers to conform to prevailing white social customs and attitudes against blacks.[4] An exclusionary racial policy, goes the argument, benefits white union members because it increases their bargaining power and income.

In evaluating this argument, however, it is important to distinguish between actual practice and the objective economic self-interest of union members. Racial exclusion increases bargaining power only when entry into an occupation or industry can be limited effectively. Industrial unions are much less able to restrict entry than are craft unions or organizations such as the American Medical Association. Historically, racial exclusion has been most practiced by skilled craft unions, and has probably benefited them, while it has

---

[2] Marshall, p. viii and chapters 1–2.

[3] Philip Taft, *Organized Labor in American History* (New York, 1964), pp. 665–670; Sterling Spero and Abram Harris, *The Black Worker* (New York: Atheneum, 1968), pass.; F. Ray Marshall, *The Negro Worker* (New York: Random House, 1967); Herbert Hill, "The Racial Practices of Organized Labor: The Age of Gompers and After," in Arthur Ross and Herbert Hill, eds., *Employment, Race and Poverty* (New York: Harcourt, Brace and World, 1967).

[4] For example, see Leonard Rapping, "Union-Induced Racial Entry Barriers," *Journal of Human Resources* (Fall 1970).

271

often weakened or destroyed industrial unions.[5] For example, many CIO unions would not have developed so rapidly in the late 1930s had they not stressed racial equality in their internal organization.

Moreover, census data indicate that the incomes of blacks and whites in labor unions are less unequal than incomes of those not in labor unions. These findings, presented in Table 7.1, are sustained even with more detailed occupational breakdowns. They are consistent with the hypothesis developed here that unions have, on the whole, a narrowing effect on racial inequality and that racial inequality inhibits unionism.

The second mechanism suggests that racial inequality creates divisions in working-class solidarity in the political arena where the level and distribution of public expenditures are determined. Racism thereby affects the distribution among whites of publicly provided services. These racial divisions reduce the ability of blacks and low- and middle-income whites to join in a united political movement that would press for the public services that benefit these groups. Two of the most important of these publicly provided services are schooling and welfare.

A certain amount of inequality in public services would exist even without racial divisions. Consider, for example, the distribution of schooling resources among social classes. The geographic segmentation of whites by social class and the tradition of local financing of school expenditures result in a high correlation between local expenditures on schooling and the per capita income of the locality. The desire of many

---

[5] Robert Analavage gives an account of a present-day example of this phenomenon: "Laurel Strike is Broken," in David Mermelstein, ed., *Economics: Mainstream Readings and Radical Critiques* (New York: Random House, 1970), pp. 131–135. In another recent case, an employer had to be enjoined by the National Labor Relations Board to cease the use of inflammatory racial arguments during union representation elections. See Sewell Manufacturing Co. 138 NLRB 66 (1963), cited in Marshall, *Labor in the South* p. 326.

TABLE 7.1   Effect of Union Membership on Relative
Incomes of Nonwhites, 1970

	Male		Female	
	In	*Not in*	*In*	*Not in*
Year-Round, Full-	*Labor*	*Labor*	*Labor*	*Labor*
Time Workers*	*Unions*	*Unions*	*Unions*	*Unions*
All Occupations	83	62	91	82
Blue Collar	90	72	95	104
White Collar	85	70	86	95
Service	73	77	101	89

* Entries refer to ratio of nonwhite to white median income.

SOURCE: U.S. Bureau of the Census, *Social and Economic Status of Blacks in the United States, 1972*, P-23 Series, no. 46, Table 43, p. 55.

teachers to work in the same neighborhoods in which they live, and their preference for students of upper social classes, biases the quality of teacher inputs within a school district in favor of the children of the rich.[6]

Racial discrimination and racial antagonisms exacerbate inequality in schooling among whites in several ways. First, black ghettos tend to be located near poor white neighborhoods more often than near rich white neighborhoods.[7] Since the inferiority of black schools often results from the fiscal deprivation of an entire school district or central city, poor whites living in the central city are simultaneously affected.

[6] Henry Levin has shown that teachers in effect charge more for their services when they teach in ghetto schools.

[7] The geographical contiguity of black and poor white neighborhoods can be deduced both from theoretical considerations and available empirical evidence. In the pure model of urban residential location, the household's decision on how far from the city center to locate depends basically on its income level and its subjective tradeoff between desire for housing space and the transportation costs of commuting to work. Given a high income elasticity of demand for housing space and the fact that transportation costs rise

273

Second, racial antagonisms dilute both the desire and the ability of poor white parents to improve educational opportunities for their children. Antagonisms between blacks and poor whites drive wedges between the two groups and reduce their ability to join in a united political movement pressing for improved and more equal education.[8] Moreover, many poor whites recognize that however inferior their own schools, black schools are even worse. This provides some degree of satisfaction and identification with the status quo, reducing

---

linearly with distance from the city center, whereas the cost of a unit of housing falls more than linearly with distance from the center, it follows that, differences in taste aside, lower-income families will reside in central cities. The poor will be concentrated in the center of cities, and the rich will live in the environs.

This pure model is not sufficient, however, to explain the concentrations of blacks in central cities. Blacks are concentrated in central cities not only because they are poor, but also because of intense racial discrimination in the residential housing market. Economic and racist forces have thus thrown lower-income blacks and whites together in the central cities. Moreover, the rapid growth of the black population in central cities and the resultant expansion of pressures on the geographical limits of the ghetto have accentuated this pattern. It has been empirically established that when ghettos expand, they tend to do so in the direction of poor white neighborhoods. The so-called deterioration of urban neighborhoods occurs first as the local housing stock ages and the average income level of its residents (mostly white) declines.

This stage always precedes the stage in which a neighborhood begins to "tip," or turn black. In other words, the geographical contiguity of blacks and poor whites is observable at the neighborhood, and even block, level, and is particularly evident at the edges of the ghetto. See Luigi Laurenti, *Property Values and Race: Studies in Seven Cities* (Berkeley: University of California Press, 1960); Karl Taeuber and Alma Taeuber, *Negroes in Cities* (Chicago: Aldine Press, 1965), and Beverly Duncan and Otis D. Duncan, *The Negro Population of Chicago: A Study in Residential Succession* (Chicago: University of Chicago Press, 1956). In a recent study, Karl Taeuber examined the extent of racial segregation in white city neighborhoods according to the social class of the neighborhood, and found that the upper-income districts showed significantly greater degrees of racial segregation. See Karl Taeuber, *Patterns of Negro-White Residential Segregation* (Santa Monica: Rand Corporation, 1970).

[8] For examples of labor union involvement in political campaigns that are intended to influence publically provided services, see David Greenstone, *Labor in American Politics* (New York: Random House, 1968).

the desire of poor whites to press politically for better schools in their neighborhoods. Finally, pressure by teachers' groups to improve all poor schools has been reduced by racial antagonisms between predominantly white teaching staffs and black children and parents.

In a similar fashion racial antagonisms reduce the political pressure on governmental agencies to provide other public services that are "pro-poor" in their distributional impact. In the case of welfare, racial inequality reduces the ability of poor blacks and whites to press for higher welfare stipends. Piven and Cloward have argued that political demands by the poor are a major determinant of legislator-determined welfare stipends as in the Aid to Families with Dependent Children program (AFDC).[9] Racial inequality, therefore, can significantly determine the average level of AFDC payments in an SMSA.

The mechanisms stated above can be expressed in the following set of equations, where the control variables are those discussed in Chapter 4.

(1) Unionism = g (racial inequality, market control variables)
(2) White schooling inequality = h (racial inequality, market control variables)
(3) Welfare payment levels = j (racial inequality, market control variables)

The greater the extent of racial inequality, the weaker will be the unions, the more unequal will be the white schooling distribution, and the lower will be the level of public welfare payments.

BARGAINING POWER AND UNIONS

The economic literature examining the influence of unions and collective bargaining on wages, productivity, and income

[9] Frances Piven and Richard Cloward, *Regulating the Poor* (New York: Random House, 1971).

distribution has become both voluminous and controversial.[10] Not surprisingly, economists disagree on how much, or even whether, bargaining power affects workers' wages. At one extreme, some economists view union strength as the sole determinant of wage rates and labor's share of income. At the other extreme, there is the view epitomized by Milton Friedman: "In a dynamic world, economic forces are always arising that tend to change relative wage rates. . . . In the absence of unions, these forces will operate more or less directly on wage rates. Given unions, the same forces will be present but they will operate indirectly on wage rates through the mediation of the union. . . . In many cases, so to speak, unions are simply thermometers registering the heat rather than furnaces producing the heat."[11]

[10] Much of the early literature is summarized and reviewed in H. Gregg Lewis, *Unionism and Relative Wages in the United States* (Chicago: University of Chicago Press, 1963). Two reviews of the controversy that also contain good bibliographies are Richard Perlman, *Labor Theory* (New York: Wiley, 1969), and Richard Perlman, ed., *Wage Determination: Market or Power Forces?* (Boston: D.C. Heath, 1964). There was little empirical research on the impact of unionism in the 1960s as research interests in microincome determination shifted from the "structural" variables of the 1940s and 1950s to individual differences in human capital endowments. However, as noted below, unionism returned to the attention of researchers in the 1970s.

For studies suggesting that unionism and oligopolistic product market structure interdependently result in higher wage increases than in non-unionized and competitive industries, see William Bowen, *Wage Behavior in the Postwar Period: An Empirical Analysis* (Princeton: Princeton University Press, 1960), and Martin Segal, "The Relation Between Union Wage Impact and Market Structure," *Quarterly Journal of Economics* (February 1964); Harold Levinson, "Unionism, Concentration and Wage Changes: Towards a Unified Theory," *Industrial and Labor Relations Review* (January 1967).

An early example of the shift to analyzing the "quality of the labor supply" is Leonard Weiss, "Concentration and Labor Earnings," *American Economic Review* (March 1966). For one explanation of the reasons for this shift, see Barry Bluestone, "The Tripartite Economy: Labor Markets and the Working Poor," *Poverty and Human Resources* (July–August 1970), and Howard Wachtel and Charles Betsey, "Employment at Low Wages," *Review of Economics and Statistics* (May 1972).

[11] Milton Friedman, "Some Comments on the Significance of Labor Unions for Economic Policy," in David M. Wright, ed., *The Impact of the Union* (New York: McGraw-Hill, 1951).

Nonetheless, it is important to examine the many empirical studies of union impact and to assess whether unions do increase workers' wages. Here I discuss some of the issues involved in this literature and indicate the implications of previous research for the structure of my cross-sectional model of income distribution.

Economists generally do agree that workers in highly unionized sectors receive higher average wages than those in nonunionized sectors. Estimates based on industry or establishment data for the 1950s indicate that wages of union workers averaged about 10 to 15 percent higher than those of comparable nonunion workers in otherwise similar environments. More recent investigations, also using industry and establishments as the unit of observation, find a greater differential; one study (by Throop) indicates a differential of 26.0 percent in 1960, and another (by Ryscavage) finds differentials ranging from 20 to 40 percent in 1973.[12] The studies

[12] Weiss, "Concentration and Labor Earnings"; Adrian Throop, "The Union, Non-Union Wage Differential and Cost-Push Inflation," *American Economic Review* (March 1968); Paul Ryscavage, "Measuring Union-Non-Union Earnings Differences, *Monthly Labor Review* (December 1974). See also Vernon Clover, "Compensation in Union and Non-Union Plants, 1960–65," *Industrial and Labor Relations Review* (January 1968).

In the 1970s large microdata sets became available that permitted using the individual worker, rather than the industry or establishment, as the unit of observation. Studies using these data sources found consistently higher union wage effects than did Lewis. Many labor economists have attributed these higher estimates not to greater union bargaining power, but to the improved quality of the new data or to upward biases created by treating an individual's union membership status as exogenous to the wage relationship.

For example, Ashenfelter and Johnson found that union effects on wages were reduced by half or more if union status is itself treated as an endogenous variable in wage determination. However, an interesting paper by Leigh critically reviews the Ashenfelter-Johnson model and a half-dozen subsequent attempts to obtain simultaneous equation estimates of union wage effects. Leigh's own estimates indicate that adjustments for simultaneity *increase* the estimated impact of unions on earnings. See Orley Ashenfelter and George Johnson, "Unionism, Relative Wages, and Labor Quality in U.S. Manufacturing Industries." *International Economic Review* (October 1972); Duane Leigh, "Racial Differentials in Union Relative Wage Effects: A Simultaneous Equations Approach," *Journal of Labor Research* (Winter 1980).

find that the size of individual union, nonunion differentials varies, depending on the type of union and industry, the age of the union, and the stage of the business cycle.

But because unionism is intertwined with other aspects of labor and product-market structures, it is not easy empirically to isolate unionism itself as the *cause* of the union, nonunion wage differentials. The presence of unions tends to be highly and positively correlated with city size, plant size, capital-intensive techniques, high levels of product market concentration, and a labor force that has a high proportion of adult white males and an above-average level of years of schooling. Since each of these variables is itself correlated positively with wage rates independently of unionism, the gross union, nonunion wage differential does not provide unequivocal evidence that unionism is the causal factor producing higher wages. This difficulty permits a wide range of interpretations on the impact of unions.

Moreover, some economists have suggested that the causality between wages and unionism may work in both directions. The labor market forces that create higher wages may also facilitate union organizing efforts. Employers may adjust to unionism by increasing the skill and educational levels of the workers they hire, by installing machinery, or by making other changes in the conditions of employment in order to augment worker productivity.

Conversely, the absence of a union, nonunion wage differential does not prove conclusively that unions have no impact on wages. Unions may exert important "spillover" effects on nonunion employers, forcing them to increase wages to the union level in order to remain competitive. Alternatively, the nonunion employers may raise wages to union levels in order to forestall incipient unionism in their own firms; to counter, in other words, the "threat effects" of unionism.[13] Unions

---

[13] Sherwin Rosen, "Trade Union Power, Threat Effects and Extent of Organization," *Review of Economic Studies* (April 1969). However, studies examining the impact of unionism on management find greater productivity in unionized plants. See Sumner Slichter, James Healy, and Robert Livernash,

may also be effective in extending union rates to an entire labor market by influencing legislative bodies.

Finally, the independent effects of unionism on wages may be difficult to identify because unionism may be necessary but not sufficient for wage increases. Some of the empirical studies suggest that unions have their greatest independent effects on wages when they are newly organized.[14] During recessions the union, nonunion differential generally increases, because unions have negotiated multiyear contracts, with wage increases scheduled in advance, while nonunion wage increases are retarded by the slowdown in the demand for labor. When recession and inflation occur simultaneously, however, as during the 1970s, multiyear contracts can retard union wages if sufficient allowances for cost-of-living increases are not included in the contract. Many unions found themselves in this predicament when inflation accelerated in the mid-1970s.

Many of the earlier analyses of union impact, beginning with Paul Douglas in 1930, compared changes in union and nonunion wages over time.[15] After 1950 most studies attempted cross-sectional comparisons of wage differences at a particular moment in time. Two early cross-sectional studies of union impact illustrate some of the difficulties mentioned in the previous paragraphs.[16] In one of the earliest empirical

---

The Impact of Collective Bargaining on Management (Washington, D.C.: Brookings Institution, 1960) and Charles Brown and James Medoff, "Trade Unions and the Production Process," Journal of Political Economy (May–June 1978).

[14] See, for example, Arthur Ross and William Goldner, "Forces Affecting the Inter-Industry Wage Structure," Quarterly Journal of Economics (May 1950); Orley Ashenfelter and George Johnson, "Unionism, Relative Wages, and Labor Quality."

[15] Paul Douglas, Real Wages in the United States, 1890–1926 (Boston: Houghton Mifflin, 1930).

[16] Harry Douty, "Union and Nonunion Wages," in W.S. Woytinsky, ed., Employment and Wages in the United States (New York, 1951); John E. Maher, "Union, Nonunion Wage Differentials," American Economic Review (June 1956). Both of these studies and others are discussed in Robert Ozanne, "Impact of Unions on Wage Levels and Income Distribution," Quarterly Journal of Economics (May 1959).

attempts to measure union impact, Harry Douty examined union and nonunion wage rates within detailed occupations across different industries. Douty found that wages of workers in unionized plants exceeded wages of workers in nonunionized plants in 87 percent of the occupations studied. This seemed to Douty to be significant proof of union impact. However, in comparing union and nonunion workers, Douty did not control for sex of the work force, region, city size, or other variables that were correlated with both wage rates and probability of unionism. In a subsequent study by John Maher, an attempt was made to control for such variables. Instead of looking at national data, Maher limited himself in his study to selected male occupations in paint and varnish plants in Cleveland and in footwear plants in one part of New England. His findings indicated a zero union, nonunion wage differential. But Maher's conclusions that unions have no impact on wages are just as open to criticism, omitting as they do the possible "spillover" effects of unionism, as mentioned above.

The Maher study also illustrates problems that arise in the measurement of the variables. How should we relate the extent of union power to the percentage of workers that are organized by the union? Maher's data required him to assume that plants where less than half of the workers are covered by wage agreements are "nonunion," while those over half organized are "union." Many other statistical studies assume that union power is simply proportional to the percentage of the workers who are organized. But what if union power faces certain threshold levels? It seems plausible that unions command relatively little influence until they have organized 60 percent of a work force, that they cross a power threshold between 60 and 80 percent, and attain little increased power beyond that level.

The more sophisticated econometricians that have followed Douty and Maher have tried to confront these problems. They employ more detailed data and more complicated models and estimation techniques. But collinearity among the independent variables continues to plague these studies.[17] In sum, attempts to isolate the independent effects of unions on wages and employment seem to have come up against many conceptual and empirical difficulties that permit continuing differences of interpretation.

Nonetheless, one can distinguish four different types of income differentials on which unions may have an impact, beginning with more micro differentials and ending with more macro effects. First, unions may have an impact on wage differentials among individuals in the same occupation. There is wide agreement that the union ethic of "equal pay for equal work," union hostility to piece rates, and the more formal structuring of labor markets that accompanies unionism have produced considerable narrowing of interpersonal wage differentials within detailed occupational categories.[18] Wages for similar work have been somewhat equalized among workers in the same plant, and among workers in different firms and industries.

Second, unions may have an impact on interoccupational and interindustry earnings differentials. Craft-type unions have generally attempted to increase interoccupational differentials between skilled and unskilled workers, whereas industrial-type unions have generally sought to narrow these

[17] For examples, see Weiss, "Concentration and Labor Earnings," Frank Stafford, "Concentration and Labor Earnings: A Comment," *American Economic Review* (March 1968); Michael Boskin, "Unions and Relative Real Wages," *American Economic Review* (June 1972); Ryscavage, "Measuring Union-Nonunion Earnings Differences"; Ronald Oaxaca, "Estimation of Union/Nonunion Wage Differentials Within Occupational/Regional Subgroups," *Journal of Human Resources* (Fall 1975); Ashenfelter and Johnson, "Unionism, Relative Wages, and Labor Quality."

[18] See Clark Kerr, "Wage Relationships—The Comparative Impact of Market and Power Forces," in John T. Dunlop, ed., *The Theory of Wage Determination* (New York: St. Martin's Press, 1957).

281

differentials.[19] Early empirical studies suggested that inter-occupational wage differentials have narrowed considerably among blue collar occupations, among white collar occupations, and between blue and white collar occupations, over the first half of this century. But little of this narrowing was considered to be a direct result of union policies.[20] However,

[19] In many basic industrial sectors, the policy of industrial unions has often been to attain equal absolute wage gains for all of its members, skilled and unskilled, thus tending to reduce relative differences in wages.

[20] The role of unions in these narrowing trends is evaluated negatively in Lloyd G. Reynolds and Cynthia Taft, *The Evolution of the Wage Structure* (New Haven: Yale University Press, 1956), p. 186, and in Kerr, "Wage Relationships," pp. 188–189.

The narrowing trends are much attenuated after 1950. The long-run decline in wage differentials among manufacturing occupations has been documented in studies by Keat and by Ober. See Paul G. Keat, "Long-run Changes in Occupational Wage Structure, 1900–1956," *Journal of Political Economy* (December 1960); Harry Ober, "Occupational Wage Differentials, 1907–1947," *Monthly Labor Review* (November 1953). Long-term trends in white collar differentials have not been systematically studied, in part because of the fragmentary data that are available. The available data suggest that at the turn of the century, clerical and other low-level white collar workers received, on the average, about double the average wage of blue collar manufacturing workers; today the average white collar clerical and sales workers earn *less* than the average blue collar worker. For example, in 1890 the average annual earnings was $848 for clerical workers in manufacturing and steam railroads and $439 for blue collar workers in manufacturing. By contrast, in 1964 the median annual earnings was $5,300 among *male* clerical and sales workers and $5,855 among skilled craftsmen. See *Historical Statistics of the United States, Colonial Times to the Present* (Washington, D.C.: U.S. Government Printing Office, 1959), p. 92, and U.S. Bureau of the Census, "Trends in the Income of families and Persons, 1947–74," *Technical Paper No. 17* (Washington, D.C.: U.S. Government Printing Office, 1968), p. 140.

The earnings gap between professional and low-level white collar work has also fallen, though again systematic data are not available. We do know that high school teachers in major cities earned nearly three times the wage of an average manufacturing production worker in 1904, but earn only 50 percent more today. See Keat, "Long-Run Changes in Occupational Wage Structure," and U.S. Bureau of the Census, *Technical Paper No. 17*. Incidentally, this narrowing is not inconsistent with the observed constancy of the rate of return to schooling, since occupational entry was much less dependent on schooling credentials in the past than it is today.

282

recent multivariate analysis by Sherwin Rosen and by Orley Ashenfelter suggests that unions have had a significant narrowing impact on interoccupational differentials.[21]

Interindustry differentials have also narrowed somewhat, but the conventional wisdom suggests that on the whole unionism had very little to do with this trend.[22] Again, the evidence is mixed. Reynolds, for example, has argued that greater union effectiveness in high-wage industries has tended to *widen* interindustry wage differentials.[23]

The effects of unionism on income differentials in a particular SMSA may differ from the effects of unionism in the nation as a whole. These differences are relevant to an examination of income distributions within SMSAs. They arise because the relative importance of craft unions and industrial unions varies across SMSAs, and because some unions in an SMSA may have strong ties to national labor unions. Interindustry differentials within the SMSA may be increased because such unions are keyed to *national* wage agreements and national labor markets, irrespective of local labor market wage levels.[24] Steel, auto, and meat-packing are examples of industries in which national labor union activity has been particularly evident.[25] On the other hand, a number of

[21] Sherwin Rosen "Unions and the Occupational Wage Structure in the United States," *International Economic Review* (June 1970); Orley Ashenfelter, "Racial Discrimination and Trade Unionism," *Journal of Political Economy* (May–June 1972).

[22] Kerr, "Wage Relationships"; Goldner, "Forces Affecting the Inter-Industry Wage Structure"; Lewis, *Unions and Relative Wages.*

[23] See Lloyd Reynolds, "The Influence of Collective Bargaining on the Wage Structure in the United States," in Dunlop, *Theory of Wage Determination.* Gail Pierson has fitted Phillips-curve-type wage equations to ten strongly unionized and several less strongly unionized manufacturing industries for the period 1953–1963. She found significantly greater wage increases in the unionized group. See Gail Pierson, "Union Strength and the Phillips Curve," *American Economic Review* (June 1968).

[24] Such unionism, it should be noted, tends to reduce inter-area differentials.

[25] See Lloyd Ulman, *The Rise of the National Trade Union* (Cambridge: Harvard University Press, 1960).

283

unions may form a coalition across industries within an SMSA. In most major cities the city-wide AFL-CIO Central Labor Councils provide at least the institutional shell of such a coalition.[26] Such a coalition might conceivably reduce inter-industry differentials within the SMSA. The net effect of unionism on interoccupational and interindustry differentials will depend, then, on the relative sizes and strength of craft unions and industrial unions, the extent to which unions are tied to national labor markets, and the extent of overall solidarity of unions in the SMSA.

A third impact of unions may impinge on the earnings differential between unionized and nonunionized workers. Differentials may arise within an industry between organized and unorganized plants as well as between industries that are organized and those that are not. As we have seen, much empirical research has examined the nature and causes of these differentials.[27]

Finally, unionism may affect the size distribution of income by changing the relative shares of labor and capital in favor of labor. Many economists express skepticism that labor can raise its share of total income, since unions represent no more than one-fourth of the total labor force, and any gains unions make for organized sections of the labor force may occur at the expense of unorganized sections. Unions are stronger in oligopolistic industries, and unorganized workers might be hurt by the capacity of such industries to pass wage increases on to consumers in the form of higher prices.

Moreover, if unions raise wages of their own members relative to nonunionized workers, capital will be substituted for labor in the unionized sector, and the resulting flow of labor into the nonunionized sector may depress the level of wages in that sector. The magnitude of this effect depends on the relative capital intensities in the two sectors as well as the elasticities of substitution between labor and capital.

[26] Greenstone, *Labor in American Politics*.
[27] See note 12 above.

284

A theoretical and empirical analysis along these lines has been carried out by Johnson and Mieszkowski. They estimate that in a competitive economy, a 1 percent increase in the union wage markup produces a gain in union wages that exceeds the loss in nonunion wages, so that the aggregate wage bill would be increased by up to 0.25 percent.[28] Insofar as the economy is not competitive and unions can extract a share of monopoly profits, the gains in labor's share will be greater and will come more at the cost of capital and less at the cost of the unorganized sector.[29]

This review of the literature suggests that although different types of unions can exert effects in opposing directions, unions on the whole probably narrow the income distribution. The magnitude of this expected impact across metropolitan areas depends on the size and strength of unions and the relative importance of craft and industrial unions. The size and strength of the unions depends in turn on their internal

[28] A statistically sophisticated attempt to examine the relationship between unionism and labor's share would employ a modern macroeconomic model so as to separate fluctuations in labor's share due to the rhythm of the business cycle from those due to the independent effect of unionism. Such an analysis should, however, account for the labor movement's political clout as one of the factors that increases the political costs of high unemployment and so shifts the nature of fiscal policy and the business cycle. I do not know of any such study, although there have been Phillips-curve-type attempts to measure the impact of the Kennedy-Johnson wage-price guideposts. See George Perry, "Wages and the Guideposts," *American Economic Review* (September 1967). There is also an emerging literature on political business cycles. See for example, Edward Tufte, *Political Control of the Economy* (Princeton: Princeton University Press, 1978).

[29] See Harry G. Johnson and Peter Mieszkowski, "The Effects of Unionization on the Distribution of Income: A General Equilibrium Approach," *Quarterly Journal of Economics* (November 1970).

In an article that is somewhat more pertinent to the present study, Clark Kerr reported that "[the] degree of unionization by SMSA is not significantly related to labor's share of manufacturing income in the SMSA's according to our calculations"; unfortunately, Kerr does not offer any clues as to his data, sample, statistical method, or quantitative results. See Clark Kerr, "Trade Unionism and Distributive Shares," *American Economic Review* (1954), pp. 279–292.

cohesiveness and solidarity (here racial divisions become important) and on the industrial structure of the metropolitan area. Areas with a high concentration of oligopolistic, capital-intensive industries are more likely to have larger union movements, and these unions will be able to win greater wage increases for their members.

Mechanisms: Econometric Evidence

I present here results of tests of the hypotheses concerning the unionism and public services mechanisms through which racial inequality operates to increase income inequality among whites. I discuss first the empirical counterparts of the variables and then turn to the findings themselves.

Variable Specification

An ideal unionization variable would account for each aspect of the phenomenon of unionism that has an impact on the distribution of income. These aspects include union structure and membership, degree of union militancy, and ties to national unions, as discussed in the previous section. Unfortunately, reliable data on unions and on union membership are very difficult to obtain. It is even more difficult to classify unions by craft versus industrial, degree of militancy, propensity to strike, and so forth. The variable used here, and the only one available for my sample, is based on union membership statistics collected by the U.S. Bureau of Labor Statistics. It is defined as the percentage of plant workers in all industries in an SMSA who are employed in establishments where a majority of workers are covered by a labor-management contract.[30] In the equations in which unionism appears

[30] These data are reported in U.S. Department of Labor, Bureau of Labor Statistics, *Wages and Related Benefits: 82 Labor Markets, 1960–61*, Bulletin No. 1285-83, Table 8-33b, p. 121; U.S. Department of Labor, Bureau of Labor Statistics, "Area Wage Surveys, Selected Metropolitan Areas, 1968–69," Bulletin No. 1625-90, Table 3. Only establishments employing fifty persons or more are included in this survey data. No data were available for seven of the SMSAs in the sample: Sacramento, San Diego, San José, Rochester, Fort Worth, Tampa, and Gary. The exclusion of these SMSAs may impart some

as a dependent variable, I expect that the coefficient of both the racial inequality and the percentage of employment in manufacturing variables will be positive. Unions will be stronger when racial inequality is low, and when manufacturing employment is high.

Turning next to schooling, an appropriate measure of schooling inequality would isolate and measure the effect of the local schooling systems on the distribution of earnings capacities among whites in the SMSA. An ideal variable would measure the degree of inequality in the distribution of postschooling individual earnings capacities *net* of the "preschool" distribution, net, that is, of the capacities relevant for later labor market years that parents transmit to their children beginning in the preschool years and continuing outside of school in later years. In this way, the effects of the schooling system alone would be isolated from those of family background.

Two sets of empirical problems are immediately present. First, how does one isolate empirically the effects of parental social-class inequality from those of schooling? Second, how does one measure the effects of schooling on individual earnings capacities? These two problems of theory and measurement have perennially bedeviled attempts to estimate educational production functions and the economic effects of schooling.[31] There is both a paucity of adequate intergenera-

---

bias into my results, but I have no strong a priori notions of the direction of the bias. Two of the seven are Southern, a proportion comparable to that for the entire sample; on the other hand, none of the seven are among the larger SMSAs in my sample. A comparison of the means, standard derivations, and correlation matrices of all the variables for this subsample of forty-one SMSAs with those of the entire sample did not reveal any significant biases in the subsample.

[31] Some of the most important studies are in W. Lee Hansen, ed., *Education, Income and Human Capital* (New York: National Bureau of Economic Research, 1972); see, in particular, Samuel Bowles, "Towards an Educational Production Function." On the issues raised in this paragraph and the following one, see also Herbert Gintis, "Education, Technology and Worker Productivity," *American Economic Review* (May 1971); Samuel Bowles, "Schooling and Inequality from Generation to Generation," *Journal of Political Economy*

tional and longitudinal data on schooling and theoretical disagreement as to the nature of the inputs and outputs of schools that are pertinent in determining earnings.[32]

It is not my purpose to examine these problems in a systematic fashion here. The only available input measures of schooling inequality in an SMSA—per pupil expenditures—are collected on a school district basis. Since much of schooling inequality occurs *within* school districts and since a school district often comprises an entire central city, the school district unit is much too aggregated for the present purposes. Moreover, a number of recent studies have cast considerable doubt on the appropriateness of per pupil expenditures as a measure of schooling inputs.

For these reasons, I use an output rather than an input measure of schooling inequality. A convenient, and for my sample, the only available, measure of schooling output is years of schooling completed. I measure schooling inequality by a Gini coefficient of years of schooling completed for a cohort of white males aged twenty-five to twenty-nine. The purpose of using a young five-year age cohort is to control for the upward secular trend in years of schooling completed and to approximate most closely inequalities among recent students.

I obtained a white frequency distribution of years of schooling by subtracting nonwhites from total frequencies for fifteen schooling classes.[33] I used midpoints of intervals as class means, and computed a Gini coefficient of years of

---

(May–June 1972); Samuel Bowles and Herbert Gintis, "IQ in the U.S. Class Structure," *Social Policy* (January 1973); Christopher Jencks et al., *Inequality: A Reassessment of the Impact of Family and Schooling* (New York: Basic Books, 1972); Martin Carnoy, ed., *Schooling in a Corporate Society* (New York: David McKay, 1972).

[32] A recent study by Peter Meyer, "The Reproduction of the Distribution of Income" (Ph.D. diss., University of California, Berkeley, 1979), advances beyond the previous literature.

[33] The data sources are *U.S. Census of the Population*, parts 2-51, Table 103 (1960), and Table 148 (1970).

schooling with the same formula used in computing Gini coefficients of income. In the equations in which schooling inequality is the dependent variable, I expect that the coefficient of the racial inequality variable will be negative; the less the racial inequality, the less will be the white schooling inequality.

Finally, I also include an equation to test the hypothesis that levels of welfare stipends are related to the extent of racial inequality. I use the average 1960 SMSA level of monthly stipends to recipient families in the Aid to Families with Dependent Children (AFDC) as the dependent variable in this equation.[34] I expect to find positive signs for both the racial inequality and the median family income coefficients in this equation.

Unions

Table 7.2 presents results for a series of tests of the unionization hypotheses, using the subsample of forty-one SMSAs for which unionization data are available. The first two equations indicate the influence of racial inequality and the control variables on the extent of unionization. PCTMFG is positive and significant in these equations, as one would expect. The racial inequality variable is also positive, as expected, and significant at the 5 percent level in equation 1 and at the 1 percent level in equation 2. According to equation 2, at the sample means, a 1 percent increase in the ratio of median black to white incomes (reduction in racial inequality) is associated with a 0.6 percent increase in the degree of unionization.

[34] The data came from a survey of state welfare agencies by Marjorie Honig, to whom I am grateful for making this data available. Data were not available for the following fourteen SMSAs: Sacramento, San Bernardino, San José, Albany, Buffalo, Rochester, Akron, Columbus, Dayton, Toledo, Gary, Minneapolis, Paterson, and Portland. A comparison of the means, standard derivations, and correlation matrix of all the variables for this subsample of thirty-four SMSAs with those for the entire sample indicated that no significant biases were introduced by the exclusion of the above SMSAs.

TABLE 7.2 Unionism Equations, 1960 (n = 41)

Equation Number	Dependent Variable	Constant	B/W	PCTMFG	WHICOL	PCTGOVT	MDWINC	UNIONISM	R^2
1	UNIONISM	-.637	.646	.863	.291		.086		.544
			(2.20)	(3.58)	(0.90)		(2.55)		
	elasticity		.52	.31	.16		.75		
	beta		.29	.17	.06		.36		
2	UNIONISM	-.491	.787	.601		-0.838	.090		.558
			(2.68)	(1.95)		(-1.40)	(2.71)		
3	G_w	.423	-.092	-.125	.098			-.038	.679
			(-2.78)	(-4.31)	(2.82)			(-2.49)	
	beta		-.30	-.47	.26			-.25	
	Non-Southern SMSAs (n = 31)								
4	UNIONISM		-.028	.450	.527				.214
			(-0.04)	(1.69)	(1.69)				
5	G_w	.406	-.093	-.086	.094			-.0312	.399
			(-2.18)	(-2.76)	(2.56)			(-1.35)	

Simple Correlations (n = 41)

	G_w	S1	B/W	PCTMFG	WHICOL	MDWINC
UNIONISM	-.60	-.50	.49	.61	.12	.40

These results both bear out my hypotheses and contradict much conventional wisdom on the relation between unions and racism. The positive sign of B/W in equation 1 indicates that, at least as far as degree of organization is concerned, unions on the whole are better off when there is less racial inequality. Although some unions—particularly craft unions—may benefit from discriminatory practices and racial exclusion, such policies do not appear to produce gains for unions in the aggregate.

Evidence on the relation between unionism and racial inequality is also provided by Ashenfelter and by Leigh.[35] Their findings are worthy of summary here.

Ashenfelter first presents evidence that unions have a narrowing effect on the interoccupational wage structure. Since blacks are concentrated in the low-skill, low-wage occupations, unions tend to reduce the average income differential between blacks and whites, holding other variables constant. According to Ashenfelter's calculations, the average black/white wage ratio of all workers is about 1 to 2 percent higher than the average black/white wage ratio of nonunion workers.[36] Ashenfelter then looks separately at the effects of craft and industrial unions, using a large microeconomic data set from the 1967 *Survey of Economic Opportunity*. His results suggest that craft unions depress the black/white wage ratio, while industrial unions increase it. The disequalizing effect of craft unions occurs for two reasons. First, craft unions are less likely to have black members than industrial unions; second, craft unions tend to increase the interoccupational wage differential, whereas industrial unions tend to narrow it. Ashenfelter estimates that craft unions in the construction industry reduce the black/white male wage ratio by 5 percent, while industrial unions tend to increase this ratio by about

[35] Orley Ashenfelter, "Racial Discrimination and Trade Unionism"; and Duane Leigh, "Racial Discrimination and Labor Unions: Evidence from the NLS Sample of Middle-Aged Men," *Journal of Human Resources* (Fall 1978).

[36] Ashenfelter, "Racial Discrimination and Trade Unionism," pp. 16 and 24.

4 percent.[37] He finds that unions, on net, increase the average black/white wage ratio by about 3 percent.

Leigh has reexamined Ashenfelter's analysis by using data for 1969 from the National Longitudinal Surveys of middle-aged men. This data set contains explicit information on the type of union—industrial or craft—representing workers. Leigh could therefore identify craft unionists directly, whereas Ashenfelter could only identify craft unionists in construction. Nonetheless, Leigh's findings are substantially the same as Ashenfelter's.[38]

Ashenfelter, Leigh, and I find similar correlations between unionism and racial inequality, but we draw opposite causal inferences. Both inferences probably have validity, although I have not tried to assess their relative importance. Both inferences are consistent with the class-bargaining-power model I have proposed. Neither inference is consistent with the Becker hypothesis that capitalists lose and white workers gain from discrimination.

Table 7.2 also provides some evidence on the direct effect of unionism on the white income distribution. The simple correlation between G_w and unionism is $-.60$, indicating that unions are strongly associated with greater income equality, but a causal interpretation requires multivariate analysis. Equation 3 in Table 7.2 shows that, controlling for the effects of industrial structure and racial inequality on the income inequality variable, an increase in unionism is still associated significantly with a reduction in income inequality. The UNIONISM variable has the expected sign, is significant at the 1 percent level, and has a beta of .25, the same order of magnitude as the betas for the other explanatory variables.

This equation significantly understates the impact of unions.

[37] Ibid., p. 23.

[38] Leigh, "Racial Discrimination and Labor Unions," pp. 572–576. These results are sustained in Leigh's simultaneous equations estimate in which union status is exogenous (not in the sense of my model, but rather of that discussed in note 12). See Leigh, "Racial Differentials in Union Relative Wage Effects."

The UNIONISM variable is highly correlated with PCTMFG, and the latter may be picking up some of the union effects. Moreover, the data underlying the UNIONISM variable contain considerable measurement error, the variable itself is an imperfect measure of labor's bargaining strength, and the overall variation in this variable is restricted by the general weakness of unions in the United States. In view of all these handicaps, I interpret these results as providing striking support (the pun is intended) of the hypothesis that unions exert a significant egalitarian effect on income distribution.

Equation 3 in Table 7.2 also shows that racial inequality affects white inequality, both directly and indirectly, through its effect on unionism. The direct and indirect effects of racial inequality on white inequality can be decomposed quantitatively by use of the following relation:

$$r_{G_w, B/W} = b_{G_w, B/W} + b_{G_w, u} \cdot r_{u, B/W} + \sum_i b_{G_w, i} \cdot r_{i\ B/W},$$

where: r_{kj} = simple correlation coefficients

b_{kj} = standardized regression coefficients (beta weights)

u = subscript for unionism

i = runs over control variables.

The direct effect of racism is then the first term on the right-hand side of the above equation, while the indirect effect through unionism is represented by the second term. The relations can be illustrated by a path diagram:

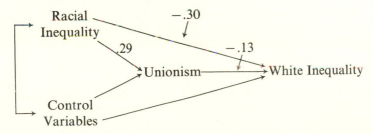

The computed results are:

Direct effects of racial inequality: $-.30$
Indirect effects via unionism: $-.13$

Finally, Table 7.2 presents estimates of the same equations for the non-South subsample. The industrial-structure variables continue to be significant in equation 4, but the B/W variable is not. The hypothesized relation between unionization and racial inequality apparently holds only on an inter-regional level. As the institutional literature suggests, the regional differences in unionization may be related to the greater degree of racial inequality in the South. The B/W variable is still significant in equation 5.

Schooling Inequality and Public Welfare

The effect of racial inequality on white schooling inequality is reported in Table 7.3. In equation 1, the coefficient of B/W is negative, as predicted, and is significant at the 1 percent level. PCTMFG has a negative sign, and is the only other variable that enters significantly into this equation. More than half of the variance is explained by the equation. Similar results obtain for the non-South subsample (see equation 3). B/W again appears with a negative coefficient, significant at the 1 percent level. The significance of the control variables in this equation again is much lower than in the G_w or S1 equations.

The high association between schooling inequality among young white males and racial income inequality in these equations supports the specific hypotheses of this chapter concerning the effects of racism on schooling inequality. The results also further support the validity of B/W as a measure of racism. A spurious correlation between B/W and EDGINW is much less likely than a spurious correlation between B/W and G_w. The much higher statistical association between B/W and EDGINW therefore diminishes the likelihood of spuriousness in the observed statistical association between G_w and B/W.

As equations 2 and 4 indicate, both B/W and EDGINW are insignificant when EDGINW is added to the G_w equation. This

294

Table 7.3 White Schooling Inequality Equations, 1960

Equation Number	Dependent Variable	Constant	B/W	PCTMFG	WHICOL	MDWINC	EDGINW	R^2	n
1	EDGINW	.563	-.563 (-6.22)	-.185 (-1.86)	.117 (-1.25)	.014 (-1.30)		.566	48
2	G_w	0.43	-.056 (-1.44)	-.123 (-4.93)	.080 (2.26)	-.012 (-3.63)	.087 (1.60)	.661	48
	beta		-.18	.46	.20	.27	.18		
	Non-Southern SMSAs								
3	EDGINW		-.321 (-2.99)	-.0475 (-0.72)	-.173 (-2.08)			.396	36
4	G_w	0.36	-.065 (-1.24)	-.086 (-2.96)	.094 (2.49)	-.0046 (-0.91)	.110 (1.36)	.358	36

Simple Correlations (n = 48)

Dependent Variable	G_w	S1	B/W	PCTMFG	WHICOL
EDGINW	.55	.55	-.77	-.44	-.25

increase in the standard error occurs because the simple correlation coefficient between the two variables is $-.77$. Moreover, EDGINW is not a truly exogenous variable in this equation, since we would expect the degree of white income inequality itself to influence the degree of schooling inequality.

The results in equations 2 and 4, together with the high correlation between B/W and EDGINW, suggest that much of the effect of racial inequality on income inequality occurs indirectly through the effect on schooling inequality. A decomposition of the direct and indirect effects, using the same technique as with unionism, produced the following results:

Direct effect of racial inequality: $-.18$
Indirect effect via schooling: $-.13$

The equation estimate relating racial inequality to the average SMSA level of monthly stipends in the Aid to Families with Dependent Children (AFDC) program is indicated in Table 7.4. The important control variable here is MDWINC, for it measures the general wage level of the SMSA and the capacity of the state and city to fund welfare programs. MDWINC has the expected sign and is significant at the 1 percent level in all the equations. PCTMFG, WHICOL, and PCTNW are not significant in these equations.

The racial inequality variable has the expected positive sign and is significant at the 1 percent level in all the equations in Table 7.4. The results indicate that SMSAs with less racial inequality have more generous transfer programs, presumably in response to greater pressure from the poor.

It is possible that the causation here works in the reverse direction: the higher AFDC benefits cause a higher B/W. This would happen if (1) AFDC stipends are high relative to median black incomes, and (2) a high proportion of black families, higher than among white families, receive AFDC payments. But underlying data clearly indicate that, in 1960, neither the average AFDC stipend nor the mean percentage of black families receiving AFDC payments was sufficiently high to produce a spurious correlation between median black income (the numerator of B/W) and the AFDC variable.

296

TABLE 7.4 AFDC Equations, 1960 (n = 34)

Equation Number	Dependent Variable	Constant	B/W	PCTMFG	WHICOL	MDWINC	PCTNW	R^2
1	AFDC	−173.	243.1 (4.28)	.071 (0.09)	−.779 (−0.38)	25.0 (2.69)		.685
2	AFDC	−197.	280.4 (3.03)			19.0 (2.80)	31.42 (0.32)	.497
			Non-Southern SMSAs (n = 22)					
3	AFDC	−207.	300.0 (3.47)	.272 (0.24)	−.655 (−0.25)	23.0 (3.47)		.521
4	AFDC	−272.	460.4 (3.24)			11.0 (6.84)	190.0 (1.17)	.375

Simple Correlations (n = 34)

	B/W	MDWINC	PCTNW
AFDC	.61	.49	−.36

Once again, the results support the hypotheses of this study: higher levels of AFDC stipends are associated with lower levels of racial inequality.

Evidence from 1970 Data

As in the investigation for 1960, I have examined two mechanisms for 1970 that link racial inequality with inequality among whites: the impact of racial inequality on inhibiting (1) the extent and strength of unionism in an SMSA, and (2) the capacity of poor and middle-income whites to unite in the political arena to obtain greater resources, such as for public schooling. I examine the first mechanism by estimating an equation with the extent of union membership in an SMSA in 1970 as the dependent variable (UNIONISM); I examine the second with an equation explaining the 1970 degree of schooling inequality among young white males, as measured by a Gini coefficient of years of schooling completed in 1970 among white males aged twenty-five to twenty-nine (EDGINW). These results are presented in Table 7.5.

In equation 1 of Table 7.5, the B/W variable appears with a positive coefficient, as expected, and is significant at the 15 percent level. At the sample means, a 1 percent increase in B/W (decline in racial inequality) is associated with a 0.33 percent increase in the extent of unionism. The coefficient, t-statistic, and elasticity at the means are each about two-thirds of that found with 1960 data. In 1970, unions were still stronger where there was less racial inequality, but the extent of the association was less than in 1960.

In equation 2 of Table 7.5, reporting the estimates of the same unionism equation for the non-Southern SMSAs only, the B/W variable does not appear significantly. This variable also did not appear significantly with 1960 data. In 1970 it still seemed to be the case that the relation between unionism and racial inequality occurred as in interregional phenomenon.

The estimates of the schooling-inequality hypotheses are reported in equations 3 and 4 of Table 7.5. The B/W coefficient in equation 1 is negative as expected, and significant at the

298

TABLE 7.5 Unionism and White Schooling Inequality, 1970

Equation Number	Dependent Variable	Constant	B/W	PCTMFG	WHICOL	MDWINC	R^2	n
1	UNIONISM	-.224	.225 (1.48)	.827 (6.61)	.009 (.048)	.0099 (1.22)	.624	44
2[a]	UNIONISM	.159	-.115 (-0.47)	.688 (4.27)	-.028 (-0.11)	.0015 (0.12)	.433	31
3	EDGINW	.218	-.048 (-1.53)	-.003 (-0.01)	-.049 (-1.27)	-.0032 (-2.07)	.199	44
4[a]	EDGINW	.193	-.045 (-0.82)	.103 (0.36)	-.518 (-1.04)	-.0014 (-0.60)	.085	32

[a] Indicates non-Southern subsample.

15 percent level. However, the magnitude and significance of this and all the other coefficients, as well as the R^2, are much lower than for 1960. I suspect that the general increase in schooling levels between 1960 and 1970 render the Gini coefficient of schooling years completed less valid as a measure of inequality in schooling resources in 1970. This may explain the changed results for the two years. Similar remarks apply to the non-South equation, where the B/W variable is not significant.[39]

Wages, Unions, Profits, and Racial Inequality

The theoretical model concerns the effects of racial inequality on workers' wages and employers' profits. Yet the empirical investigations have made use of and examined the relation between racial inequality and the size distribution of income in an SMSA. A more direct test of the model would be desirable. While the most direct test would employ the relevant data on individual firms, such data unfortunately are not available for a statistically adequate sample. Relevant data from the Census Bureau and the Internal Revenue Service are available, however, for three-digit detailed industries in 1970. A brief discussion will indicate how I use industry data on wages, unions, and profits to make more direct tests of the model.

My argument states that greater racial inequality between black and white workers makes alliances between them more difficult, hindering the development of joint bargaining power against employers. At the microeconomic level of the firm or, better yet, at the establishment or shop-floor level, racial inequality in annual earnings is due more to occupational and seniority differences then to the pure wage discrimination of unequal pay for equal work. Nonetheless, the differences that exist can and often do affect the solidarity of the workers in negotiating wages and working conditions.

---

[39] The 1960 results I obtained concerning the relation between racial inequality in an SMSA and average AFDC stipend levels drew on data gathered by Marjorie Honig. I have not been able to obtain comparable data for 1970 and therefore could not repeat this analysis.

300

I therefore expect that *lesser* racial inequality should be associated with (1) *higher* earnings for white workers and (2) stronger unions. These implications are the opposite of what one would expect to find if white workers and their unions were thought to benefit from racial inequality.

A bargaining-power model of wage determination suggests, at the same time, a bargaining-power model of profit determination. Holding productivity and output prices constant, an increase in wages will come out of profits. I therefore also expect to find that lesser racial inequality is associated with lower profit rates.

Table 7.6 reports results for three equation, relating racial inequality to wages, unionism, and profit rates, respectively.[40] These equations are estimated across those industries for which data are available, including data for control variables. Note that since my hypotheses concern the establishment or firm, while the data are at the industry level, the estimates are

---

[40] Some of the variables, such as union membership, are not available with as much disaggregated detail as others. To make efficient use of the available data and permit inclusion of independent control variables, I constructed a conformable set of observations for each equation by employing weighting procedures to reaggregate some observations. This explains the different sample sizes for each of the equations in Table 7.6.

White and nonwhite workers' earnings refer to median annual wage and salary income in the industry for males who are in the experienced civilian labor force. The B/W variable is the ratio of nonwhite-to-white earnings. The unionism variable refers to proportion of employees in labor unions and is based on household-survey data. The profit rate is measured as the ratio of after-tax profits to stockholders' equity in the industry. AGE is median age of male workers, PCTNW refers to the percentage of nonwhites in the industry labor force, and PCTYR refers to the proportion of the industry labor force that worked fifty or more weeks in 1969.

Data sources for these variables are: U.S. Bureau of the Census, *Census of the Population, 1970*, "Subject Reports: Industrial Characteristics," Tables 5, 6, and 7 (earnings, percent year-round workers); 32 (age); 33 (percent nonwhite); U.S. Internal Revenue Service, *Corporation Returns, 1970*, Table 1 (profit rate); U.S. Department of Labor, Bureau of Labor Statistics, *Selected Earnings and Demographic Characteristics of Union Members, 1970*, Bulletin No. 417 (union membership).

Table 7.6 1970 Industry Equations

Equation Number	Dependent Variable	Constant	B/W	Age	PCTNW	PCTYR	R^2	n
1	Median White Earnings	5197	3178 (2.16)	-138.3 (-1.90)	-63.6 (-2.13)	83.4 (4.36)	.542	47
2	Unionism	-1.03	1.15 (3.15)	.014 (1.27)	-.252 (-0.36)	.019 (0.04)	.336	27
3	Profit Rate	.205	-.140 (-2.61)		-.217 (-2.15)		.145	83

likely to understate the true relationships among the variables I am studying.

As equations 1 and 2 in Table 7.6 indicate, racial inequality in an industry appears to be a significant determinant of white male workers' annual earnings in the industry and of the proportion of union members among workers in the industry.[41] A reduction in racial inequality (higher B/W) is associated with higher earnings for white workers and with more unionism, controlling for other variables in both cases. At the sample means, the elasticity of the B/W variable is .29 in the earnings equation, and 2.30 in the unionism equation. Each of these results is consistent with the conflictual bargaining-power model.

Equation 3 indicates that a reduction in racial inequality is associated with a fall in the industry profit rate. A 1 percent decline in racial inequality produces a 0.44 percent decline in the profit rate. This result is again consistent with my model.

These results, taken together with the 1970 SMSA equations in Tables 7.4 and 7.5, provide further confirmation of my hypotheses. Capitalists benefit and most white workers lose from racial inequality. Whether or not these effects are apparent to the respective agents is not clear, but they seem to be still present in the United States in 1970.

CONCLUSION

The class conflict analysis of racial inequality identifies specific and testable mechanisms through which racial inequality works to hurt most white workers and benefit capitalists. Unions are weaker and the supply of public services to low- and middle-income whites are lessened by racial divisions.

---

[41] A years-of-schooling variable could not be included in the earnings equation because these data are only available at a very high level of aggregation. The same is true for weekly hours and weeks worked, though these influences are picked up to some extent by the PCTYR variable. Data limitations thus precluded the inclusion of a number of control variables in these equations.

These mechanisms are tested here econometrically using the cross-SMSA model developed in Chapter 4, and applying a cross-industry model as well. The empirical findings generally support the class conflict theory. These results thus complement the econometric evidence presented in Chapter 4, the theoretical analysis presented in Chapter 5, and the historical evidence presented in Chapter 6. Racial inequality benefits capitalists and hurts most whites.

CHAPTER EIGHT

Conclusions and Implications

RACIAL INEQUALITY in the United States has persisted since the slaves won emancipation in 1865. The patterns of inequality continue not only in the South, with its state-sanctioned and enforced history of discrimination and segregation, but also in the North, where racial-based government policies have exerted less impact on the operation of markets. The persistence of racial inequality thus cannot be explained simply as the results of past and present coercion exercised through the channels of the state. It appears that the market economy has also worked in a manner that is consistent with continuing racial inequality.

The persistence of racial inequality is particularly striking in view of the major changes that have taken place in the economic and political position of blacks in the United States in the post-World War II era. Since 1945 most racial barriers to equal political and civil rights have been torn down and, at the Federal level at least, government activity has shifted from promoting discrimination to combating it. There also have been some improvements at the state and local levels. The oppressive sharecropping system of the agrarian South that reproduced black poverty and racial inequality for so many decades has diminished to a fraction of its former size and importance. A majority of blacks in the United States now reside in metropolitan areas, many of them in the North, and work for a wage or salary for private industry or government. A small but significant number of these blacks have professional and managerial jobs, but the majority of them are employed in low-level clerical, blue collar, or service positions, and some survive through welfare, unemployment compensation, and other transfer payments.

In the post-World War II era the intersectoral shift of the economy from agriculture to industry and services reduced the number of blacks in agrarian classes and expanded their number in an urban working class with a large secondary labor force component and a small professional-managerial stratum. This structural change and the equalizing governmental activities together account for most, if not all, of the aggregate improvement in the relative position of blacks that has taken place since 1945. But this structural change has not reduced levels of racial inequality in private industry or in metropolitan areas. The incorporation of blacks into the metropolitan economies has occurred with the reproduction of entrenched patterns of racial inequality. However, government employment has provided greater opportunities for black advancement.

Before we can understand how to combat the forces that have reproduced racial inequality in the urban setting, we must understand what these forces are. The best-known economic explanations of racial inequality have been developed in the discrimination models of neoclassical economists. But these neoclassical attempts have not proven successful. They are either logically incomplete or inconsistent, or they require strong empirical assumptions that are extremely implausible. This conclusion holds whether the main discriminating agent is the individual capitalist, the white worker, or whites acting collectively as a conspiracy. One way or another, in a neoclassical world, competition among economic agents should be expected to break down structures of racial discrimination.

These failings of the neoclassical economic discrimination theories reflect more general failings of neoclassical economic theory. This theory has a general, market-determined income distribution analysis that contains very few specific conclusions regarding the observed patterns of income inequality in every capitalist economy. One of its few results predicts that non-productivity-related differences in economic returns to productive factors will be competed away by the operation of the market.

Neoclassical theorists rarely analyze conflict among individuals and groups who are engaged in collective action, largely because the logical structure of neoclassical analysis turns attention away from the existence of such activity. Although imperfect product markets have been analyzed empirically and, with less success, theoretically by neoclassical writers, the study of collective action within firms, in the labor market, and in the determinants of government activity remains underdeveloped. Neoclassical economics thus focuses unduly on individualistic behavior in explaining income distribution.

Once we jettison the view that individuals are only self-interest-maximizing individuals who rarely engage in coalitions, and begin to examine the social relations in firms and political and governmental units in a manner that places conflict, power, and collective activity at the center of our vision, an alternative political-economic analysis can easily be conceptualized. This alternative approach takes the analyses of class conflict and of markets as the starting points of its understanding of political and economic processes. It views the determination of income distribution as resulting both from market processes and processes of power and conflict between workers and capitalists. The workplace is now understood to be a contested terrain, where capitalists organize work and workers with the objective of extracting the most work for the least amount of pay, while workers resist these efforts, both individually and collectively. Profitability therefore depends on limiting worker collective action. The organization of jobs, including bureaucratic structures that exploit the existence of racial and other divisions among workers, becomes a key variable. Government activity is now seen as determined by economic and political power. This activity is organized through political parties and a variety of formal and informal pressure groups.

The class conflict theory indicates the outlines of a formal analysis that suggests why racial inequality is reproduced over time in a capitalist economy. The result holds both for competitive and monopsonistic labor markets and does not depend on employers' conscious intentions. The class conflict theory thus challenges the neoclassical theories of racial discrimination. It offers an explanation of why the market by itself does not eliminate racial inequality and suggests, in contrast to neoclassical theories, that most white workers do not benefit from racial inequality while capitalists do.

An econometric investigation of who benefits from racism permits a uniform test of the neoclassical and class conflict theories. The evidence presented here contradicts the neoclassical theories and supports the class conflict analysis. Racial inequality disproportionately benefits rich whites, in the sense that their share of the white income distribution increases. This pattern holds both for the entire nation and for the non-South, in 1960 and 1970. This econometric evidence thus suggests that racism is best understood in the class conflict perspective that is presented here.

Historical investigation yields the same conclusions. The divisive effects of racism on coalition formation are apparent both in the agrarian history of the postbellum South and in the industrial history of both the South and the North. Historical examples indicate that the capacity of farmers and workers to organize interracial coalitions depends upon macroeconomic conditions affecting the unemployment rate, upon the role of the state, and upon differences in the economic positions of blacks and whites.

In recent decades blacks have been incorporated into industry in large numbers, and since the 1930s the industrial union movement has attempted, with some success, to counter racial inequality. Since the late 1940s, however, organized labor in the private sector has stagnated; this stagnation constitutes both cause and consequence of the stagnation of the position of blacks in industry. The inability of the labor movement to organize unions or to extend welfare-state

308

programs to workers in the low-wage competitive periphery, or secondary segment of the labor market, has hurt both black and white workers. Perhaps not coincidentally, unionism has developed most during the postwar period among public employees. Many of these unions include high and growing proportions of black members.

The class conflict theory proposes two testable mechanisms that link racial inequality with income inequality among whites: the effects on unionism and the effects on inequality in public services. Econometric tests indicate that these mechanisms do operate. In 1960 unionism was inhibited and schooling inequality among whites was exacerbated by racial inequality. These mechanisms became the focus of considerable public policy efforts during the 1960s, and their strength apparently diminished by the end of the decade. However, the distribution of benefits from racism remained unchanged during the 1960s. In 1970 white workers' wages, the extent of unionism, and profit rates of manufacturing industries were each significantly influenced by racial inequality. Wages and unionism were lower and profits were higher where racial inequality was greater. Given the limitations of available data and the resulting considerable gap between the conceptual definitions of variables and their empirical counterparts, the econometric evidence proves remarkably unambiguous in supporting the contentions that are suggested by the theoretical and historical inquiry.

The econometric investigations in this book do not directly reveal the extent to which the processes that currently produce racial inequality are located within firms or outside the workplace, in schooling, housing, and other community settings. This somewhat different question has been the focus of considerable research efforts made by others, and the results suggest that the processes are located in both workplace and the community. However, the interpretation of the evidence presented in this book, I have argued, does not depend on identification of the actual processes that produce racial inequality. The divisive effects of racial inequality on coali-

309

tion formation are the same whatever those associated processes are.

The theoretical, historical, and econometric investigations in this book notably all point in the same direction. The combination of these separate inquiries therefore reinforces the main conclusions of each. Despite the claims of neoclassical economists, income distribution is determined by the conflictual exercise of power between workers and capitalists, and racism benefits capitalists while hurting most white workers.

Implications for Economic Theory and Public Policy

The findings of this book contain important implications for economic theory and important suggestions for blacks and whites who are concerned with formulating strategies to combat racial inequality.

The results presented here suggest that economic analysis is better served by a class conflict and power analysis than by the individualistic and market-oriented emphasis of neoclassical economics. This does not imply throwing out all aspects of market analysis. Markets do function in a capitalist economy, and no economic analysis of capitalism can be complete without a discussion of these market forces. But equally important, no analysis of a capitalist economy can be complete without a discussion of class conflict and power forces. Although only a limited quantity of the evidence in this book pertains directly to the determinants of government policy, the results also suggest the importance of class power in the political process.

The two analytical foci of market and power forces can and must be united to form a complete and coherent political-economic analysis. This unity, however, cannot be created successfully by simply labeling market phenomena as the economic realm, and class conflict and power as the political or governmental realm. Class conflict occurs within firms, and government policy frames worker-capitalist relations at both the microeconomic and macroeconomic levels. Therefore, political variables enter fundamentally into what is usually

310

specified as the realm of economic analysis. Similarly, economic power is used to influence government policy within the constraint that governments functioning in capitalist economies must maintain profitable conditions for private investment. Consequently, economic variables enter into the conventional realm of political analysis. Thus, both market and class forces must be incorporated into the economic and the political analysis.

In this book I have suggested some ways that market and power variables can be integrated into a unified theory. These suggestions only begin the needed discussion, however, since there are many additional aspects of markets and power factors to consider.

The theoretical, econometric, and historical findings in this book contain important strategic implications for the continuing struggle against racial inequality in the United States. The finding that racism works against most whites' economic interests suggests that most whites need not be hostile to campaigns against racism. On the contrary, it should be possible to mobilize a coalition against racism that encompasses broad segments of the American population. To succeed, however, such efforts must indicate to whites that the achievement of racial economic equality need not occur at their cost.

At the present time, white racism in the United States remains deeply rooted. Most whites are either unaware of the unequal distribution of benefits that arise from racial inequality or feel unable to respond collectively with other whites and blacks in a manner that would benefit both. The perception that fighting racism means sacrifice is understandable, if not inevitable. So too are individualistic reactions to the economic and psychological insecurities of life in a capitalist society.

While racism continues to divide workers, it is not created solely or even primarily today by conscious efforts of capitalists to trick their workers. The racism of whites is being reinforced

311

today by the insecurities created by the decline of the American economy, by the decline of individual autonomy in craft and professional occupations, by the strains that affect family structure, and by the increase of individualism in our culture. In this context, racist appeals and responses can and do appear attractive to broad segments of the white population. Racism provides a vulnerable scapegoat group upon whom the frustrations of life in a capitalist society can be directed.

The struggle for racial equality thus must stress the collective situation of most workers and the efficacy of solidarity and collective action. The economic pie that gets divided between black and white workers does not have a fixed size. Both blacks and whites can make and share a larger pie by appropriating a share of what capitalists now receive, and they can increase the total economic pie by pressuring government to institute economic policies that stress full employment and social welfare programs. Such objectives may seem distant. But they can be achieved through broad economic and political reforms.

Given the likely continuing difficulties facing the American economy, the presence or absence of antiracism as a popular theme will be crucial not only for the immediate economic interests of blacks and whites, and not just for the realization of reformist programs, but also for the entire social and cultural character of coming decades. There are signs that the social meanness that has already appeared against blacks and other racial minorities can easily spill over into broader currents of American life.

Yet the range of possible responses remains quite broad. The recent experience of the various northern European nations with immigrant workers of dark complexion reveals the range of possible outcomes. Among these countries Sweden and Holland contain the most established labor movements and exhibit the most egalitarian income distributions. Sweden and Holland have pioneered in extending political and economic rights to immigrant workers and in actively opposing racial intolerance and discrimination. France and West Germany,

312

by contrast, have weaker labor movements and greater degrees of income inequality. They have done little to incorporate foreign workers into their mainstream; in France, particularly, overt racial violence has erupted repeatedly.[1]

Within the United States, we have, at one extreme, the important example of the antiracist struggles conducted by the Left and the labor movement in the 1930s, and the associated progressive victories of that era. At perhaps the other extreme, we have the racist violence surrounding school busing controversies in cities such as Boston, and the associated conservative turn of the 1970s. This range of experiences suggests that until the Left and the labor movement become capable once again of creating a popular collective vision, culture, program, and movement, the reproduction of racism will be one of the consequences.

[1] See Stephen Castles and Godula Kosack, *Immigrant Workers and Class Structure in Western Europe* (New York: Oxford University Press, 1973).

Bibliography

Ackerman, Frank, and Zimbalist, Andrew. "Capitalism and Inequality in the United States." In Edwards, Reich, and Weisskopf, eds. *The Capitalist System.*

Aigner, Dennis. "A Linear Approximator for the Class Marks of a Grouped Frequency Distribution with Special Reference to the Unequal Interval Case." Systems Formulation, Methodology and Policy Workshop Paper 6708. University of Wisconsin, 1967.

―――. "On a Calculation Technique for the Moments of a Frequency Distribution in Grouped Forms." *Proceedings of the American Statistical Association* (August 1966).

―――, and Heins, A. J. "On the Determinants of Income Equality." *American Economic Review* (March 1972).

―――, and Heins, A. J. "A Social Welfare View of the Measurement of Income Equality." *Review of Income and Wealth* (March 1967).

Akerlof, George. "The Economics of Caste, the Rat-Race and Other Woeful Tales." *Quarterly Journal of Economics* (November 1977).

―――, and Soskice, David. "The Economics of Sanctions." Unpublished paper, Department of Economics, University of California, Berkeley, no date.

Aldrich, Mark. "Post-Bellum Southern Income: A Response to Ransom and Sutch." *Review of Black Political Economy* (Summer 1979).

Al-Samarrie, Ahmad, and Miller, Herman. "State Differentials in Income Concentration." *American Economic Review* (March 1967).

Analavage, Robert. "Laurel Strike is Broken." In Mermelstein, ed. *Economics: Mainstream Readings and Radical Critiques.*

315

Anderson, Bernard, and Wallace, Phyllis. "Public Policy and Black Economic Progress: A Review of The Evidence." *American Economic Review* (May 1975).

Arrow, Kenneth. "Some Mathematical Models of Race Discrimination in the Labor Market." In Pascal ed. *Racial Discrimination in Economic Life.*

———, and Debreu, Gerard. "Existence of Equilibrium for a Competitive Economy." *Econometrica* (1954).

———, and Hahn, Frank. *General Competitive Analysis.* San Francisco: Holden Day, 1971.

Ashenfelter, Orley. "Changes in Labor Market Discrimination Over Time." *Journal of Human Resources* (Fall 1970).

———. "Racial Discrimination and Trade Unionism." *Journal of Political Economy* (May–June 1972).

———, and Johnson, George. "Bargaining Theory, Trade Unions, and Industrial Strike Activity." *American Economic Review* (March 1969).

———, and Johnson, George. "Unionism, Relative Wages, and Labor Quality in U.S. Manufacturing Industries." *International Economic Review* (October 1972).

Askew, Reuben. "Busing is Not The Issue." *Inequality in Education.* Harvard Graduate School of Education (March 1972).

Atkinson, A. B. "On the Measurement of Inequality." *Journal of Economic Theory* (1970).

Baron, Harold. "The Demand for Black Labor: Historical Notes on the Political Economy of Racism." *Radical America* (March–April 1971).

Barrera, Mario. *Race and Class in the Southwest.* South Bend, Ind.: Notre Dame University Press, 1979.

Batchelder, Alan. "Decline in the Relative Income of Negro Men." *Quarterly Journal of Economics* (May 1966).

Becker, Gary. *The Economics of Discrimination.* Chicago: University of Chicago Press, 1957.

Bennett, Lerone. *Before the Mayflower: A History of the Negro in America, 1619–1964.* Baltimore: Penguin

Books, 1966.

Bergmann, Barbara R. "Occupational Segregation, Wages and Profits When Employers Discriminate by Race or Sex." *Eastern Economic Journal* (April–July 1974).

———. "The Effect on White Incomes of Discrimination in Employment." *Journal of Political Economy* (January–February 1971).

———, and Lyle, Jerolyn R. "Occupational Standing of Negroes by Areas and Industries." *Journal of Human Resources* (Fall 1971).

Blaug, Mark. *Economic Theory in Retrospect.* 3rd ed. New York: Cambridge University Press, 1973.

Bluestone, Barry. "The Tripartite Economy: Labor Markets and the Working Poor." *Poverty and Human Resources* (July–August 1970).

Blum, John M., et al. *The National Experience.* 3rd ed. New York: Harcourt Brace Jovanovich, 1973.

Bolce, Louis, and Gray, Susan. "Blacks, Whites and Race Politics." *Public Interest* (Winter 1979).

Bond, Horace Mann. *Negro Education in Alabama: A Study in Cotton and Steel.* New York: Atheneum, 1969.

Boskin, Michael. "Unions and Relative Real Wages." *American Economic Review* (June 1972).

Bowen, William. *Wage Behavior in the Postwar Period: An Empirical Analysis.* Princeton: Princeton University Press, 1960.

———, and Finegan, T. Aldrich. *The Economics of Labor Force Participation.* Princeton: Princeton University Press, 1969.

Bowles, Samuel. *Planning Educational Systems for Economic Growth.* Cambridge: Harvard University Press, 1969.

———. "Migration as Investment: Empirical Tests of the Human Investment Approach." *Review of Economics and Statistics* (November 1970).

———. "Schooling and Inequality from Generation to Generation." *Journal of Political Economy* (May–June 1972).

317

————. "Unequal Education and the Reproduction of the Social Division of Labor." In Carnoy, ed. *Schooling in a Corporate Society.*

————. "Towards an Educational Production Function." *In* Hansen, ed. *Education, Income and Human Capital.*

————, and Gintis, Herbert. "IQ in the U.S. Class Structure." *Social Policy* (January 1973).

————, and Gintis, Herbert. *Schooling in Capitalist America.* New York: Basic Books, 1976.

Bowman, Mary Jean. "A Geographical Analysis of Personal Income Distribution in the United States." In American Economic Association, *Readings in the Theory of Income Distribution.* Philadelphia: Blakiston, 1946.

Braverman, Harry. *Labor and Monopoly Capital.* New York: Monthly Review Press, 1974.

Briggs, Vernon; Fogel, Walter; and Schmidt, Robert. *The Chicano Worker.* Austin: University of Texas Press, 1977.

Brody, David. *Steelworkers in America: the Nonunion Era.* Cambridge: Harvard University Press, 1960.

————, *Labor in Crisis: the Steel Strike of 1919.* Philadelphia: Lippincott, 1965.

Bronfenbrenner, Martin. *Income Distribution Theory.* Chicago: Aldine, 1967.

Brooks, John Graham. *The Social Unrest.* New York, 1903.

Brown, Charles, and Medoff, James. "Trade Unions and the Production Process." *Journal of Political Economy* (May–June 1978).

Brunt, E. A. "Reflections on British and Roman Imperialism." *Comparative Studies in Science and History* (1965).

Butler, Richard, and Heckman, James. "The Government's Impact on the Labor Market Status of Black Americans: A Critical Review." In Hausman et al., eds. *Equal Rights and Industrial Relations.*

Cain, Glen, and Watts, Harold, eds. *Income Maintenance and Labor Supply: Econometric Studies.* New York: Academic Press, 1973.

Cantor, Milton, ed. *Black Labor in America.* Westport: Negro Universities Press, 1970.

318

Carleton, Frank. *Economic Influences Upon Educational Progress in the United States, 1820–50*. New York, 1908.

Carnoy, Martin, ed. *Schooling in a Corporate Society*. New York: David McKay, 1972.

Castles, Stephen, and Kosack, Godula. *Immigrant Workers and Class Structure in Western Europe*. New York: Oxford University Press, 1973.

Chamberlain, Neil. *Collective Bargaining*. New York: Mc-Graw-Hill, 1951.

Chase, Samuel, ed. *Problems in Public Expenditure Analysis*. Washington, D.C.: Brookings Institution, 1968.

Cherry, Robert. "Racial Thought and the Early Economics Profession." *Review of Social Economy* (October 1976).

Chiswick, Barry. "Racial Discrimination in the Labor Market: A Test of Alternative Hypotheses." *Journal of Political Economy* (November–December 1973).

Clover, Vernon. "Compensation in Union and Non-Union Plants, 1960–65." *Industrial and Labor Relations Review* (January 1968).

Cohen, David, and Lazerson, Marvin. "Education and the Modern Labor Force." In Edwards, Reich, and Weisskopf, eds. *The Capitalist System*, 1972.

Comanor, William. "Racial Discrimination in American Industry." *Economica* (November 1973).

Condran, John. "Changes in White Attitudes Toward Blacks, 1963–1977." *Public Opinion Quarterly* (Winter 1979).

Cox, Oliver. *Caste, Class, and Race*. New York: Monthly Review Press, 1968.

Cremin, Lawrence. *The Transformation of the School: Progressivism in American Education*. New York: Knopf, 1964.

Dalton, Hugh. "The Measurement of the Inequality of Income." *Economic Journal* (September 1920).

Davis, Allison, et al. *Deep South*. Chicago: University of Chicago Press, 1941.

Davis, David Brion. *The Problem of Slavery in Western Culture*. New York: Pantheon, 1969.

Debreu, Gerard. *A Theory of Value*. New York: Wiley, 1953.

319

Dobb, Maurice. *Theories of Value and Distribution.* New York: Cambridge University Press, 1973.

Doeringer, Peter, and Piore, Michael. *Internal Labor Markets and Manpower Analysis.* Lexington, Mass.: D. C. Heath, 1971.

Dooley, Peter. "The Interlocking Directorate." *American Economic Review* (June 1969).

Doolittle, Fred. "Intergovernmental Relations in Federal Grant Programs: The Case of Aid for Families with Dependent Children." Berkeley: Institute of Business and Economic Research, 1977.

The Life and Times of Frederick Douglass. Hartford, 1883; reprint ed., New York: Collier-Macmillan, 1962.

Douglas, Paul. *Real Wages in the United States, 1890–1926.* Boston: Houghton Mifflin, 1930.

Douty, Harry. "Union and Nonunion Wages." In W. S. Woytinsky, ed. *Employment and Wages in the United States.* New York: Twentieth Century Fund, 1951.

DuBois, W. E. B. *Black Reconstruction in America, 1860–1880.* New York: Harcourt, Brace and World, 1935.

———. *The Negro Artisan.* Atlanta, 1902.

Duncan, Beverly, and Duncan, Otis D. *The Negro Population of Chicago: A Study in Residential Succession.* Chicago: University of Chicago Press, 1956.

Duncan, Otis D. "Inheritance of Poverty or Inheritance of Race." In Daniel P. Moynihan, ed. *On Understanding Poverty.* New York: Basic Books, 1970.

Dunlop, John, ed. *The Theory of Wage Determination.* New York: St. Martin's Press, 1957.

Edel, Mathew. "A Note on Marxism, Collective Action and the Prisoner's Dilemma." *Journal of Economic Issues* (September 1979).

Edwards, Richard. *Contested Terrain: The Transformation of the Workplace in the Twentieth Century.* New York: Basic Books, 1979.

———, Reich, Michael, and Weisskopf, Thomas, eds. *The*

320

Capitalist System. 2d ed. Englewood Cliffs, N.J.: Prentice-Hall, 1978.

Farley, Reynolds. "Trends in Racial Inequalities: Have the Gains of the 1960s Disappeared in the 1970s?" *American Sociological Review* (April 1977).

Fein, Rashi, and Michelson, Stephan. "Social and Economic Conditions of Negroes in the United States—A Critique." *Washington Post*, 14 January 1968.

Fine, Sidney. *Sit-Down: The General Motors Strike of 1936–1937*. Ann Arbor: University of Michigan Press, 1969.

Finley, Moses. "A Critique of David Brion Davis." In Laura Foner and Eugene Genovese, eds. *Slavery in the New World*. Englewood Cliffs, N.J.: Prentice-Hall, 1969.

Flanagan, Robert. "Racial Wage Discrimination and Employment Segregation." *Journal of Human Resources* (Fall 1973).

———. "Actual vs. Potential Impact of Government Anti-discrimination Programs." *Industrial and Labor Relations Review* (July 1976).

Foner, Laura, and Genovese, Eugene, eds. *Slavery in the New World: A Reader in Comparative History*. Englewood Cliffs, N.J.: Prentice-Hall, 1969.

Foner, Phillip. *History of the Labor Movement in the United States*. Vol. 3. *The Policies and Practices of the American Federation of Labor 1900–1909*. New York: International Publishers, 1964.

———. *Organized Labor and the Black Worker, 1619–1973*. New York: Praeger, 1974.

Franklin, Raymond. "A Framework for the Analysis of Interurban Negro-White Economic Differentials." *Industrial and Labor Relations Review* (April 1968).

Freeman, Richard. "The Role of Educational Discrimination." Mimeographed, 1972.

———. "Overinvestment in College Training?" *Journal of Human Resources* (Summer 1975).

———. "The Changing Labor Market for Black Americans,

1948–72." *Brookings Papers on Economic Activity*, no. 1 (1973).

———. *Black Elite: The New Market for Highly Qualified Black Americans.* New York: McGraw-Hill, 1977.

———. "Black Economic Progress Since 1964." *Public Interest* (Summer 1978).

Friedman, Milton. "Some Comments on the Significance of Labor Unions for Economic Policy." In David M. Wright, ed. *The Impact of the Union.* New York: Mc-Graw-Hill, 1951.

———. *Capitalism and Freedom.* Chicago: University of Chicago Press, 1962.

Frolich, Norman, and Oppenheimer, Joe. *Modern Political Economy.* Englewood Cliffs, N.J.: Prentice-Hall, 1978.

Genovese, Eugene. *The Political Economy of Slavery.* New York: Random House, 1965.

———. "Yeoman Farmers in a Slaveholder's Democracy." *Agricultural History* (April 1975).

———. "The Treatment of Slaves in Different Countries." In L. Foner and E. Genovese, eds. *Slavery in the New World.*

Georgakas, Dan, and Surkin, Marvin. *Detroit: I Do Mind Dying, A Study in Urban Revolution.* New York: St. Martin's Press, 1975.

Geschwender, James. *Class, Race and Worker Insurgency: The League of Revolutionary Black Workers.* New York: Cambridge University Press, 1977.

Gilman, Harry J. "Economic Discrimination and Unemployment." *American Economic Review* (December 1965).

Gintis, Herbert. "Education, Attitudes and Worker Productivity." *American Economic Review* (May 1971).

———. "The Nature of Labor Exchange: Toward a Radical Theory of the Firm." *Review of Radical Political Economics* (Summer 1976).

Goldin, Claudia. *Urban Slavery in the American South 1820–1860.* Chicago: University of Chicago Press, 1976.

———. "'N' Kinds of Freedom." *Explorations in Economic History* (January 1979).

Goldsmith, Selma. "Changes in the Size Distribution of Income Since the Mid-Thirties." *American Economic Review* (May 1957).

Goodwyn, Lawrence. *Democratic Promise: The Populist Movement in America.* New York: Oxford University Press, 1976.

Gordon, David. "From Steam Whistles to Coffee Breaks." *Dissent* (Winter 1972).

Gossett, Thomas. *Race: The History of An Idea in America.* New York: Schocken, 1965.

Greenstone, David. *Labor in American Politics.* New York: Random House, 1968.

Greer, Edward. "Racial Employment Discrimination in the Gary Works, 1906–1974." Unpublished paper, 1976.

Griliches, Zvi. "Notes on the Role of Education in Production Functions and Growth Accounting." In Hansen, ed. *Education, Income and Human Capital.*

Gurley, John. "Federal Tax Policy." *National Tax Journal* (September 1967).

Gutman, Herbert. "The Negro and the United Mine Workers." In Jacobson, ed. *The Negro and the American Labor Movement.*

Gwartney, James. "Changes in the Nonwhite/White Income Ratio—1939–67." *American Economic Review* (December 1970).

Hackney, Sheldon. *Populism to Progressivism in Alabama.* Princeton: Princeton University Press, 1969.

Hall, Robert E. "Why Is the Unemployment Rate So High at Full Employment?" *Brookings Papers on Economic Activity,* no. 1 (1969).

Hansen, W. Lee, ed. *Education, Income and Human Capital.* New York: National Bureau of Economic Research, 1972.

Harcourt, G. C. *Theory of Capital: Some Cambridge Controversies.* New York: Cambridge University Press, 1972.

———, and Laing, N., eds. *Capital and Growth.* Baltimore: Penguin Books, 1972.

323

Harris, Donald. *Capital Accumulation and Income Distribution*. Stanford: Stanford University Press, 1978.

Harrison, Bennett. *Education, Training and the Urban Ghetto*. Baltimore: Johns Hopkins University Press, 1972.

Hausman, Leonard, et al., eds. *Equal Rights and Industrial Relations*. Madison: Industrial Relations Research Association, 1977.

Haworth, Joan; Gwartney, James; and Haworth, Charles. "Earnings, Productivity and Changes in Employment Discrimination during the 1960s." *American Economic Review* (March 1975).

Heckman, James. "Simultaneous Equation Methods with and without Structural Shift in the Equations." In Steven Goldfeld and Richard Quandt, eds. *Studies in Nonlinear Estimation*. Cambridge, Mass: Ballinger, 1976.

Henle, Peter. "Exploring the Distribution of Earned Income." *Monthly Labor Review* (December 1972).

Herbst, Alma. *The Negro in the Slaughtering and Meatpacking Industry in Chicago*. Boston: Houghton Mifflin, 1932.

Herriott, Roger, and Miller, Herman. "Who Paid the Taxes in 1968?" *Conference Board Record* (1972).

Hibbs, Douglas. "Political Parties and Macroeconomic Policy." *American Political Science Review* (December 1977).

Higgs, Robert. *Competition and Coercion, Blacks in the American Economy 1865–1914*. New York: Cambridge University Press, 1977.

Hill, Herbert. "The Racial Practices of Organized Labor: The Age of Gompers and After." In Arthur Ross and Herbert Hill, eds. *Employment, Race and Poverty*. New York: Harcourt, Brace and World, 1967.

Hoffman, Saul. "Black-White Life Cycle Earnings Differences and the Vintage Hypothesis: A Longitudinal Analysis." *American Economic Review* (December 1979).

Hunt, E. K., and Schwartz, Jesse, eds. *A Critique of Economic Theory*. Baltimore: Penguin Books, 1972.

Hyman, Herbert, and Sheatsley, Paul. "Attitudes Toward Desegregation." *Scientific American* (July 1964).

Jacobson, Julius, ed. *The Negro in The American Labor Movement*. New York: Anchor, 1968.

Jencks, Christopher, et al. *Who Gets Ahead? The Determinants of Economic Success in America*. New York: Basic Books, 1979.

————, et al. *Inequality: A Reassessment of the Impact of Family and Schooling*. New York: Basic Books, 1972.

Johnson, Harry G., and Mieszkowski, Peter. "The Effects of Unionization on the Distribution of Income: A General Equilibrium Approach." *Quarterly Journal of Economics* (November 1970).

Joint Center for Political Studies. *Black Political Participation: A Look at the Numbers*. Washington, D.C., December 1975.

Jordan, Winthrop. *White Over Black, American Attitudes Toward the Negro, 1550–1812*. Baltimore: Penguin Books, 1968.

Kain, John. "The Journey-to-Work as a Determinant of Residential Location." *Papers and Proceedings of the Regional Science Association*, 1962.

————, ed. *Race and Poverty*. Englewood Cliffs, N.J.: Prentice-Hall, 1969.

Katz, Michael. *The Irony of Early School Reform*. Cambridge: Harvard University Press, 1968.

Kau, James, and Rubin, Paul. "Self-Interest, Ideology, and Logrolling in Congressional Voting." *Journal of Law and Economics* (October 1979).

Kaun, David. "Negro Migration and Unemployment." *Journal of Human Resources* (Spring 1970).

Keat, Paul G. "Long-run Changes in the Occupational Wage Structure, 1900–1956." *Journal of Political Economy* (December 1960).

Kelley, E. W. "Bargaining in Coalition Situations." In Sven Groennings, E. W. Kelley, and Michael Leiserson, eds. *The Study of Coalition Behavior*. New York: Holt,

325

Rinehart and Winston, 1970.

Kerr, Clark. "Trade Unionism and Distributive Shares." *American Economic Review* (1954).

―――. "Wage Relationships—The Comparative Impact of Market and Power Forces." In Dunlop, ed. *Theory of Wage Determination.*

King, Alan. "Labor Market Discrimination Against Black Women." *Review of Black Political Economy* (Summer 1978).

Kolchin, Peter. "Scalawags, Carpetbaggers and Reconsturction: A Quantitative Look at Southern Politics, 1868–1872." *Journal of Southern History* (February 1979).

Kousser, J. Morgan. *The Shaping of Southern Politics, Suffrage Restriction and the Establishment of the One-Party South, 1880–1910.* New Haven: Yale University Press, 1974.

Krueger, Anne. "The Economics of Discrimination." *Journal of Political Economy* (October 1963).

Lampman, Robert. *The Share of Top Wealth-Holders in National Wealth, 1922–1956.* New York: National Bureau of Economic Research, 1962.

Landes, William. "The Economics of Fair Employment Laws." *Journal of Political Economy* (July–August, 1968).

―――. "The Effects of State Fair Employment Laws on the Economic Position of Non-whites." *American Economic Review* (May 1967).

Laurenti, Luigi. *Property Values and Race: Studies in Seven Cities.* Berkeley and Los Angeles: University of California Press, 1960.

Leibenberg, Maurice, and Kaitz, Hyman. "An Income Size Distribution From Income Tax and Survey Data, 1944." In *Studies in Income and Wealth.* Vol. 13. New York: National Bureau of Economic Research, 1951.

Leigh, Duane. "Racial Discrimination and Labor Unions: Evidence from the NLS Sample of Middle-Aged Men." *Journal of Human Resources* (Fall 1978).

―――. "Racial Differentials in Union Relative Wage Effects:

326

A Simultaneous Equations Approach." *Journal of Labor Research* (Winter 1980).

Levinson, Harold. "Unionism, Concentration and Wage Changes: Towards a Unified Theory." *Industrial and Labor Relations Review* (January 1967).

Levitan, Sar; Mangum, Garth; and Taggart, Robert. *Still a Dream: The Changing Status of Blacks Since 1963.* Cambridge: Harvard University Press, 1975.

Lewis, H. Gregg. *Unionism and Relative Wages in the United States.* Chicago: University of Chicago Press, 1963.

Litwack, Leon. *North of Slavery.* New York: Knopf, 1960.

Lydall, Harold. *The Structure of Earnings.* Oxford: Oxford University Press, 1968.

Lynd, Staughton. "Workers' Control and Workers' Rights." *Radical America* (September–October 1976).

———. "Employee Speech in the Private Workplace: Two Doctrines or One?" *Industrial Relations Law Journal* (1977).

McLaurin, Melton. *Paternalism and Protest: Southern Mill Workers and Organized Labor, 1897–1905.* Westport: Greenwood Press, 1971.

Madden, Janice. "Discrimination—A Manifestation of Male Market Power?" In Cynthia Lloyd, ed. *Sex, Discrimination and the Division of Labor.* New York: Columbia University Press, 1975.

Maher, John W. "Union, Nonunion Wage Differentials." *American Economic Review* (June 1956).

Mandle, Jay. "The Economic Underdevelopment of the Post-Bellum South." *Marxist Perspectives* (Winter 1978).

———. *The Roots of Southern Black Poverty.* Durham: Duke University Press, 1978.

Marshall, Ray. *Labor in the South.* Cambridge: Harvard University Press, 1965.

———. *The Negro Worker.* New York: Random House, 1967.

Marx, Karl, *Capital: A Critique of Political Economy.* Vol. 1. New York: Vintage, 1977.

————, and Engels, Friedrich. "The Communist Manifesto." In Edwards, Reich, Weisskopf, eds. *The Capitalist System.*

Masters, Stanley. *Black-White Income Differentials.* New York: Academic Press, 1975.

Mathewson, Stanley. *Restriction of Output Among Unorganized Workers.* Carbondale, Ill.: Southern Illinois University Press, 1969 (originally published in 1931).

Meier, August. *Negro Thought in America, 1880–1915.* Ann Arbor: University of Michigan Press, 1963.

Menshikov, S. *Millionaires and Managers.* Moscow: Progress Publishers, 1969.

Mermelstein, David, ed. *Economics: Mainstream Readings and Radical Critiques.* New York: Random House, 1970.

Meyer, Peter. "The Reproduction of the Distribution of Income." Ph.D. diss., University of California, Berkeley, 1979.

Miers, Suzanne, and Kopytoff, Igor, eds. *Slavery in Africa, Historical and Anthropological Perspectives.* Madison: University of Wisconsin Press, 1977.

Miller, Glenn. *Government Policy Toward Labor: An Introduction to Labor Law.* Columbus, Ohio: GRID, 1975.

Miller, Herman. *Income Distribution in the United States.* A Census Monograph. Washington, D.C.: U.S. Government Printing Office, 1966.

Montgomery, David. *Beyond Equality, Labor and the Radical Republicans, 1862–1872.* New York: Knopf, 1967.

Moore, Barrington. *Social Origins of Dictatorship and Democracy.* Boston: Beacon, Press, 1967.

Morgan, Edmund. *American Slavery, American Freedom.* New York: Norton, 1975.

Morishima, Michio. *Marx's Economics: A Dual Theory of Value and Growth.* New York: Cambridge University Press, 1973.

Moynihan, D.P. "Memo to Nixon on the Status of Negroes, January 16, 1970." *New York Times,* 1 March 1970.

Myrdal, Gunnar. *An American Dilemma, The Negro Problem*

and Modern Democracy. New York: Harper and Row, 1944, reprint ed., 1962.

Naison, Mark. "The Southern Tenant Farmers Union and the C.I.O." *Radical America* (September–October 1968).

———. "Harlem Communists and the Politics of Black Protest." *Marxist Perspectives* (Fall 1978).

Newberry, D. M. G. "A Theorem on the Measurement of Inequality." *Journal of Economic Theory* (1970).

Newby, I. A. *Jim Crow's Defense: Anti-Negro Thought in America 1900–1930*. Baton Rouge: Louisiana State University Press, 1965.

Northrup, Herbert, ed. *Negro Employment in Basic Industry: A Study of Racial Policy in Six industries*. Philadelphia: University of Pennsylvania Press, 1970.

Oaxaca, Ronald. "Estimation of Union/Nonunion Wage Differentials Within Occupational/Regional Subgroups." *Journal of Human Resources* (Fall 1975).

Ober, Harry. "Occupational Wage Differentials, 1907–1947." *Montly Labor Review* (November 1953).

Olson, James. "Race, Class, and Progress: Black Leadership and Industrial Unionism, 1936–1945." In Cantor, ed. *Black Labor In America*.

Olson, Mancur. *The Logic of Collective Action*. Cambridge: Harvard University Press, 1964.

Omvedt, Gail. "Towards a Theory of Colonialism." *Insurgent Sociologist* (Spring 1973).

Oshima, Harry, and Ono, Mitsuo. "The Size Distribution of Family Incomes, by States and Industries." Mimeograph prepared for the Conference on Income and Wealth, National Bureau of Economic Research, March 1967.

Ozanne, Robert. *A Century of Labor-Management Relations at McCormick and International Harvester*. Madison: University of Wisconsin Press, 1967.

———. "Impact of Unions on Wage Levels and Income Distribution." *Quarterly Journal of Economics* (May 1959).

Pascal, Anthony. *The Economics of Housing Segregation*.

329

Santa Monica: RAND Corporation, Memorandum RM-5510-RC, November 1967.
———, ed. *Racial Discrimination in Economic Life*. Lexington, Mass.: D. C. Heath, 1972.
Perlman, Richard. *Labor Theory*. New York: Wiley, 1969.
———, ed. *Wage Determination: Market or Power Forces?* Boston: D. C. Heath, 1964.
Perry, George. "Wages and the Guideposts." *American Economic Review* (September 1967).
Pettigrew, Thomas, ed. *Racial Discrimination in the United States*. New York: Harper and Row, 1975.
Phelps, Edwin. "The Statistical Theory of Racism and Sexism." *American Economic Review* (September 1972).
Pierson, Gail. "Union Strength and the Phillips Curve." *American Economic Review* (June 1968).
Piven, Frances, and Cloward, Richard. *Regulating the Poor: The Functions of Public Welfare*. New York: Random House, 1971.
Preston, Michael. "Black Elected Officials and Public Policy: Symbolic or Substantive Representation?" *Policy Studies Journal* (Winter 1978).
Price, Daniel. *Changing Characteristics of the Negro Population*. A 1960 Census Monograph. Washington, D.C.: U. S. Government Printing Office, 1969.
Procope, John. "The New Political Power Among Blacks." *Journal of the Institute for Socioeconomic Studies* (Spring 1978).
Ransom, Roger, and Sutch, Richard. *One Kind of Freedom: The Economic Consequences of Emancipation*. New York: Cambridge University Press, 1977.
———. "Growth and Welfare in the American South of the Nineteenth Century." *Explorations in Economic History* (April 1979).
Rapping, Leonard. "Union-Induced Racial Entry Barriers." *Journal of Human Resources* (Fall 1970).

Reich, Michael. "The Development of the Wage Labor Force." In Edwards, Reich, and Weisskopf, eds. *The Capitalist System.*

———, and Devine, James. "The Microeconomics of Conflict and Hierarchy in Capitalist Production." *Review of Radical Political Economics* (Winter 1981).

———, and Edwards, Richard. "Political Parties and Class Conflict in the United States." *Socialist Review* (May–June 1978).

———; Edwards, Richard; and Gordon, David. *The Segmentation of Labor in U.S. Capitalism.* New York: Cambridge University Press, 1981.

Reynolds, Lloyd. "The Influence of Collective Bargaining on the Wage Structure in the United States," In J. Dunlop, ed. *Theory of Wage Determination.*

———. *Labor Economics and Labor Relations.* Homewood: Irwin, 1975.

Reynolds, Lloyd G., and Taft, Cynthia. *The Evolution of the Wage Structure.* New Haven: Yale University Press, 1956.

Robinson, Joan. *The Economics of Imperfect Competition.* London: MacMillan, 1933.

Rosen, Sherwin. "Trade Union Power, Threat Effects and Extent of Organization." *Review of Economic Studies* (April 1969).

———. "Unions and the Occupational Wage Structure in the United States." *International Economic Review* (June 1970).

Rosen, Sumner. "The C.I.O. Era, 1933–55." In Jacobson, ed. *Negro and the American Labor Movement.*

Ross, Arthur. "The Negro in the American Economy." In A. Ross and H. Hill, eds. *Employment, Race and Poverty.* New York: Harcourt Brace, 1967.

———, and Goldner, William. "Forces Affecting the Inter-Industry Wage Structure." *Quarterly Journal of Economics* (May 1950).

Rothschild, Michael, and Stiglitz, Joseph. "Some Further Results on the Measurement of Inequality." *Journal of Economic Theory* (1973).

Rowan, Richard. "The Negro in the Steel Industry." In Northrup, ed. *Negro Employment in Basic Industry.*

Rowthorn, Robert. "Neo-Classicism, Neo-Ricardianism and Marxism." *New Left Review* (July–August 1974).

Roy, Donald. "Quota Restrictions and Goldbricking in a Machine Shop." *American Journal of Sociology* (March 1952);

————. "Efficiency and the 'Fix': Informal Intergroup Relations in a Piecework Machine Shop." *American Journal of Sociology* (1954–1955).

Ryscavage, Paul. "Measuring Union-Nonunion Earnings Differences." *Monthly Labor Review* (December 1974).

Schirmer, D. B. *Republic or Empire, American Resistance to the Philippine War.* Cambridge: Schenkman, 1972.

Schnare, Ann. "Residential Segregation by Race in U.S. Metropolitan Areas: An Analysis Across Cities and Over Time." Washington, D.C.: Urban Institute, 1977.

Schuman, William. "Sociological Racism." *Trans-Action* (December 1969).

Schumpeter, Joseph. *History of Economic Analysis.* New York: Oxford, 1951.

Segal, Martin. "The Relation Between Union Wage Impact and Market Structure." *Quarterly Journal of Economics* (February 1964).

Sheatsley, Paul. "White Attitudes Toward the Negro." *Daedalus* (Winter 1966).

Shepherd, William G. *Market Power and Economic Performance.* New York: Random House, 1970.

Sheshinski, Eytan. "The Relation Between a Social Welfare Function and the Gini Index of Inequality." *Journal of Economic Theory* (1972).

Shugg, Roger. *The Origins of Class Struggle in Louisiana.* Baton Rouge: Louisiana State University Press, 1939.

332

Sitkoff, Harvard. *A New Deal for Blacks.* New York: Oxford University Press, 1978.

Slichter, Sumner. *Union Policies and Industrial Management.* Washington, D.C.: Brookings Institution, 1940.

————; Healy, James; and Livernash, Robert. *The Impact of Collective Bargaining on Management.* Washington, D.C.: Brookings Institution, 1960.

Smith, J. D. and Franklin, S. D. "The Concentration of Personal Wealth, 1922–1969." *American Economic Review* (May 1974).

Smith, James, and Welch, Finis. "Black-White Male Wage Ratios: 1960–1970." *American Economic Review* (June 1977).

Smith, Marvin. "Industrial Racial Wage Discrimination in the U.S. *Industrial Relations* (Winter 1979).

Sorenson, Annemette; Taeuber, Karl; and Hollingsworth, Leslie. "Indexes of Racial Residential Segregation for 109 Cities in the United States, 1940 to 1970.' *Sociological Focus* (April 1975).

Sovern, Michael. *Government Restraints on Discrimination.* New York: Columbia University Press, 1965.

Spady, William G. "Educational Mobility and Access: Growth and Paradoxes." *American Journal of Sociology* (November 1967).

Spence, Michael. *Market Signalling.* Cambridge: Harvard University Press, 1974.

Spero, Sterling, and Harris, Abram. *The Black Worker.* New York: Atheneum, 1968.

Stafford, Frank. "Concentration and Labor Earnings: A Comment." *American Economic Review* (March 1968).

Stampp, Kenneth. *The Peculiar Institution: Slavery in the Ante-Bellum South.* New York: Random House, 1956.

————. *The Era of Reconstruction, 1865–1877.* New York: Knopf, 1963.

Starobin, Robert. *Industrial Slavery in the Old South.* New York: Oxford University Press, 1970.

333

Stein, Judith. "'Of Mr. Booker T. Washington and Others': The Political Economy of Racism in the United States," *Science and Society* (Winter 1974–1975).

Stent, Madelon. "Education for Black Americans on the 25th Anniversary of the Brown Decision." In Williams, ed. *The State of Black America, 1979.*

Strauss, Robert, and Horvath, Francis. "Wage Rate Differences by Race and Sex in the U.S. Labor Market: 1960–1970." *Economica* (August 1976).

"Symposium" *Quarterly Journal of Economics* (November 1966).

Szymanski, Albert. "Racial Discrimination and White Gain." *American Sociological Review* (June 1976).

————. "White Workers' Loss from Racial Discrimination: Reply to Villemez." *American Sociological Review* (October 1978).

Taeuber, Karl. *Patterns of Negro-White Residential Segregation.* Santa Monica: Rand Corporation, 1970.

————, and Taeuber, Alma. *Negroes in Cities: Residential Segregation and Neighborhood Change.* Chicago: Aldine, 1965.

Taft, Philip. *Organized Labor in American History.* New York: Harper and Row, 1964.

Takaki, Ronald. *Iron Cages: Race and Culture in the Nineteenth Century.* New York: Random House, 1979.

Taylor, Garth; Sheatsley, Paul; and Greeley, Andrew. "Attitudes Toward Racial Integration." *Scientific American* (June 1978).

Theil, Henri. *Economics and Information Theory.* Amsterdam: North-Holland, 1967.

Thompson, Wilbur, and Matilla, John. "Toward an Econometric Model of Urban Development." In Harvey Perloff and Lowdon Wingo, eds. *Issues in Urban Economics.* Baltimore: Johns Hopkins University Press, 1968.

Throop, Adrian. "The Union, Non-Union Wage Differential and Cost-Push Inflation." *American Economic Review* (March 1968).

Thurow, Lester. *Poverty and Discrimination*. Washington, D.C.: Brookings Institution, 1969.

Trelease, Allen. "Who Were the Scalawags." *Journal of Southern History* (November 1963).

———. *White Terror: The KKK Conspiracy and Southern Reconstruction*. New York: Harper and Row, 1971.

Tufte, Edward. *Political Control of The Economy*. Princeton: Princeton University Press, 1978.

Ulman, Lloyd. *The Rise of the National Trade Union*. Cambridge: Harvard University Press, 1960.

U.S. Bureau of the Census. *Census of Manufactures, 1963*. Washington, D.C.: U.S. Government Printing Office, 1965.

U.S. Bureau of the Census. *Census of the Population, 1950*. Washington, D.C.: U.S. Government Printing Office, 1953.

U.S. Bureau of the Census. *Census of the Population, 1960*. Washington, D.C.: U.S. Government Printing Office, 1963.

U.S. Bureau of the Census. *Census of the Population, 1970*. Washington, D.C.: U.S. Government Printing Office, 1973.

U.S. Bureau of The Census. *Census of Population, 1970*. "Subject Reports: Industrial Characteristics." Washington, D.C.: U.S. Government Printing Office, 1973.

U.S. Bureau of the Census. "Characteristics of Families Residing in 'Poverty Areas,' March 1966," *Current Population Reports, Technical Studies*. P-23 Series, no. 19. Washington, D.C.: U.S. Government Printing Office, 24 August 1966.

U.S. Bureau of the Census. "Income of Families and Persons in the United States." *Current Population Reports*. P-60 Series. Washington, D.C.: U.S. Government Printing Office, various years.

U.S. Bureau of the Census. *Historical Statistics of the United States, Colonial Times to 1957*. Washington, D.C.: U.S. Government Printing Office, 1960.

U.S. Bureau of the Census. "Negro Population: March 1966." *Current Population Reports, Population Characteristics.* P-20 Series, no. 169. Washington, D.C.: U.S. Government Printing Office, 22 December 1967.

U.S. Bureau of the Census. "Trends in the Incomes of Families and Persons, 1947–64." *Technical Paper No. 17.* Washington, D.C.: U.S. Government Printing Office, 1968.

U.S. Department of Health, Education and Welfare, Office of Education. *A Survey of Equality of Educational Opportunity.* Washington, D.C.: U.S. Government Printing Offiice, 1966.

U.S. Department of Labor. *Manpower Report of the President, 1970.* Washington, D.C.: U.S. Government Printing Office, 1970.

U.S. Department of Labor, Bureau of Labor Statistics. *Area Wage Surveys, Selected Metropolitan Areas, 1968–69.* Bulletin no. 1625–90. Washington, D.C.: U.S. Government Printing Office, 1970.

U.S. Department of Labor, Bureau of Labor Statistics. *Economic Status of Nonwhite Workers 1955–1962.* Special Labor Force, Report no. 33. Washington, D.C.: U.S. Government Printing Office, 1964.

U.S. Department of Labor, Bureau of Labor Statistics. *Selected Earnings and Demographic Characteristics of Union Members, 1970.* Bulletin no. 417. Washington, D.C.: U.S. Government Printing Office, 1972.

U.S. Department of Labor, Bureau of Labor Statistics. *The Social and Economic Status of Negroes in the United States, 1966.* Bulletin no. 332. Washington, D.C.: U.S. Government Printing Office, October 1967.

U.S. Department of Labor, Bureau of Labor Statistics. *The Social and Economic Status of Negroes in the United States, 1969.* Report no. 375. Washington, D.C.: U.S. Government Printing Office, 1970.

U.S. Department of Labor, Bureau of Labor Statistics. *The Social and Economic Status of Negroes in the United*

States, 1970. Washington, D.C.: U.S. Government
Printing Office, 1971.

U.S. Department of Labor, Bureau of Labor Statistics. *Wages
and Related Benefits: 82 Labor Markets, 1960–61.*
Bulletin no. 1285-83. Washington, D.C.: U.S. Government Printing Office, 1963.

U.S. Department of the Treasury, Internal Revenue Service.
Corporation Returns, 1970. Washington, D.C.: U.S.
Government Printing Office, 1971.

U.S. Department of the Treasury, Internal Revenue Service.
*Statistics of Income, 1966: Individual Income Tax Re-
turns.* Washington, D.C.: U.S. Government Printing
Office, 1967.

Vander Zanden, James. "The Ideology of White Supremacy."
In Barry Schwartz and Robert Disch, eds. *White Racism.*
New York: Dell, 1970.

Varian, Hal. *Microeconomic Analysis.* New York: Norton,
1978.

Van Valey, Thomas; Roof, Wade Clark; and Wilcox, Jerome.
"Trends in Residential Segregation 1960–1970." *American Journal of Sociology* (January 1977).

Vickery, Clair. "The Impact of Turnover on Group Unemployment Rates." *Review of Economics and Statistics*
(November 1977).

Vietorisz, Thomas, and Harrison, Bennet. *The Economic
Development of Harlem.* New York: Praeger, 1970.

Villemez, Wayne. "Black Subordination and White Economic
Well-Being." *American Sociological Review* (October
(1978).

Vroman, Wayne. "Changes in the Labor Market Position of
Black Men Since 1964." *Proceedings of The Twenty-
Seventh Annual Winter Meeting.* Industrial Relations
Research Association. Madison: The Association, 1975.

Wachtel, Howard, and Betsey, Charles. "Employment at Low
Wages." *Review of Economics and Statistics* (May 1972).

Wade, Richard. *Slavery in the Cities: The South, 1820–1860.*

337

New York: Oxford University Press, 1964.

Walton, Richard, and McKersie, Robert. *A Behavioral Theory of Labor Negotiations*. New York: McGraw-Hill, 1965.

Ward, Benjamin. *The Ideal Worlds of Economics*. New York: Basic Books, 1979.

Weaver, Robert. *Negro Labor—A National Problem*. New York: Harcourt Brace, 1943.

Weber, Arnold. "The Craft-Industrial Issue Revisited: A Study of Union Government." *Indistrial and Labor Relations Review* (April 1963).

Weiss, Dorothy et al. "Survey of Financial Characteristics of Consumers." In Lee Soltow ed. *Six Papers on the Size Distribution of Income*. New York: National Bureau of Economic Research, 1969.

Weiss, Leonard. "Concentration and Labor Earnings." *American Economic Review* (March 1966).

——, and Williamson, Jeffrey. "Black Education, Earnings and Interregional Migration: Some New Evidence." *American Economic Review* (June 1972).

Welch, Finis. "Black-White Differences in Returns to Schooling." *American Economic Review* (December 1973).

——. "Labor Market Discrimination: An Interpretation of Income Differences in the Rural South." *Journal of Political Economy* (June 1967).

Wells, Dave, and Stodder, Jim. "A Short History of New Orleans Dockworkers." *Radical America* (January–February 1976).

Wesley, Charles. *The Negro Laborer*. New York, 1924.

Widick, B. J. *Detroit: City of Class and Race Violence*. Chicago: Quadrangle, 1972.

Wiener, Jonathan. *Social Origins of the New South*. Baton Rouge: Louisiana State University Press, 1978.

Wilkerson, Doxey A. "The Negro School Movement in Virginia: From 'Equalization' to 'Integration.'" In August Meier and Elliott Rudwick, eds. *The Making of Black America*. Vol. 2. New York: Atheneum, 1969.

338

Williams, Eddie. "Black Political Participation in 1978." In Williams ed. *The State of Black America, 1979.*

Williams, Eric. *Capitalism and Slavery.* New York: Capricorn, 1966.

Williams, James, ed. *The State of Black America, 1979.* New York: National Urban League, 1979.

Wolters, Raymond. "Closed Shop and White Shop: The Negro Response to Collective Bargaining, 1933–35." In Cantor, ed. *Black Labor in America.*

Woodward, C. Vann. *Tom Watson: Agrarian Rebel.* New York: Macmillan, 1938.

———. *Origins of the New South, 1877–1913.* Baton Rouge: Louisiana State University Press, 1951.

———. *The Strange Career of Jim Crow.* New York: Galaxy, 1966.

Worthman, Paul. "Black Workers and Labor Unions in Birmingham, Alabama, 1897–1904." In Cantor, ed. *Black Labor in America.*

———, and Green, James. "Black Workers in the New South, 1865–1915." In Nathan Huggins et al., eds. *Key Issues in the Afro-American Experience.* Vol. 2. New York: Harcourt Brace, 1971.

Wright, Erik Olin. *Class, Crisis and the State.* London: New Left Books, 1978.

———. *Class Structure and Income Determination.* New York: Academic Press, 1979.

Wright, Gavin. *The Political Economy of the Cotton South.* New York: Norton, 1978.

———. "Freedom and the Southern Economy." *Explorations in Economic History* (January 1979).

Index

affirmative action, 5
AFL-CIO Central Labor Councils, 284
Aigner, Dennis, and Heims, A. J., 135
Alabama Iron and Steel Workers, 244–246
Al-Samarrie, Ahmad, and Miller, Herman, 135
American Federation of Labor, 243, 245, 246, 250, 256
American Medical Association, 271
Arrow, Kenneth, 98–102, 102–107; and Debreu, Gerard, 172, 178, 180
Ashenfelter, Orley, 291–292
Asians, 12–13
Askew, Reuben, 10

Bakke, Allen, 6
bargaining power, 268–269
Bergmann, Barbara, 81, 94–97
Becker, Gary, 76, 80, 88. *See also* discrimination theories
bituminous coal mining, 239–241
black: communities, as colonies, 93; elected officials, 73–74; labor force participation rates, 30–31, 36; labor mobility, 229; landownership, 228; migration, 227, 252; nationalists, 93; professionals and managers, 29, 30, 34, 36; strikebreakers, 241, 251, 253, 254; urbanization, 62–65; wageworkers, 227; women, 23, 29, 30, 41, 61
blacks: college-educated, 60; in northern industry, 254
Bowen, William, and Finegan, T. Aldrich, 130
Brody, David, 255

Brooks, John Graham, 247
Brotherhood of Sleeping Car Porters, 258
Bruce, Philip, 248
Bureau of Labor Statistics, 17–18
Butler, Richard, and Heckman, James, 36

capital accumulation, 188–189
capitalism and discrimination, 78
capitalist firms: conflict theory, 191–198; neoclassical theory, 171–172
cartel behavior, 183
CETA, 72
Chicanos, 13ff.
Chinese workers, 228
civil rights, 7; movement, 4, 73
class and race, 3
class conflict: among whites, 221; and racial inequality within the firm, 204–215
class structure: of blacks, 7–8, 20; in South, 219
classical economists, 169–170
Cleveland, 279
collective action, 183–185; by workers, 196–197, 206–210
collective bargaining, 183, 191–192, 204–209
colonial system, 15
Committee for Industrial Organization (CIO), 256–262, 272; changing employment practices, 259; Committee to Abolish Racial Discrimination, 258; Constitutional Conventions of 1938, 257; in the 1930s and 1940s, 256–262
Commonwealth v. Hunt, 199

341

LIBRARY OF CONGRESS CATALOGING IN PUBLICATION DATA

Reich, Michael.
    Racial inequality.

    Bibliography: p.
    Includes index.
    1.   United States—Race relations.   2.   Race dis-
crimination—Economic aspects—United States.
3.   Labor and laboring classes—United States.
4.   Race discrimination—Political aspects—United
States.   5.   United—Economic conditions.
I. Title.
E185.61.R34   305.8′00973   80-8573
ISBN 0-691-04227-6
ISBN 0-691-00365-3 (pbk.)